HOW TO WRITE A NOVEL

The Fundamentals of Fiction

By Bryan Thomas Schmidt

ALSO BY BRYAN THOMAS SCHMIDT

NOVELS

The Worker Prince (Saga of Davi Rhii 1)
The Returning (Saga of Davi Rhii 2)
The Exodus (Saga of Davi Rhii 3)
Simon Says (forthcoming)

CHILDREN'S BOOKS

102 More Hilarious Dinosaur Jokes
Abraham Lincoln-Dinosaur Hunter: Land of Legends

ANTHOLOGIES (AS EDITOR)

Infinite Stars II (forthcoming)
Joe Ledger: Unstoppable (with Jonathan Maberry)
Predator: If It Bleeds
Infinite Stars: Definitive Space Opera and Military Science Fiction
The Monster Hunter Files (with Larry Correia)
Maximum Velocity (with David Lee Summers, Carol Hightshoe, Dayton Ward, and Jennifer Brozek)
Little Green Men—Attack! (with Robin Wayne Bailey)
Decision Points
Galactic Games
Mission: Tomorrow
Shattered Shields (with Jennifer Brozek)
Raygun Chronicles: Space Opera for a New Age
Beyond the Sun
Space Battles: Full-Throttle Space Tales

To my teachers who've stuck with me like Bill Pierson, Joy Patrick, Barbara Sackrider, and Larry Ward, and writing mentors like Mike Resnick, Robert Silverberg, and Jonathan Maberry. Great teachers all.

Contents

FOREWORD

from Inkitt Founder Ali Albazaz

A few years ago, when I met the CEO of one of the largest book publishers in the world, I was astonished to find out that less than 5 percent of their new publications were by debut authors, while 95 percent were by previously published authors. He explained to me that the reason they were reluctant to invest in new talent was because, generally speaking, previously published authors possess fan bases whose support ensures them the security of at least breaking even and the likelihood of earning a small profit on top of that. Publishing new authors, on the other hand, is a riskier endeavor because there's no way to tell in advance whether the book will find an audience. This is why *Harry Potter* was rejected by 12 different publishers before a 13th, Bloomsbury, finally accepted the book for a modest advance. Stephanie Meyer's *Twilight* was originally rejected by 14 literary agents. Stephen King's *Carrie* was rejected by 30 publishers, and James Patterson's *The Thomas Berryman Number* was rejected by 31 publishers. This led me to wonder how many authors there are worldwide who wrote amazing books which would have resonated with millions of readers but gave up after being rejected by a handful of publishers. This thought stayed with me for a long time until I found a solution.

In 2013 I was building an invite-only manuscript-sharing platform for authors that would enable them to give each other

I

feedback. I had seen a host of other platforms become overruled by trolls, so I wanted to keep the quality of the community I was building high and exclusively for professional authors. Therefore, we restricted membership to those who other members believed could add value to our community. After just a few months, the community was growing exponentially as thousands of writers and readers became active on Inkitt. That's when I started to think about debut authors having a hard time getting their books published. Sure, self-publishing is a viable route for some, but you have to be a marketing genius—which most authors aren't—to succeed with self-publishing.

In mulling this issue over at length, it occurred to me that I could analyze the reading behavior of readers to determine which books were performing better than others. I could identify which books were loved by the community without even reaching a viral stage. I was also able to see how many people stayed up all night to finish reading a particular book, how fast they would finish, how often they would come back to read, and more. That's when I decided to turn Inkitt into a modern, customer-centric publishing house. Our guiding principle was that if readers loved a book, we'd publish it. Since then we've raised more than 5 million dollars from investors to help realize this dream. Last year alone, we published 50 books and, of those, 46 became bestsellers in their category. Most of them ranked in the Top 50 of all 6 million books available on Amazon. One of them even ranked ahead of Harry Potter. This shows us that we are on a great path towards building the future of publishing.

At Inkitt we believe that every author deserves an equal chance to succeed, and we want to build the fairest and most objective publishing house in the world. We also want to discover hidden talents and help turn them into globally successful authors.

I'm very happy that we partnered with Bryan Thomas Schmidt, who previously applied his editorial skills to help Andy Weir publish his bestseller, The Martian, to teach you about writing. I'm confident that Bryan will not only teach you valuable lessons for all stages of the writing process but that he will also give you the motivational push you need to take on the project of completing your first novel. It is my sincere hope that this book can help you write your own bestseller so that your story can finally be told.

INTRODUCTION

You say you want to write a novel. You've got a story that just has to be told. You dream of the day you walk into your local bookstore or library and pull your own book off the shelf.

Well, writing a novel is hard work. It's a big commitment. It takes a specific knowledge of craft and a specific skill set. I'm not convinced everyone can do it, but it is indeed a worthy goal, and this book is designed as a tool to help you succeed in that task. Filled with lessons on craft, interviews with successful novelists, and more, *How to Write a Novel* aims to be a partner in your successful writing career. Whether you are a beginner or have a few books under your belt, the information you find here can be an ongoing resource for your writer's journey.

Do you have what it takes? Are you up to the challenge? There's only one way to know—by doing it. So, let's get started, shall we?

This book will cover everything from basics of craft like structure and outlining, dialogue and setting to editing and research, and lots in between. There will be sidebars by some skilled author-teachers on various topics that expand on what I'm covering as well as interviews on various topics to give you practical insight. *How to Write a Novel* is aimed at giving you everything you need to launch your career as a novelist. Whether you are successful after that is up to talent, luck, and your dedication to hard work. Successful writing is a full-time job, even though many successful novelists do it on the side of regular full-time day jobs. It's no quick path to fame and fortune, though a lucky few do achieve that. For most, the satisfaction comes from stories well told, passionate readers, and the fun journeys into character, setting, and the inner mind that all novelists take. Regardless of your outcome, this book can help you learn to write and write well, and provide tips on what to do once you're holding that finished manuscript in your hands.

So, if you've got a story to tell, the pages that follow will help you do it. The book is designed to be read the first time straight through and then serve as a future reference to revisit as needed by subject matter. It's an expansion of the *Fundamentals of Fiction* teaching videos I've done for Inkitt, and it is intended to cover the subject broadly, with some topics in depth and others more generally. Whatever your experience or interest level in professional writing, there will be material in here to interest you and help you expand your knowledge. There's also a great list of other books you may find indispensable as you launch your writing career. I wish you the best of success. After all, the only reason to write a book like *How to Write a Novel* is to encourage and help other writers, so consider us your first fans and cheerleaders. Your success is our success.

The journey begins in Chapter 1. Here's to the future novel we all look forward to reading.

CHAPTER 1
WHAT IS A NOVEL?

Definitions

A novel is the long-form fictional prose storytelling form of Western literature. Dictionary.com defines it as "a fictitious prose narrative of considerable length and complexity, portraying characters and usually presenting a sequential organization of action and scenes." Modern novels tend to run from 50,000 to 300,000 words, with an average range of 80,000 to 120,000 being most common. Length requirements depend upon factors like genre, market, audience, etc. But a novel is generally more epic and complex in scale with more characters and settings than shorter fiction forms like short story, novelette, and novella.

As I said in the introduction, writing a novel may not be for everyone. Some will find themselves more gifted at poetry or nonfiction, short form than long. Novel writing is certainly rewarding but also a major undertaking. It is not generally something one tends to do on a whim or on the fly. It requires deliberate effort, concentrated focus and thought, and complicated planning of theme, characters, and so on. But that being said, writing a novel is the dream of many, and while not all novels become hits that provide fame and fortune or even get published, there is still great satisfaction to be found in completing one, and much to learn.

It all usually starts with an idea or a character—a setting, a concept, a conflict, or some combination thereof; something that leads to questions the writer wants answers to and is willing to undertake the long journey required to discover them. In speculative fiction, we commonly refer to this as the "What If" question, but the same types of questions apply to any genre. Whatever form it takes, the result is a longing to discover and tell, a feeling that the answer or answers are important and worthy undertakings, and that sharing them with others is somehow a noble cause. Lofty goals perhaps. But artists cannot work without passion and inspiration, and so lofty or not, whether the end result lives up to the dreamed-of lofty heights or not, it all begins with a story that must be told.

Stories are complex beasts—living organisms, you might say. They are not often envisioned complete and fully realized. Most of the time, they require exploration and investigation even to uncover and reveal their details, nuances, and full depths. For some, a certain amount of planning is necessary to undertake this work. For these writers, outlines, character sketches, and much research are usually the first order of business before the writing. Others prefer working organically, allowing the story and characters to reveal themselves as they go, researching as needed, perhaps even outlining or sketching a bit when required, but mostly just opening the heart to the muse and letting the words flow. These discovery writers, or "pantsers" as some call them, feel too boxed in by such restrictions that heavy planning and organization tend to place upon them. They require the freedom and openness to see where the story leads and follow it, rather than try to define and chart its course beforehand. Both are quite valid approaches, time-tested by many, many writers before you, so fear not whatever path you choose. Regardless, both ultimately begin in the same place: the premise, which is the concept on which every novel is based. So, before anything, to create a novel, you must first devise a premise.

The Premise

In his bestselling book *How to Write a Damn Good Novel*, James N. Frey describes a premise as "the $E = mc^2$ of novel writing." The premise, he contends, "is the reason you are writing what you are writing … the core, the heart, the center, the soul of your expression." He defines it as "a statement of what happens to the characters as a result of the core conflict in a story." Agent Donald Maass defines a premise as

> any single image, moment, feeling or belief that has enough power and personal meaning for the author to set her story on fire, propel it like a rocket for hundreds of pages, or perhaps serve as a finish line: an ending so necessary that every step of the journey burns to be taken.

While you might say to yourself: *What's the big deal? A premise is an idea*—a premise is so much more than that. Ideas are common. Original ideas are almost nonexistent these days. Everything's been done. So, what makes your premise special is not the basic simple idea but the unique spin and angle you bring to it. A premise is as much in the execution and unique approach to a concept as it is the idea itself.

Again, in *How to Write a Damn Good Novel*, James N. Frey compares a novel to an argument and writes:

> The premise of an argument is a statement of the conclusion that will be reached through the argument. Each part of the argument must contribute to the premise if the argument is a good one … the premise of a work of fiction is not provable or arguable in the real world … not a universal truth. In a novel, the premise is true only for the particular situation of that novel.

3

But nonetheless it is proven by all that leads to it. Your novel's premise is the conclusion everything in your story leads to.

In his bestseller *Writing the Breakout Novel*, mega-agent Donald Maass writes of a premise: "Not just any idea, though, but one with soil rich enough to grow a highly memorable novel; one that will both feed the author's imagination, and, finally, nourish millions of readers." An idea is not enough. It must be backed up by all the details of character, setting, conflict, and theme. It's an idea with something unique and special to say, something we haven't seen, told in a way we haven't encountered that pops off the page. Maass calls it "a breakout premise," implying that truly hit, breakout novels start with something special at their core. I'm sure we'd all love to write a hit novel that breaks out. So, what is it that makes "something special"?

First, a premise should describe an experience that is unusual, one not encountered by everyone, at least not firsthand. The experience also takes place in a vivid, wholly realized world that is compelling in its details and stands apart as unique yet real and fascinating on multiple levels.

Second, a premise should involve a character or characters who are larger-than-life, who talk, think, and act in ways not everyone does or can. These types of characters have a boldness, drive, and determination to pursue journeys we only dream about and take risks and actions we only wish we had the courage to take ourselves. In the process they undergo growth and changes we admire greatly, that inspire us, embolden us, and leave us breathless with admiration.

To create such a premise takes effort. It may not arrive fully formed right off the bat. Some great premises are discovered in the course of writing and discovering a story, but all successful writers learn to identify them and cling to them with all their might when

4

they do. The best premises have the power to illuminate and confront, challenging our most deeply held beliefs, our hopes, our fears, our faith, even our very wills and nature. They engage readers' imaginations and emotions and raise questions, hopes, fears, and more that have them yearning to turn the pages, cheer for the heroes, boo the villains, and reach the inevitable climactic confrontation that sets everything right again and resolves the mystery and uncertainty it evoked when it began.

Such a premise is so much more than just boy meets girl and falls in love or boy sets out to save the world. There's something unique and special about the boy and the girl, what draws them together, where and how they come together, and why they are willing to fight for their love. The boy is someone special who believes he might actually save the world, after all. No ordinary Joe would dare undertake such a noble quest. It takes a certain level of courage, even determination, a refusal to surrender to insecurity and incredible odds, and an undeterred drive to keep going no matter what. I don't know about you, but while I have met such people, I have found them to be few and far between. And those few-and-far-between people are the heart of good, successful stories. So, your premise requires one. Character is story. Story is character. Story flows from character. There really is no chicken or the egg question here about who came first. *Who* always leads into *What*.

So, to write your novel, you first need a really good idea with premise potential. You may not devise all the pieces before you write, but you must write looking for them to fall into place, and you will certainly need a solid concept to get you started. How you come up with it is something I cannot teach. It really is between you and your muse. Singer-songwriter John Denver used to say the ideas for his songs came from the aether—just floating out there waiting to be discovered, and he was the lucky soul who connected at the right moment to find them and give them life. In some ways, this is the way stories tend to work as well. Your ideas will come from your life, people you know, places you've been or want to go, things you've done or want to do, etc., and then your imagination should take over and start working on the rest. There is a certain magic to storytelling that can be neither easily described nor taught. That's where the talent comes in. But it will take more than talent to write your novel. It will also take determination and a drive to push through the struggles and keep going no matter what. And so, the more passionate you are about your premise, the more likely you are to succeed. If nothing else, pick a premise that fires you up, not just the first seemingly viable one that comes in your head. Find the one that hooks you and won't let you go. That's where your great novel will surely come from.

Let's look at some examples Frey gives of premises from famous novels:

The Godfather by Mario Puzo (the story of the Corleone Mafia family over generations): family loyalty leads to a life of crime.

The Old Man and the Sea by Ernest Hemingway (the story of an old Cuban fisherman who struggles against a marlin far out in the Gulf Stream off the Cuban coast): courage leads to redemption.

A Christmas Carol by Charles Dickens (the story of a miserable, cheap, bitter man who is visited by ghosts of past, present, and future and learns the meaning of Christmas): forced self-examination leads to generosity.

One Flew Over the Cuckoo's Nest by Ken Kesey (the story of patients oppressed at a mental hospital): even the most determined and ruthless psychiatric establishment can't crush the human spirit.

In effect, a premise is like an argument. A story can have only one premise, because you cannot prove two arguments well at once. Your story's conclusion will have a cause-and-effect relationship with what came before. In most cases, the argument within the premise is about a dilemma the characters confront. If you start first with characters and think about your premise, you may come up with it as you consider the characters' flaws and the obstacles they face, as well as their goals and needs. Frey writes: "There is no formula for finding a premise. You simply start with a character or situation, give the character a dilemma, and then meditate on how it might go." By opening your imagination and letting it run, usually the possibilities are endless, and your premise will come to light in the process. Frey quotes Egri as saying: "Every good premise should contain an element of character which through conflict leads to a conclusion." So in essence, what are your three Cs (Character, Conflict, Conclusion)? Identify them and you have your premise. Since the story of characters changing because of dramatic conflict makes good fiction, your premise will define such a situation. Old high school friends meet after 20 years and fall in love despite her terminal illness. The coach of a small-town basketball team with a history of losses recruits the first black player to help lead the team to a championship. A tough technophobic cop must team with an android partner to solve his partner's murder. Can you see the three Cs at work in all these examples?

A good premise will give your novel focus and power that carries readers through to the end. It will hold their attention. Keep them turning pages. Make them long to know what happens next. And it may well do the same for you as you write. In fact, it should, even for the dedicated outliners. Everything in good fiction propels and leads you to the conclusion of the story, which is also a decisive conclusion or answer to the argument of the premise. Anything else should be cut and dropped. So a well-conceived premise is inherent to a well-written novel and key to your success. You must know where you are going to successfully complete any journey. The premise is the target on the map of your storytelling journey. Start without it at your own peril.

The concept, idea, or premise is a start. Craft and work will do the rest. Before we move on, let's take a look at *theme*, which is closely tied to premise and key to good story structure.

Theme

"If a powerful problem is a novel's spine," Donald Maass writes in *The Breakout Novel*, "then a powerful theme is its animating spirit ... It starts with you having something to say." Theme is one of those topics that makes many people's eyes glaze over. They think of the theme papers they hated writing in school, perhaps. Or find it abstract and hard to conceive. But theme can and should form the unifying narrative structure of your well-written novel. What is theme? Theme is what a story, at its heart, at its moral core, is really trying to say, what it's about. It's why you are telling the story. It is what you have to say. Theme, in essence, is not the argument, but the moral derived from it. It is the lesson(s) and life truth(s) embedded and demonstrated through your story.

In *Theme and Strategy*, Ronald B. Tobias defines theme as "the *central concern* around which a story is structured." He writes, "Theme is your inertial guidance system. It directs your decisions about which path to take, which choice is right for the story and which isn't." In essence, theme is what unifies the whole and informs it beyond just a story about a guy or girl who did so-and-so into something memorable with lasting impact that speaks to the human condition. Choosing the right theme will help you unify your story. It isn't something you should just wing or make up as you go, but something you should think about early on, even as you plan your story, and keep in your mind with every scene you write.

Maass suggests three facts to keep in mind:

1. All stories are moral.
2. Readers tend to seek out stories that are in line with their beliefs.
3. Fiction is most compelling when it pulls readers into points of view that are compelling, detailed, and different.

Readers crave insight on the world around them. They want to be pushed to expand their minds and see things differently, through different eyes. Readers become most engaged when the characters' beliefs capture their attention and make them think. Whether you know it or not, you have something to say, and having the courage to say it through your story and characters will imbue your novel with power that makes it memorable and lasting. Deep down, all writers believe they have something that must be said, some insight on the human condition the world cannot do without, and these demonstrate their own morality and views of right and wrong in the universe. Ask yourself what that is, and let your story speak to that. Have it in mind as you write. This will create a unified story with resonance far beyond just entertainment. As Maass writes, "stories without fire cannot fire readers."

Because readers are moral people, they inherently look for the moral compass that drives characters in fiction. Whether they agree with it or not is not the primary concern—understanding it is. Powerful beliefs and messages imparted through characters are far more effective than writers preaching or teaching directly, because characters who have beliefs that drive them will take concrete actions that reflect those beliefs. The consequences of these actions then speak powerfully about life, people, and more in ways that direct lessons can never accomplish. The key is embedding these morals and beliefs in the characters' actions. When characters live what they believe, readers will accept the validity of those beliefs and be impacted by the results.

Tobias suggests several major patterns, which can be summarized as follows:

Plot as Theme—Much of popular fiction is driven by this theme, in which plot is paramount over any other concerns. Escapism is the goal here, and as such, while the novels may not carry long-lasting moral messages, they earn big points with readers and generate bestseller after bestseller. They are not striving for great literature but rather great entertainment, and this has made them hugely successful. Agatha Christie, George Lucas, Steven Spielberg, Dan Brown, John Grisham, and many more create works that fall readily into this category.

Emotional Effect as Theme—Terror, Suspense, Romance, Comedy—in this case the emotional effect of the story is the driving theme. Works by authors such as Stephen King, Peter Straub, Gini Koch, Christopher Moore, John Grisham, Heather Graham, Nora Roberts, Nicholas Sparks, and more deal with this theme.

Style as Theme—This theme encompasses a small minority of movies and books because the theme is the artistic style and approach rather than other concerns. The art films and literary novels by auteurs such as John Hawkes, Ingmar Bergman, Federico Fellini, Margaret Atwood, and more have this focus.

Character as Theme—Character studies, like style-themed art, also lend themselves to literary concerns. The focus here is the characters, their growth, and how the world and events of the story affect them. Mark Twain's *The Adventures of Huckleberry Finn*, Charles Dickens's *David Copperfield*, Gustave Flaubert's *Madam Bovary*, and films like *Raging Bull*, *The Great Santini*, *Taxi Driver*, and *The Godfather* embody this approach.

Idea as Theme—Of all the patterns, this one is most successful at creating memorable events and characters that jump off the page. Idea-themed works affect us profoundly, change the world, change lives, start wars, or at the least, make us think because the whole point of ideas is to make us ponder them, ask questions, discuss, and draw new conclusions. These are often the books whose themes are erased during conversion to movies, leaving us to complain that "the book was better." Idea as theme is less cinematic, less exciting, but its power cannot be denied. Examples include *Robinson Crusoe*, *Don Quixote*, *The Graduate*, and *Shane*.

Moral Statement as Theme—The most dangerous of theme categories, this one is most likely to become preachy and heavy handed and turn readers off, so it must be used with great care and attempted only by skillful hands. If the characters are sincere and the plot gripping and storytelling is your focus, though, you can pull this off. According to Tobias, *Fatal Attraction* and *Wall Street* are two examples of films that fall in this category. In both cases, the moral results from the story rather than the other way around.

Human Dignity as Theme—These are the stories where the fight to hold on to dignity in spite of circumstances is the focus. Stories like *One Flew Over the Cuckoo's Nest*, *Rocky*, *On the Waterfront*, *Gladiator*, and even *Roots* employ this type of theme.

Social Comment as Theme—Criticizing or shining a light on our culture can be accomplished with great power using fiction. The trick here is finding the right story. Great examples are *The China Syndrome* and *The Grapes of Wrath*. The key is to let the characters' convictions argue for you.

Human Nature as Theme—"What is Man?" is a question that has been explored for centuries and still captures readers' interest. Stories that fit here include *Deliverance*, *Lord of the Flies*, and *Robinson Crusoe*. (Note: Stories can combine more than one theme. More on that later.)

Human Relations as Theme—Terms of Endearment, Ordinary People, Love Story, many a Nicholas Sparks book like The Notebook or The Wedding, and more all explore this theme where the relation of humans in community, small or large, is the focus.

Coming of Age as Theme—This one I know a lot about as it has been the theme of six of my novels and several short stories to date. The exploration of finding one's self and confidently staking one's place or recognizing one's role and purpose in the universe is a theme found in Star Wars, Rocky, Harry Potter, The Hunger Games, Ender's Game, and many, many more.

Once you know your theme or themes, you must then decide several things:

1. Who are the characters who can best embody this theme?
2. What plot is best suited for the theme?
3. What kind of setting will best fit the characters and actions necessary to portray the theme?
4. What voice and style is best suited to the theme?

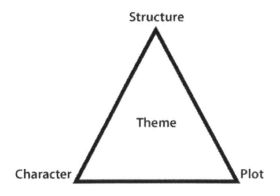

Figure 1-1 All together, structurally, Theme works with Plot and Character as shown in this diagram.

Your theme informs all these decisions, which is why knowing the theme first is so important. As the diagram in Figure 1-1 demonstrates, theme is at the center of the core elements of your story's structure. Additionally, many stories explore more than one theme. If the themes are compatible, this is a very powerful and easy thing to do. As moral people, readers will turn to fiction for affirmation of their values or the values that underpin the world as they see it. They seek deeper understanding, answers to questions, and more in great stories, driven by the desire to know that what they believe is right. Maass suggests it matters less whether the moral is widely accepted than that it is developed in depth. "The key is your antagonist," he writes. "If we believe in him, we will believe what he believes." We buy into *Star Wars* because Luke Skywalker believes so passionately in his cause—the Force, the right of the Rebels over the Empire, good versus evil, and what is just. The same can be said of *Rocky* and many other films, even *The Godfather*, wherein the protagonist is a criminal corrupted by his world and relationships over the course of the film. The viewer's agreement with the decisions being made is less important than the conviction of the character. It is in the

14

character's anger, weeping, fear, and determination that we are inspired to believe, that readers feel it is imperative to know their stories. This is how knowing your theme and developing every scene from that perspective can transform a simple, ordinary story into a life-changing, memorable classic.

So, whether you are a planner or a pantser, outliner or discovery writer, thinking about theme and allowing it to inform your writing will make the difference between your novel being plain or something special, blending in or standing out from the pack. Theme is that vital, that key. And so, as you move forward to plan your premise and the structure that will best bring it to life, theme is an important component of your process which must be considered and carefully weighed.

Once you have the premise and theme, the next step is to come up with a plan or structure to help undergird the concept—a set of guideposts to lead you on the journey. That's what Chapter 2 is all about.

CHAPTER 2
OUTLINING AND DRAMATIC STRUCTURE

Before you write your novel, it is vital to understand the dramatic structure of Western storytelling. There are several structures many will use, but the two most common are three-act and four-act structures. We will look at a few others in a sidebar, but we'll focus on these two here. While pantsers prefer organic writing, and outliners work in more detail, for both, identifying the story's dramatic structure is essential, and outlining structure is not the same as outlining a novel, which we will talk about later in the chapter. So, let's look at what I mean by structural outlines, starting with the three-act structure, probably the most commonly used dramatic structure in Western storytelling.

Three-Act Structure

A sketch that will inform your outline, the three-act structure nonetheless identifies the core dramatic points of a story. Some of you may be discovery writers like me, preferring to let the story unfold organically. But at some point, you will be required to outline as a professional writer. And when faced with a tight deadline, the more organized you are, the more efficient you can be. The first thing you need to do is understand the dramatic structure that underpins your story. So we are going to talk about a very simple, basic way to identify key points that can help you write more quickly and efficiently to meet a deadline.

While outlines are multiple pages of detail, the structural diagram will be no more than a brief paragraph or a few sentences describing each required point accompanied perhaps by a paradigm sketch. The paradigm shown in Figure 2-1 is based on *Screenplay* by Syd Field, a classic writing teaching book employed by many film schools, but in Western literature, the principles also apply to any dramatic story, including those told in prose. The outline is for three acts. In a screenplay, those are act one, which is 30 pages, or a quarter of the text; act two, which is 60 pages, or half; and act three, which is 30 pages, or a fourth. Your page numbers will vary, but the fractions for each portion should wind up roughly the same.

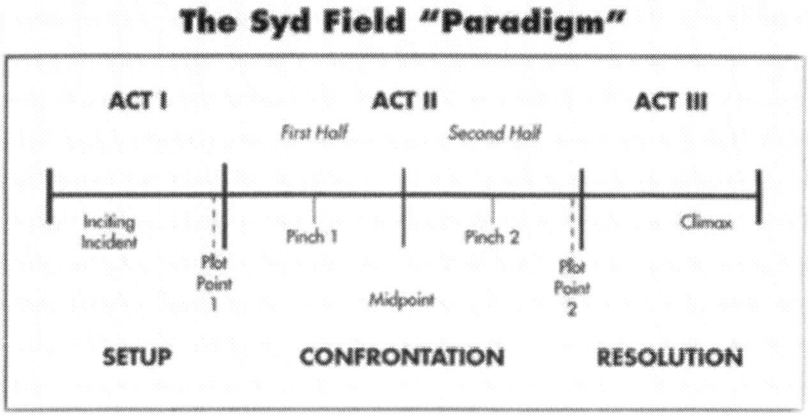

The Syd Field "Paradigm"

Figure 2-1

The key turning points between acts are called plot point 1 and plot point 2. These are events which force the protagonist, and sometimes the antagonist too, to turn in new directions and take new action in pursuit of resolving the conflict. Plot point 1, at the end of act one, will require agency, or action, from the protagonist in pursuit of finding the solution and determining what must be done. Plot point 1 propels the protagonist into act two, which is an ascending action involving discovery and a journey to find the solution and achieve the goal without yet knowing all that is required. In the course of act two, the questions will be answered until you reach plot point 2. Plot point 2, at the end of act two, will occur when the protagonist discovers what must be done and where, and with whom, to resolve the conflict and achieve the goal. And thus, it propels him or her into act two, which is the climactic, descending action to reach that point.

When I write any story, I always start with some idea of what my plot points will be and how it will end, to give me a sense of focus and direction as I write, even when allowing it to unfold organically. Now, just as the overall story has three acts, so will each plot and subplot, and each act. As such, each has a mini turning point called the midpoint or pinch that twists the action a bit and propels us into the second half. In the first act, this is called the inciting incident. This inciting incident often provokes a change in the protagonist's routine—something new they experience that could either challenge or encourage them. In *The Silence of the Lambs* (1991), FBI trainee Clarice Starling (Jodie Foster) meets with Dr. Hannibal "the Cannibal" Lecter (Anthony Hopkins). The confrontation of both parties is nerve-wracking. But it intrigues us and sucks in Clarice and leads to the rest of the story. Other examples are Indiana losing the golden idol to Belloq at the opening of *Raiders of the Lost Ark*, which then sets up a rivalry that drives the later journey as Indiana Jones seeks to get the Ark before Belloq. Morpheus choosing Anderson in *The Matrix* sets up all that follows after. In *The Sixth Sense*, without the opening confrontation and gunshot, nothing else that follows could occur.

In act two, you have a pinch point for each half, and in act three, you have the climactic confrontation before the denouement. These may not be as dramatic as the inciting incident of act one, but they nonetheless inspire the protagonist or antagonist to take further action and move forward on the journey. Whereas the plot points are both major dramatic developments, the inciting incident, midpoint, and pinches can be more internal than external but of significance to the characters' hearts and minds such that they cause them to change course and move in a new direction or with renewed vigor toward the goal. These are like lesser plot points, in a way, but nonetheless significant points in the framework of the overall dramatic arc that drives your story.

Let's talk examples. In *Star Wars: A New Hope*, the inciting incident starts with Darth Vader's ship attacking Princess Leia's rebel ship and forcing her to load the Death Star plans into R2-D2, the droid, and send him to escape. He lands on the planet with his companion, C-3PO, and they wind up in the hands of the hero, Luke Skywalker. When Luke discovers a message from a princess that reports danger and points him to a mysterious figure named Obi-Wan Kenobi, he sets off to find out what it means, and that leads him to Old Ben Kenobi, whose shared surname is an obvious clue. Kenobi rescues Luke from Sand People at the midpoint of act one and takes him back to his own home. There, they view the message and Kenobi gives Luke a lightsaber and tells him about the murder of his father, a story Luke never knew. The Empire and a Rebellion, which until now have been mostly rumors far away, have entered Luke's life, and when Kenobi takes him home, they find that the Jawas who sold Luke's family the droids have been murdered and torched. Fearing the worst, they race to Luke's home and find Luke's aunt and uncle have been murdered and their homestead torched. Plot point 1 is when Kenobi tells Luke they must go rescue the princess together and find a way to deliver the plans hidden in R2-D2.

Act two starts with their trip to Mos Eisley spaceport where they must find passage, and they end up recruiting Han Solo, evading Stormtroopers searching for the droids, and head off for Alderaan. Then, we see Luke in training for the inevitable confrontation, while Vader and Tarkin attempt to extract information from Leia, and ultimately destroy Alderaan. Luke, Han, and Kenobi's discovery of this is our pinch point for act one. That determines they must rescue Leia themselves and deliver the plans. Then they are caught in a tractor beam and pulled aboard the Death Star. The midpoint comes during the attempted rescue in the Detention Block when they are trapped. The pinch point for act two is when Kenobi confronts Vader to help his friends escape with the droids to the rebellion. Plot point 2 is after they fight their way clear and escape to the rebel base, where the plans reveal the Death Star's flaw. The Rebels unveiling their attack plan propels us into act three. Act three is the Rebel attack and the Imperial counterattack, and the climax comes as Luke faces off against Vader in the trench run and ultimately destroys the Death Star with surprise help from Han.

So, now that we have seen how this plays out in a story we are all familiar with, it's time to identify this structure for your story. Keep in mind that this is only a blueprint. Plans can change. As the story evolves, if required, your plot points, as well as pinches and midpoints, and even your climax, may change. The point of this is not to set anything in stone but to have goals to guide your work. It will help direct you as you write and set up each character and point required to reach each marker. If that ultimately requires the markers to change, it's okay because these are tools to help you achieve a whole.

Here are the things you'll need to know to develop this paradigm outline.

- Who is your protagonist?
- Who is your antagonist?
- What are their goals?
- What are the obstacles each faces in reaching that goal?
- What growth must each undergo to make success possible?
- And finally, what do you think the final confrontation needs to be?

Answering these questions is just a temporary means to an end. The answers may change, but the idea is to think through key elements of your story to allow you to write with blinders off and have some goal points along the way to work toward. That will allow you to write faster and spend less time wondering what the heck you should do next. As you actually write, these goal points may need to change, and that is okay.

Four-Act Structure

The four-act structure is a more recent rethinking of three-act structure. Proponents claim it is much better and more effective because it more naturally follows the flow of dramatic story. I certainly agree that for motion pictures this is probably the case, but I am not sure about novels. Regardless, the rule in writing is to use what works for you, so I present it here as an option that might be more helpful to some of you than the three-act structure.

Four Act Structure

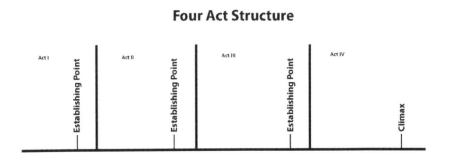

Figure 2-2

Fundamentally, the difference between the three-act and four-act structures is that act two is now two acts, with each ending in a plot point or establishing point. Act one ends with an establishing point where the hero has a life-changing event that spurs him or her to action, essentially enabling circumstances that lead the hero to launch into the quest or journey that makes up the rest of the story and results inevitably in a confrontation with the antagonist in act one. In act one, there is no midpoint but instead an establishing point that generally consists of a hero-ally confrontation in which the hero is forced to give up his or her flaw. Act two becomes about establishing a relationship with the ally while the hero tries to hold onto his or her flaw and still complete

22

the quest. The establishing point here reveals that the flaw is an obstacle which must be overcome to achieve success.

After that establishing point, instead of a second half, we enter act three, which ends with an establishing point where the flaw is finally resolved, and the hero enters the ring against the opponent in preparation for act four's final confrontation. Act three thus consists of the hero demonstrating the growth of overcoming the flaw or at least conquering and controlling it as he or she prepares with the ally to take on the antagonist. Act four is the climbing into the ring where the hero faces his or her opponent to see who will triumph.

In theory, using four acts makes writing the longer middle easier for writers by breaking it into two logical halves. It also puts more emphasis on a hero-ally confrontation where the flaw is confronted and overcoming begins. This can be a physical or emotional confrontation, but it is a key turning point that functions much like the midpoint in the three-act structure. This often serves to strengthen the relationship between the hero and his or her key ally.

A great example of this four-act structure can be found in the film *Rocky*, which is considered one of the best-structured films of all time. In act one, Rocky is on the mean streets of Philly and considers himself a loser, but is a nice, bright guy who won't even stoop to breaking legs for work with loan sharks or other things. Then he gets the chance to fight for heavyweight champion of the world, his establishing point or life-changing event.

In act two, Rocky tries to react to this challenge but is dragged down by his lack of self-confidence. Allies come in the form of his wife, Adrian, and manager, Mickey, who push him to believe in himself, but he can't do it until he finally confronts the memory of his father telling him he was too ugly and stupid to be anything but a boxer, so he'd better be good. Once he articulates and faces this, he regains a sense of purpose and confidence in an establishing point wherein he determines to prove his father wrong.

Act three is then the training surge when Rocky prepares for the fight with Apollo Creed and begins to think of himself as capable and strong and smart, not a loser, mentally changing and transforming into being ready for the fight.

Act four is the final fight against Creed.

As you can see here, the four-act structure depends more on character development for its turning points than the three-act structure does and really defines and clarifies the characters in a different way, which may be helpful to some of you in structuring your story and thinking it through before writing.

Before moving on to outlining, let's take a look at a few more structural approaches outlined in the Sidebar by my friend and bestselling author—editor Peter J. Wacks.

———————————————

SIDEBAR: OTHER STRUCTURES by Peter J. Wacks

When approaching plotting, it helps to understand not only the overall structure of the acts, but also how the story moves through those acts. Cognitive studies performed by both McCombs and Stanford have shown that learning curve is directly related to plot structure, and the brain connects the stories we read to our own experiences. It draws those connections through certain key elements like:

- Is the story (or lesson) "interesting"?
- Is the story easily understood?
- Is the story easily remembered?

At the heart of each of those elements is structure. How does structure work? Beyond looking at the three-act structure—most commonly organized as setup, confrontation, resolution—there are pinches, subplots, character arcs, reversals, and several other elements that can be used by storytellers to weave a story.

The methodology used to organize the movement of the story and various tools being used is often referred to as a plot structure rather than an act structure. While the acts make a story easily remembered and understood, the plot structure will help it be understood and interesting. Here is a list of three basic types of plot structures used to move stories through their acts, organized by historical period:

- **Classical:** Classical plots have been around for millennia and helped build the first genres.
- **Modern:** Modern plots are a wave of new structures implemented since the invention of the printing press.
- **Post-modern:** Post-modern are more recent (the last century or so) innovations in structure, which still stand apart and are uncommon.

The following structures help organize stories into shapes that can be visualized and will help give you—the storyteller—more tools to work with in your "how to organize my outline" toolbox.

Classical Plot Structures

There are four classical plot structures, and they have been around since Aristotle's 335 BC bestseller *Poetics*. We can see them in the plays of Aristophanes and thousands of pieces of literature since then.

25

The first is the dramatic, or progressive, plot. This is a chronological plot that moves characters through the story based upon time. The structure is to:

1. Establish setting
2. Rapidly introduce a conflict
3. Follow the characters through rising action
4. End in a climax that resolves the conflicts
5. A denouement (basically, tying off any loose ends)

The second structure is a mutation of the first, called the Mountain (you can also find these by looking up Freytag's Pyramid), which utilizes a rapid series of reversals to build increasing tension as follows:

1. Reveal the story elements
2. Introduce a complication
3. Provide a resolution of part of the conflict, which allows the story to move back to element 2 or forward to element 4
4. Resolve the conflicts with a climax
5. Denouement

The third structure is the Hero's Journey, most commonly found in myths and epics. It is the foundation for the more widely known *The Hero with a Thousand Faces'* interpretation by Joseph Campbell of the Monomythic Hero's Journey. It unfolds as follows:

1. Call to adventure
2. The journey (and the test)
3. The supreme ordeal
4. The reward
5. The return home and denouement

See a pattern here? Don't worry, not all stories are broken into five elements. Patterns repeat because that simple structure helps connect the story to the reader.

The final of the classical structures is the episodic plot. In modern storytelling, this is most commonly used in television. Rather than a five-point progression, the episodic plot is a simple progression of reversals that allow the story to reach a climax. Most notably, this plot is considered to most closely match real life and rarely has a denouement.

Modern Plot Structures

Throughout the centuries, storytellers have polished and honed the craft of making stories interesting. The most common post-classical plots are looping plots, segmenting plots, overlapping plots, backwards momentum plots, and flashback plots. Though some of these are centuries old, they are still new enough to have many names. The names chosen for these were selected for motion implied (remember, a plot moves!).

- **Looping (nodal) plots** are defined by reversals, as are many movements in classical plots, but then by repetitions. Each loop reveals a larger story until the climax, which reveals that the story was apparent in the first loop all along. A looping plot does not use a denouement, but rather ends immediately after the climax.
- **Segmented plots** rely on hooks and turns, told out of order. By connecting the hooks through a series of discovery moments and reversals, the climax is approached by resolving "confusion of audience" until a denouement, which confirms and clarifies all hooks and turns.
- **Overlapping (modulated) plots** show a story that is never told. By weaving a plot as a series of subplots and background points in surrounding perspectives, an invisible story is told. Each story is often a complete story, yet the entire plot is not revealed until all overlaps are complete.
- **Backwards momentum plots** (a form of open plot) begin with a resolution and move backwards through a story. The

27

resolution (or denouement) builds a complex picture that leaves the reader wondering how the story could have possibly ended there. As the plot moves backwards, each movement ties off another question, setting right a reversal, until the entire originating conflict is revealed and tied back to the resolution, revealing one final piece of information in a second climax.

- **Flashback plots** are generally a frame built around a second structure (usually a progressive plot) and are exactly what they sound like. In a glimpse of the future, characters will look to the past and remember the events of the story. A quick side note: subplots can be structured within other plots, and frequently are. Superstructures and substructures can complement or clash, so be careful as you build!

Post-Modern Plot Structures

This series of plots is a combination of very recent techniques extracted from writers like Joss Whedon, Dan Harmon, and others, combined with the series I created to devise the true nonlinear plot.

- **Gravity-pull plots** create separate character and story arcs that can be structured with any plotting techniques. Each arc ends with a reversal, leaving a question of how the arc will resolve. Unlike the overlapping plot, these arcs do not create a separate story, but rather each leads to the same resolution, even though they appeared unconnected at first.
- **Spiderweb plots** are an evolution of the gravity-pull structure. Spiderwebs follow character actions and interactions, connecting them in a similar fashion to a web. Often, they will treat the rising action and reversals as a discovery mechanism. By focusing on the interactions, it is only through time in the story that the true plot (and resolution) can be revealed.
- **Ghost plotting** is a spiderweb in which the characters are not pulled toward a central resolution. Ghost plots allow a greater scope of nonlinear interactions to drive characters

28

through active and reactive arcs without making every decision plot oriented.

- **Tesseracting plots** get a little "mathy" and are by far the most complex form of visual plotting. Only a small percentage of storytellers will get this one initially. If you are unfamiliar with charting, Google "X, Y, Z Axis." This plot charts motion through setting against character actions as X and Y axes, while using the story to push back on the characters and setting as the Z axis. This will create a spiral. Time forms a line to move the story between the three axes. Any time the line intersects the spiral, write a scene, finishing with the climax in which all motivations have been resolved.

Some of these will have spoken to you, some will not. While these are not all of the structures out there (not by a long shot), they are some of the more common, and a few of the more clever. Whichever you use, keep them all in your toolbox and use them as the useful story builders they are. Always remember that the real goal is to develop your own tools so that you can always answer yes to:

- Is the story "interesting"?
- Is the story easily understood?
- Is the story easily remembered?

Good luck and happy writing!

PETER J. WACKS is a cross-genre writer and world traveler. In his spare time, he enjoys Scotch, beer, swords, magic, and absurdist philosophy. Over the course of his life, he has worked across the creative fields and in the pursuit of character research has done side jobs ranging from IT break-fix to private detective. You can find him online on both Twitter and Facebook, where he occasionally pops in to crack jokes about the state of the world. Or if you just want to stalk him a little, you can go to www.peterjwacks.net.

Outlining

Numerous blog posts, books, and more have been written on outlining, and what your outline looks like depends on who it's for, what it's for, and other factors. So, I'm only going to cover outlining generally here. When we talk about outlining, I am not talking about plotting, but conceptualizing. While knowledge of plot, characters, and setting helps your outline, in many cases, the bulk of plotting will be done after the outline as you write. Instead, you just need to know a few basics about plots and subplots to outline, because the goal is to get an overview conception of your novel—create a conceptual guide, if you will. Chapter 3 will cover plotting in detail, but this is about outlining—part of your prewriting, planning phase.

Different writers approach outlining differently, sometimes varying it for each book. If you sell a book on speculation, sending a 50-page sample of the unwritten book to a publisher, you will have to outline the whole book as part of that pitch. Generally, publishers want beat-by-beat scene summaries minus dialogue and flowery setting descriptions. These outlines can be anywhere from 15 to 35 pages or more. But the outline you use for your book may be simpler or more complex. You may want, for example, to write some partial scenes as they come to you, including dialogue and descriptions and action. You may want to note key dialogue without writing a full scene as you describe the main action. You may include character lists for each scene, notes on which plot or subplot the scenes line up with, etc. You may include character sketches and prehistories, scene sketches and prehistories, and more. All of this depends on how much you depend on your outline to write.

The idea of an outline is to block out the key moments, dramatic beats, and characters of your story along its timeline so that you can sit down and write it with a solid plan in place. Like anything else, outlines are fluid. They can be expanded or revised as required in the course of writing, even when submitted to a publisher. The idea is to demonstrate you have a plan, to establish a clear sense of what your story will be—either for yourself or for the publisher—not to lock everything in stone before you write. Some outlines are very sparse. For example, as a pantser, I only outline a few scenes ahead, and usually mostly in my sequels. I write a *TV Guide*–style one- or two-sentence description of a few scenes ahead of where I am and which characters they need to include, and I usually designate the plots represented by letters: A, B, C, etc. This helps me keep in my mind where the story is going generally, how often I am using the key characters to be sure none disappear for long stretches, and balance the plot lines so I keep them all flowing and running throughout just like the key characters. I keep a lot of notes in my head, but if key dialogue or settings seem important, I may also note them on my outline. These outlines are usually a page, maybe two, of five to fifteen scenes ahead, sometimes divided by chapter. Many, many times I will change the order of scenes or revise the character list or setting as the story develops. But having bare-bones sketches helps me, particularly when writing sequels to novels I already pantsed.

I am not here to advocate for any particular approach. Your outline, again, needs to suit the needs of its purpose: to guide you or reassure your publisher. The exception is when writing media tie-ins where every beat of the story must be approved by the movie studio executives before you write the book. In that case, outlines are pretty locked. But fleshing out will always occur in the writing. You just have to be prepared for the possibility they will reject anything they didn't approve in advance or ask for big changes and rewrites. Most of the time, your outline is just for you, so make it what you need to write the best book you can. No one else has to see it or use it, so it can be as organized, sloppy, or chaotic as you choose.

The next figures (Figures 2-3 and 2-4) are sample pages from two different outline forms for an actual novel by my friend Jonathan Maberry, a *New York Times* bestselling author. He's had 28 novels published to date, numerous comics, some nonfiction, hundreds of short stories, and more. And these are three approaches he uses in outlining to give you examples. Again, these are just examples. Make them your own as needed, but they serve to give you an idea of what we are talking about.

OUTLINE FORMAT 2/ Novel with many short chapters

Prologue: 1- The Extinction Clock
             2- They're Coming

PART 1: HUNTERS
1. NSA fronts Joe at cemetery
2. Joe at Helen's grave; Joe tells Church about NSA; Church tells him of VP plan
3. Intro of Cyrus and Otto/the Deck/Dodo meat
4. VP and JP Sunderland at the White House
5. Joe beats the crap out of NSA; flees
6. The Jakoby Twins
7. Sickle Cell outbreak in Benin
8. Joe uses PK to elude NSA
9. Cyrus and Otto talk about Denver; extinct animals
10. Joe ruminates on danger and his anger at NSA
11. Outbreak of communicable Tay Sachs in Louisiana
12. Joe on phone with Rudy; Joe's dream
13. Echo Team is ambushed in Wilmington; Big Bob is shot
14. Panjay and Smithwick tell Dr. Hlesak at WHO about plague; she calls Otto
15. Joe at Druid Hill Park; talks with Church
16. Church calls Linden Brierly
17. Otto and Cyrus: the production floor
18. Paris on phone with Sunderland
19. Joe at Druid Hill Park; talks with Grace
20. Grace and the NSA in a stand-off
21. Sunderland and VP
22. Rudy picks up Joe at Druid Hill Park; they drive to jet pickup
23. Hester Nichols; the MacNeil-Gunderson bottling plant in Asheville, NC
24. N'Tabo and the ape men in Somalia
25. Joe on jet; talks with Hu re: cryptozoology
26. Computer Virus at the CDC part 1
27. Cyrus and the Twins
28. Joe –the unicorn video

Etc.

Figure 2-3

This outline, as you can see, is basically short chapter descriptions with a layout of the novel's structure. It doesn't tell us much about the novel itself, but it is a guideline for how the story will flow that will trigger things in the author's mind as he writes. It is almost barely more than a table of contents might include, but sometimes this may be all you want or need.

Ghost Road Blues by Jonathan Maberry / Outline

GHOST ROAD BLUES

By Jonathan Maberry

CHAPTER OUTLINE / First Draft

PROLOGUE -1976

1. The Bone Man killed the devil with a guitar.
2. Bone Man buries Griswold; is blamed and lynched
3. John Guthrie buries Morse; season ends

MODERN DAY

PART I: DOWN AT THE CROSSROADS

1. September 30 -Morning
   a. Guthrie Farm - Val working; Crow & Val smooching
   b. Terry waking up after bad dream; puts on his Mayor face.
   c. Crow driving; Pine Deep wakes up.
   d. Breakfast with Vic, Lois and Mike
   e. Tow-Truck Eddie listening to God
   f. Crow stops at Hayride to do some repairs; as he works he keeps humming *Black Ghost Blues.*
2. September 30 -Sunset
   a. That was the year the monsters came to town
   b. Morse rises; Ruger's car passes
   c. Ruger & co in car
3. September 30
   a. Ferro & LaMastra at shoot-out scene
   b. Vic naps -has dream
   c. Ruger's accident; Griswold's ghost
4. Just past sunset
   a. Griswold & the Bone Man
   b. Crow at his store with Terry
   c. Ruger & Co after the crash
   d. Tony after the shooting

5. Just past sunset; around 8
   a. Crow & Val on the phone
   b. Terry walking through town toward sheriff's office; Mandy's ghost appears
   c. Iron Mike Sweeney
   d. Terry at sheriff's office; meets Ferro & LaMastra

Figure 2-4

This outline is broken out by timeline with descriptions of chapters and the scenes that make it up. Again, these are very sparse descriptions that trigger key memories for the author as he writes—nothing long and detailed. Some outlines may follow this pattern but have paragraph or multiparagraph descriptions of the scenes or chapters. Some may have key scenes partially sketched out or just have sample dialogue and description or action. Some may have research notes with scenes, etc. Basically, you can do what works for you in making an outline. The outline is a tool, like the paradigm. Its purpose is to aid writing, not to get in the way or slow you down or in any way create an obstacle. Outlines should include what you feel you need to write your story well and nothing more.

A reminder: outlining is not for everyone. In no way is it required. It is merely one tool of many in some authors' arsenals. Unless you are required to write one by circumstances, you may never plan your novel in this much detail, letting it unfold as it goes like an organic pantser. That's fine. Whatever works for you. It is included here because many writers find it very helpful, and I want to provide you with as many tools and options as I can to help you write your novels successfully. That is the focus of everything in this book: not to tell you what to do and lay out requirements but to provide you the tools you need and can choose in order to write in the way that works best for you and makes you most comfortable and successful.

In his book *Million Dollar Outlines, New York Times* bestselling author David Farland identifies the following things you need to know to successfully outline your novel:

1. **Lock Down Your Settings:** Settings determine economic and social status, education levels, and history of characters and thus are necessary before creating characters.

2. **Identify Your Main Characters**: Everyone the story is about, and anyone you will follow through the story.

3. **Identify Your Main Conflicts:** Between whom and whom are the conflicts that drive the main plot arc of the story?

4. **Identify Conflicts for Each of Your Characters:** All good novels are filled with many conflicts and many plots and subplots. Each of these has conflicts of its own, as do the characters. Identify them before you begin.

5. **Embellish on the Conflicts by Brainstorming How Your Characters Will Try to Resolve Them:** What's the worst that can happen? What are the possibilities? We'll discuss this more in the next chapter on plot and scene structure.

6. **Merging Characters onto a Plot Chart:** Doing this shows where the various characters and their conflicts will intersect and also ensures you do not have long stretches where your characters seem to have little going on. Then you can adjust to keep the tension and pace flowing well. We'll look at plot charts in the next chapter as well.

Once you have your dramatic structure and outline in place, you are ready to move on to the writing phase. But in order to make an outline, part of your process will involve plotting. So, Chapter 3 will examine plotting—what it is and what some ways to approach it effectively are.

CHAPTER 3
PLOT AND SCENE STRUCTURE

People do not give it credence that a fourteen-year-old girl could leave home and go off in the wintertime to avenge her father's blood, but it did not seem so strange then, although I will say it did not happen every day. I was just fourteen years of age when a coward going by the name of Tom Chaney shot my father down in Fort Smith, Arkansas, and robbed him of his life and his horse and $150 in cash money plus two California gold pieces that he carried in his trouser band.

— Charles Portis, *True Grit*

What Is Plot?

If only it was always so easy to sum up one's plot in the first paragraph as Charles Portis does here. Usually, it's not quite so simple. In her book *Plot*, Ansen Dibell writes: "The common definition of plot is that it's whatever happens in a story... Plot is built of significant events in a given story—significant because they have important consequences." That's as good a definition as any for the next element you need as you write your novel. Whether you outline, use the paradigm, or just wing it, plotting will consume a lot of your thoughts and time as you create. Plot is different from incidents. Incidents have less weight. Per Dibell, for example, a scene with a girl washing her long hair seems mundane and meaningless, unless that girl is Rapunzel and the hair is the long tresses she's going to use to escape from the tower. That's when the scene becomes about something significant. And scenes are the building blocks of plot. Every scene should flow into and out of another scene, raising the stakes, building the tension and pressure as you go. Without significance, scenes become just mildly diverting incidents with no gravitas. They don't matter much. And in dramatic storytelling, everything must matter.

An oft-heard tip of experienced writers is "show, don't tell." This little three-word phrase is thrown about so much it is almost a cliché, and the problem is, it is not often readily explained, so it is easy to blow off. The truth is that showing is exactly what scenes are: demonstrating dramatically your ideas with something happening, someone talking and doing, that has conflict, tension, and asks questions we want to follow through scene after scene to a conclusion. Dibell defines scenes as

> one connected and sequential action together with its embedded description and background material. It seems to happen just as if the reader were watching and listening to it happen. It is built on talk and action. It is shown, rather than being summarized or talked about.

This is what showing versus telling is all about.

Every scene has a point. It leads somewhere and has an impact on what follows. Just like building blocks, each subsequent scene adds layers to what the one before it established, like pieces in a puzzle that slowly unveil the meaning and direction of the story and keep us interested and turning pages to find out what happens next. Each scene leads to consequences, establishes character and/or setting, and shows action. Plotting, thus, is the way of showing what is important in the way you reveal it, order it, and connect it to other pieces throughout your story so it all leads somewhere. So how do you make a scene?

How to Structure a Scene

The scene is the basic building block of dramatic structure for any story. If written correctly, each scene leads to another scene and another. According to Jack M. Bickham, in his book *Scene & Structure*, all well-written scenes use the following pattern:

- Statement of goal
- Introduction and development of conflict
- Failure of character to reach his goal or a tactical complication/disaster which creates a new goal

Notice how these parallels the three-act dramatic structure of the entire story. It is not an accident. Scenes have three acts just as the entire story will. Scenes are not static. At their heart lies conflict. One character or group has a goal and others have other goals, and these meets and create obstacles to be overcome. Hence, conflict. Most scenes start with the point-of-view (POV) character walking into a place with a clear goal in mind. (As discussed in Chapter 4 the point-of-view character is the character from whose vantage point a particular scene is told.) Success of the scene dramatically depends upon your ability to interpose obstacles between your hero/heroine and the obtainment of this goal. Sometimes the goal carries over from the previous scene. Sometimes it is the overall goal in the story. Other times, it is a sub-goal required as part of the many steps to reaching the overall story goal. In any case, usually the goal is stated early on either through internal monologue or dialogue of the character.

For example, Luke Skywalker enters the workshop and cleans the droids per Uncle Owen's instructions (goal). In the process, he finds something jammed in a slot on R2-D2 and tries to free it, unleashing the video of Leia pleading for help. When the message is unclear, he asks R2 to play the whole message and R2 refuses by first pretending not to know what he is referring to, then saying that the restraining bolt is preventing it in order to get the bolt taken off (obstacles). The disaster comes as R2-D2 escapes, forcing Luke to chase him down.

To work well and increase dramatic tension, all scenes must end badly. Whatever the goal going in, whatever the action taken, the result must be a failure of some sort. It can be an actual failure, a twisty complication, or additional unexpected tasks, but it constitutes a delay to success regardless.

But there is another key element at play as well. When the character's goal is stated, the reader asks a question.

> **Goal:** To get the golden key to the temple where I can retrieve the sacred scroll.
>
> **Reader Question:** Will (character) get the key?

Whatever the question, the resolution (or answer) must be a negative. Sometimes a character does the get the key, but other objects are required to find the temple or open the door, and the character must go seek them before getting the scroll. The answer to the question, the disaster, the end of the well-written scene, always creates further complication on the character's journey through that story.

There are several key points to keep in mind when determining goal, conflict, and resolution:

1. The goal of each scene must clearly relate to the larger story question; the question evoked in readers by the stated goal of the character for the major story arc.

2. The conflict must be about the goal.
3. The conflict must be external, not within one's self. Either with an object, animal, or person or more than one.
4. Point of view should be maintained from goal to resolution in the same scene. It is best not to break it up into different points of view to avoid confusion and loss of tension.
5. Disaster always works by pushing the character away from his or her goal.
6. Readers will tolerate much if you keep making things worse and worse in every scene. This is how you build tension and suspense and create a compelling read.
7. Since the end of each scene dictates what will happen after, scenes cannot be written in isolation from the overall arc, goals, conflict, etc. of the story itself if they are to work well.

Plots are made up of a series of interconnected scenes that create a larger story. Since a plot is the storyline arc of the overall book, and the book is a story that is like an argument with a premise, a plot consists of a series of questions asked and answered. What you ask when, and how soon you answer it, affects the tension and pacing of the overall story. Some questions get asked and answered in the same scene or chapter. Some carry over multiple scenes and chapters. Some may carry over to another book. Some carry from chapter 1 to the final chapter. The questions have various levels of stakes to them. More intense, important questions tend to take longer to answer. One great way to figure out if your story makes sense and has good pacing is to go through and identify all the questions asked and answered and when and where they are asked and answered. If you are missing any answers or questions, you have a problem that needs fixing.

Since some stories have several plots—usually an overarching main plot and subplots—and not all scenes relate to each plot, but all relate to the main arc in some way or affect it. All plots and subplots have three acts just like the overall story, so sometimes identifying which plot and subplot(s) relate to each scene is key to making them work and determining in what order the scenes need to occur to best tell the story. To be clear, a subplot is a lesser plot that is less important than the main driving plot and sometimes focuses around a specific character, location, or aspect of that larger plot and points readers back to it. I'll say more on that at the end of this chapter.

It is also important to know which characters are in a scene. Too many characters can make a scene confusing. And too few can make it ineffective. Most importantly, the person with the most to lose is usually the best POV character for that particular scene, so keep in mind whether you have multiple POV characters or not. That will determine your character use in each scene. Remember also that individual characters can have conflicting goals, and that can further complicate scenes by creating competing tensions or conflicts that add layers and depth to the scene and further obstacles to the resolution as well.

In Medias Res

The last point I'll make is the number one rule of good dramatic writing I learned in film school: **Get into a scene as late as possible in its action, and end the scene as soon as you can after that.** The literary term for entering a scene when the action has already begun is *in medias res*.

Scenes are more dramatic when they start within tense moments of action or conflict, so skip all the slow buildup and setup like greetings and small talk, how the characters got there, etc. which would slow things down, and instead get right into it.

Telephone scenes, scenes sitting around a table, on couches, or in a car, etc. have a casual, slow feel that does not lend itself well to drama, so these use sparingly. The pacing and power of your story will go up in spades, and your readers will thank you for it.

Here's another example, one of my favorites: the opening scene from the film *Lethal Weapon 2*.

The film opens with Riggs yelling and pounding his palms on a dashboard as horns honk and traffic roars. Then he and Murtaugh are arguing about speed and strategy. They are in a car chase. We don't yet know who they are chasing or why, but we are immediately thrust into the center of tense, fast-paced action, and the details will come. We soon learn there are two car chases with two teams of cops, and as they fight traffic and near misses with other vehicles and race to keep up with the fleeing criminals—Murtaugh driving his wife's station wagon, which hardly seems up to the task—the bad guys start shooting and taking more and more chances. The goal is to catch the bad guys. The conflict comes from disagreements between cops and from all the obstacles.

When the bad guys ditch them in airport traffic, Riggs jumps out and continues the chase on foot until Murtaugh untangles the station wagon and catches up. Riggs then insists on driving, and he pushes the car even more to its limits, practically destroying it in the process. So now they are fighting each other as well (more conflict). Then the other chase ends at an intersection, where cars collide and a helicopter comes in to rescue the bad guys with automatic gunfire leading to a shootout with cops (Failure 1). Riggs and Murtaugh, meanwhile, continue their chase until their baddie flips his car over a black-and-white cop car that blocks its path and crashes into a building. By the time Riggs and Murtaugh get to the car, the bad guy is gone (Failure 2), but they find

Krugerrands, the currency of South Africa, and so their quest begins.

This is a great example of getting in as late as possible and out as soon as possible (*in medias res*) while still including all three core building blocks of a great scene.

Plotting

So now that we have talked about scenes, the basic building blocks, let's talk more about plotting and some methods and techniques to use in doing it.

In *Writing the Breakout Novel*, Donald Maass identifies five basic plot elements that all plots must have. They are:

1. A sympathetic character
2. Conflict
3. Complication
4. Climax
5. Resolution

So, every good plot starts with character, specifically a character we can care about. Then that character encounters obstacles that create conflict. This can be another person or group of people, some natural or other issue, etc. Then the conflict is complicated by various other obstacles and barriers that stand in the way of the character resolving it. This leads to a climax wherein the character must confront the opponent—person, animal, or thing—head on and see who will win. This leads to a resolution. These five elements make up any solid, well-developed plot.

We've already talked about how the plot is a series of questions asked and answered, so now let's look at a key question we must always ask to make our plots stronger: **What's the worst that can happen?**

You start with conflict and then consider what the complications might be. In doing so, there may be a temptation to like the character too much and not want to make things too hard on him or her. But that is the death of good drama. Instead, you need to ask yourself, "What's the worst that can happen?" and consider the more dire possibilities. This is what makes good drama. Maass writes: "What makes a breakout novel memorable are conflicts that are deep, credible, complex, and universal enough so a great number of readers can relate." So, don't go off the deepest end necessarily, choosing something so dire and outrageous that it seems too hard to believe. You want to complicate and create disasters and dangers, not create incredulity in readers.

What you do want to do is push your problem far beyond what readers might imagine. Maass suggests: "Push your characters into situations that you yourself would never go near in your own life." Remember that the characters should speak and act in ways we only wish we had the courage to do. This is what inspires us to admire and follow them. So they will be capable of facing situations we wouldn't dare take on ourselves. The key is to push things to utter extremes while still managing to make them feel familiar to readers. Not outlandish, then, but familiar. In other words, possible.

When we create conflict that is credible, relatable, and familiar, we create stories with tension on every page. These are the kinds of stories that keep readers turning pages and coming back time and again to the same authors for more. John Grisham, Nicholas Sparks, Michael Connelly, Jonathan Maberry, Stephen King, Joyce Carol Oates, Heather Graham, J.K. Rowling, Rachel Caine—these are examples of authors who have mastered this technique. **If you want your plots to become breakout, hit stories, you must create tension on every page.** Make us desperate to know what happens next. Create urgency in the questions the plot asks. This will drive the story forward, increasing the stakes and tension with each scene and page, until readers may feel they or the characters can't possibly take anymore, but they do every time. And we are dying to know how they manage it and can possibly survive, so we stay up all night reading to find out. We've all read and loved books like that, right? Imagine what it would be like to write one.

One technique that aids this kind of tension is nonlinear narrative. Grisham is a master of this: constantly holding information back from his readers to surprise them with later. Nonlinear narrative is storytelling that increases tension by telling the story in a nonchronological fashion, using flashbacks and other such techniques. Basically, you start telling the story in the center of the action at the most dramatic place and then go back and fill in the backstory and details as necessary through the course of the novel.

Recently, in his novel *Parallel Lines*, my friend Steven Savile demonstrated a tour de force of such plotting, so I sat down to talk with him about his unique approach to this dynamic, character-driven heist.

---

6 QUESTIONS WITH STEVEN SAVILE ON NONLINEAR PLOTTING

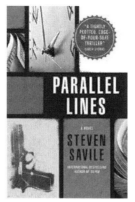

Premise: Eight people, twelve hours, one chance to cover up a murder.

The explosive new thriller from the bestselling author of *Silver*.

Adam Shaw is dying, and knows he'll leave his disabled son with nothing. His solution? Rob a bank. It's no surprise that things go wrong. What *is* surprising is that when another customer is accidentally shot, no one in the bank is in a hurry to hand Adam over to the police. There's the manager who's desperate to avoid an audit, the security guard with a serious grudge, and the woman who knows exactly how bad the victim really was …

Eight people, twelve hours, one chance to cover up a murder. But it's not just the police they have to fool. When many lives intersect, the results can be deadly.

Bryan Thomas Schmidt: I have described *Parallel Lines* as a heist with a tour de force of nonlinear plotting. Tell us about the premise and how that determined your approach to the plotting.

Steven Savile: I had this idea, probably 20 years ago, about using Brownian random motion as a plot structure for a novel, taking a dozen lives and following a story that shifted perspectives every time one character bumped into another, our way into the story a bit like a hot potato being passed from one to the next and the next, working back around as, say, character seven interacted with character one, character one interacts with character four, etc. I ended up constructing an elaborate web of stories that I never did write, but one aspect of that was a bank heist. That became *Parallel Lines*. The thing is it took probably 18 years from the genesis of the idea to the finished book, and in that time it kept growing as an idea without growing in terms of page count. I think it's deceptive to think of writing time as the hours spent at the keyboard; a lot of the most important stuff for me happens long before I sit down at the computer.

> *Live fast, die young, and leave a good-looking*
> *corpse. One out of three wasn't a great showing on*
> *the old scoreboard of life. 33.3% recurring. A big*
> *fat fail in mathematical terms. It certainly wasn't*
> *the deal he'd wanted to make with the universe*
> *back when the universe was up for making deals.*
>
> —Steven Savile, Parallel Lines

BTS: Okay. So, you start the book with the heist. The middle of the action with almost all the characters assembled together. Then start going back to reveal how they came together, one at a time, based on various interactions between them. It really works so well. And allows for such great character development. Tell us a bit about the characters, please.

SS: Yeah, so once I realized there was this core event, the heist, the shape of the story became obvious. It couldn't be the random motion I'd wanted but rather because it was about fixed points and how these dozen people all ended up in the wrong place at the wrong time. Weirdly at this stage, Adam, the actual hero of the novel, the bank robber with ALS, wasn't even in the story. The first people I came up with were Richard Rhodes, the Robin Hood bank manager, Archer, the pimp, and Sasha, the teller. I kept thinking how can you make this worse? Who would be the worst people to be locked in this situation with? I mean a bank manager who is robbing his own bank hardly wants to call the police in, does he? I always knew Archer would have one of his girls with him, but not how important she'd be as things played out. The thing is I tried to write this Anne three or four times down the years and couldn't do it. It stalled out, it was dull. For whatever reason I wasn't getting it right. Then my father-in-law was diagnosed with ALS and we were out having a pizza and his hand was shaking uncontrollably and he was getting more stressed because he felt ashamed, and the more stressed he got the more he shook. I cracked a joke that he'd be the worst person to rob a bank … and suddenly the missing piece fell into place.

I rushed home and wrote the first chapter, and knew that the gun in this first chapter was definitely going off, but not in the third act. It was going off nice and early … and Archer was a dead man, and I was suddenly looking at a locked-room mystery. The thing is by this point I knew these people. I never considered it a thriller and was really annoyed when that was put on the cover. It isn't. It's a character study. Hell, it's as close to literary fiction as you come, but it is dressed in the trappings of the crime genre. Once that gun went off, the writing died right along with Archer. All of my plans went out of the window because I kept thinking of it as a bank heist, and the reality is you are never getting away with it, not in the digital age.

It wasn't until a few years later that I'm walking along the Thames with my friend Jane (who the book is dedicated to) when she says, "You are a writer, tell me a story" … and for no reason I can explain I started to tell the stories of all of these characters. And just like with the book, I stalled out. We sat on this park bench and suddenly I was up on my feet all excited because I'd cracked it: it wasn't a book about a bank robbery, it was a book about how to get away with murder. Here was Adam, this really sympathetic villain, and

Archer, this complete bastard of a victim … and all of these bystanders with intersecting lives … and this Agatha Christie–like locked-room mystery … that realization is what informed the structure. I needed you to know why all of these hostages would help the killer … so it became obvious we needed to see how their lives were shaped up to this connection.

The title is a bit of a joke, too … not just that parallel lines never meet, and here is this story of a tangled knot of plot where these seemingly random lives all tangle, but there's so much untruth in it … escape based on a foundation of lies … Parallel Li es … I really wanted the cover designer to obscure the "N" … as a hidden Easter egg kind of thing…

> *"Shall I tell you what I see? I see lives, hundreds of thousands of them, lit up like fireflies. And for every light, I see an opportunity. You can be anyone you want to be out there, can't you?"*
>
> *"I suppose."*
>
> *"All you have to do is pick a light, you can try on its life like a new outfit, maybe a comfortable pair of jeans or some crisp Italian threads. Is that what you've done, Milo? … I don't think you're who you say you are. I think you're wearing someone else's life, trying to impress."*
>
> —Steven Savile, Parallel Lines

BTS: Well, it came together beautifully. And what happens is a tapestry of character development bound together by the heist that sets up eight very different people from different walks of life who are bound by a single moment and one man's desperate love for his son and decision to rob the bank to ensure he is taken care of. And then various decisions and conflicts arise that bind them in result and lead them down a path. It is similar to Stockholm Syndrome in some ways but not really that as much as a realization that they all want the same thing and have more in common than they could have imagined, and they come to care about each other due to being thrown together. Did you write linearly and then mix it up? How much did you plan ahead or outline?

SS: There's only one scene, divided over two chapters, that was written as a whole and split, and that was the telephone call where you have first the hostage side of the conversation and then outside we hear the hostage negotiator's side of things. And boy did I have a fight over that. First my editor joined it back together, then the copyeditor insisted it would be better if it was presented as a single chapter all from one POV. I dug my feet in. It's one of my favorite parts of the book. Now, plan, yes, outline no. I've written rigorous outlines with some of the tie-ins, but I wanted this to feel more organic, so I worked out my main anchors for the story, my big reveals, but beyond that every day I allowed the sense of discovery to run wild. The big thing for me is always know your characters, they are the source of the story. Trust you know them well enough. That's another reason why I consider this more of a character study than a thriller.

BTS: Did you do character studies then? The bank is the through line and keeps the tension and stakes high. How did you decide how often to go back to the bank between other scenes?

SS: Yes, in this case I did a fair bit of backstory stuff getting to know my hostages. I really wanted some odd and unexpected connections that could fly in the face of that title. There's no real way to construct such an elaborate Gordian knot of a plot and not work a lot under the hood. I know I got frustrated when this one review just dismissed it as, "Oh, it's just a lot of coincidences," and really didn't grasp that it was so much more.

But as you say, the bank is our locked room, and it's essential the majority of the plot functions through it. So, we look at Archer, for instance, and think, Ah, he's got his own pet bank man, why? Why would he need that? And why would he be there at that moment? Then you have to flip it and think, Okay, so we've got Archer and he's a complete S.O.B.; what stuff is he involved in outside of this bank scheme? Where does he have to be next? And then it's all about the stakes. One of the first things I found when I was researching guns in crimes was that Chicago was a bit of a hotbed for these straw men, the guys who would buy legit guns that would end up on the streets involved in crimes, and I loved the irony of the guy being killed by one of the guns he'd sold, you know? It was that lovely collision point, so that was there right from the beginning when I knew I wanted the gun to go off in the bank, I knew I wanted that feedback loop that made Archer actually in many ways responsible for his own death.

In terms of actual structure and choices, I've talked about this a bit, and if you'll indulge me I'll get a little personal. My dad died right in the middle of writing this book. I had only written the first 50 or 60 pages when it happened, and for a good six months I couldn't work. There was no creativity in there. I actually began to wonder if I was done. And even as I started trying to write again and began to have my first ideas in months, my concentration was so fragmented and damaged I could sit and stare at the screen for six hours and write six sentences. I went on a bit of a personal pilgrimage in search of the perfect writing tool... The thing about Scrivener for me was that it forced a complete change in how I saw books. I used to see them in terms of chapters, each chapter with two or three parts to it, ending on the rising action to carry you into the next. But instead, almost taking a lesson from the movie structure, I found myself looking at the 100,000[-word] novel as maybe 85 scenes. Each scene had to pay for its place in the book. Something important had to happen in each scene. Knowing that, it became easier to be a little mathematical about it, considering you have about 12 hours, not much more, so you need a sense of momentum to the scenes as well, and a ticking clock.

Originally, I actually had a time next to each switch of POV, but that was more for me than the reader so I could be sure things were advancing quickly enough.

Of course, after edits, I think I chopped the 115K manuscript down to 88K give or take, so in a few places where I'd allowed things to build a more natural slow-burn tension, the edits ratcheted up the pace and if anything rushed through a few key landmarks in terms of making the hostages become more and more sympathetic with Adam's plight. In the original MS, for instance, it had always been my intention that the prostitute would survive. And she did. She went into witness protection to testify against the mob boss. But my editor kept saying, "I don't buy it," and I don't know if it was that I wasn't selling it well, or what, but she kept getting really confused by stuff I thought made perfect logical sense. Thing is when that happens, you have to trust they have at least highlighted an issue even if they've not given the answer. But, once she couldn't hide from the Dane, there was only one way her story could end. So of course my editor came back: "Can't you … I don't know, give her a happy ending? Poor woman…" but that's the price of logical consistency. You can't hide from a guy like the Dane.

Anyway, sidetracked myself a bit there, it becomes obvious where one scene ends, and once you have that shift in how you view the story you can start using tricks. Here's the thing—we read because we are curious, we keep reading not because we get answers but because we keep getting questions we don't have the answer to. And every time you think, Here's an answer, you turn it on its head and make it another question instead, and hold back on the satisfaction of giving an answer, instead providing more questions so you're left thinking, How the hell are they going to get out of this mess, what's the guard's big secret, why isn't the bank manager calling the cops, etc., so structurally you end a scene with another hint at a deeper question or bigger issue for the first two-thirds of the novel, making it worse with every switch, and don't start giving answers until the sheer momentum of the story carries you into them naturally.

> *It was all on camera. The death of the man called Archer. They'd play it in court at his trial and he'd be damned by it. There were no circumstances in the world that could ever be extenuating enough to save him. Adam's mind raced: Did Illinois have the death penalty? Did it even matter? His own body would execute him long before the state ever could.*
>
> —Steven Savile, Parallel Lines

BTS: I am really glad you stuck to your instincts on splitting the scene too. It ramped up the tension. And I imagine the organic/discovery writing choice lent itself to twists and turns and the whole plotting approach as well.

SS: Indeed, the organic discovery approach was just right. It wouldn't necessarily have worked on a different book, but that's the joy of writing. It's a process of exploration. You get to push yourself as a creative, trying out different structures, different themes and voices. It's not just set dressing. If you don't push yourself into new directions, you don't develop. You end up churning out 10 identical versions of the same novel you've already published. The good thing is the more you do it, the better your instincts get in terms of where it's not working. Of course, when you go for this kind of discovery process it's not hard to write yourself into a corner and screw things up; that's why I think it's so vital you know your people, and more so that you will ever put on the page. Let them keep you out of trouble. Or get themselves into it.

BTS: Well, as you know, I love the result. It speaks for itself. It's one of the best novels I have read in ages. Anything else you want to add about your plotting approach before I go?

SS: I think one thing something as complex as this taught me is that often my first instinct is too easy. That doesn't mean it's wrong, only that there are levels to it. That first instinct can be the key that unlocks deeper ideas. The thing I've learned is I have to listen to myself and trust that after doing this for so long the good stuff is down there waiting to be mined. Don't just think, Okay, that's my idea. Sorted. Give it room to breathe. That thinking time is priceless when it comes to plotting. The more time you spend thinking about stuff before you commit it to paper, the better chance you are giving yourself of getting it right.

STEVEN SAVILE has written for Doctor Who, Torchwood, Primeval, Stargate, Warhammer, Slaine, Fireborn, Pathfinder, Arkham Horror, Risen, and other popular game and comic worlds.

His latest novels include *Parallel Lines*, a bank heist novel, and *Glass Town* and *Coldfall Wood* from St. Martin's Press, and he is currently working on Lost Heroes, a role-playing campaign in the incredibly popular Trudvang world of Drakar & Demoner published by RiotMinds in his native Sweden. His novels have been published in eight languages to date, including the Italian bestseller *L'eridità*.

He won the International Media Association of Tie-In Writers award for his Primeval novel, *Shadow of The Jaguar*, in 2010, and the inaugural Lifeboat to the Stars award for

Tau Ceti (coauthored with Kevin J. Anderson), and writing as Matt Langley was a finalist for the People's Book Prize in the United Kingdom.

Silver, his debut thriller, reached #2 in the Amazon UK charts in the summer of 2011 and was among the UK's top 30 bestselling novels of 2011 according to *The Bookseller*.

He has lived in Sweden for the last 20 years and can be found online at http://stevensavile.com/

As you can tell from this interview, writing nonlinear plots can be very effective, if challenging, and really help keep readers guessing and turning pages by ramping up the tension and pace. Again, John Grisham and many thriller writers are masters of this. And it is an option you can use to great effect as well. Donald Maass writes: "The guiding principle of any nonlinear plot is that the story is not organized in terms of chronological time but according to some other logical progression." The key is rising tension. If time-hopping or moving backwards through time can more effectively ramp up the tension of your story, then that should be the approach you choose. If not, don't do it on a whim. Most of the time, effective nonlinear stories use a marker—a point in time they periodically return to as an anchor—as Savile uses the bank heist. This roots the story in a familiar home base readers can use to assess and evaluate what's been happening in the context of the larger picture. The choice to use nonlinear plotting or not should be determined solely by what works best to tell this particular story, not by some creative desire to mix it up or experiment. Storytelling is all about communication. And craft is about having the right tools to communicate as clearly and effectively as possible with readers.

Plot Charts

Let's look at one more helpful plotting tool before moving on to subplots. Here's a plotting chart from David Farland's *Million Dollar Outlines* that charts the main plot for J.K. Rowling's *Harry Potter and the Half-Blood Prince*.

Half-Blood Prince

1. In Potions class, Harry doesn't have a textbook, so he borrows one from the classroom. It has notes scribbled on all of the pages. With the extra notes, he outdoes everyone in Potions, including Hermione, who gets jealous. They find out the book belonged to someone called "The Half-Blood Prince."

2. The book not only has notes on potions, but various spells that Harry experiments with; some prove helpful, others don't. Harry, Ron, and Hermione try to find out who the Half-Blood Prince is, but fail.

3. Harry uses one of the Prince's spells on Malfoy. It fatally injures him. Harry immediately gets rid of the book, acknowledging it may have belonged to a Dark Wizard. Snape is able to heal Malfoy.

4. Snape reveals that he is the Half-Blood Prince. The book belonged to him, and he invented the spells found in it. He presents himself as a Death Eater.

Figure 3-1

As you can see from the chart, once you have your key plot points and climax, it is very easy to line them up on an ascending and descending arc chart like so. And if you do this for every plot and subplot, you can then make a master plot chart for your entire novel as shown in Figure 3-2.

With all of these plot lines overlapping, you will ultimately have something like this:

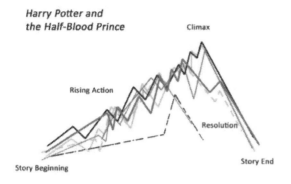

Figure 3-2

Subplots

Most novels have subplots that accompany and lead back to the main plotline, filling out details, building characters, etc. Subplots are still plots. They still require the same structure (three- or four-act or otherwise) and basic five elements as the main plot does. Subplots always must affect the main plotline in some way. Subplots also should range over the milieu of the world in which you are telling your story, but they should still make sense in context and thus involve characters who have reasons to interact and come together. So, your subplots will be largely determined by your setting and characters.

Two to three subplots are usually about all a novel can effectively maintain. Too many, and readers will lose track and become bored or confused. They may mix up characters with one another, or even lose track of the novel's premise and main plot throughline, thus weakening the emotional impact of your overall story. Narrative art has essential simplicity. So even doorstop novels of epic size must maintain simplicity or lose their readers amidst their depths. So limit the subplots. Otherwise you may wind up telling the same story from multiple angles and become repetitive. Also, readers grow most attached to one, central sympathetic character whom they care about and root for. Keep the story centered there to maintain the emotional power and drive the pacing and drama throughout.

In the end, all subplots should amplify themes of the main storyline. So, if your subplots are not thematically related to the main plotline in some way, cut them and choose something else or just skip them altogether. Not all novels need subplots. Not all stories need multiple points of view.

The next thing you need to plan and write your novel are characters, which is the subject of Chapter 4.

CHAPTER 4
CHARACTERS

At five eleven, Adam Shaw was an unremarkable man. He was thinner than he had been in the last decade thanks to the wasting disease eating away at his muscles; the hair at his temples and the stubble on his cheeks was graying. The only thing that made him stand out that day was the long raincoat he wore in spite of the heat. He was always cold these days. That was one of the side effects of his lack of body heat.

With this passage, Steven Savile introduces the protagonist of his brilliant novel *Parallel Lines*. Note how every detail is vivid and evokes not just images but emotions. We feel like we know both his appearance and state of mind after just a few sentences. Vividly realized characters, as you will see, are key to much of the success of any novel—connecting to plot, setting, theme, suspense, dialogue, and everything else. Powerful novels are always about characters, characters with problems, characters in conflict with other characters, characters with needs. Characters, and characters alone, drive everything in a winning story. Make no mistake. Starting with characters after other elements of craft is not meant to downplay their importance to storytelling. Characters are the key to every story, and more often than not, your premise and story idea will begin with them. This is especially true of your protagonist and antagonist.

Protagonists and Antagonists

Good or bad, however flawed, your protagonist is the center of your story and usually your main point-of-view (POV) character through whom we follow and experience the story. His or her opponent, the antagonist, is often the second biggest POV character. Readers want your characters to seem like real people, whole, alive, believable, and worth caring about. People become, in our minds, what we see them do, so first thing first, your character is what he or she does.

But just seeing what someone does isn't enough in good storytelling. To truly know a person, we need to understand their inner self, their motives. Motive is what gives moral value to their actions. And what a character does, no matter how good or bad, is never morally absolute. A character is what he or she means to do, but we all make mistakes, we all have flaws. So, the intention they have and the ideal they desire to be and will become by the end of your story is even more important. Even if their motive is concealed from readers for much of the book, as often is the case with the antagonist, and even if they themselves are not always certain what is driving them due to some psychological trauma or issue, you need to know their motive clearly as you write, and they need to have one.

Here are some key things you need to know about your characters to write them well:

> **Their Name**—This may seem obvious. But every once in a while, you get some person who thinks they are clever and decides to write a mysterious unnamed character. This is very hard to pull off and poses and number of problems, but even if you try it, you still need to know their name. Names tell us lots about a person, from their background and

history to ethnicity, culture, age, and more. A name is invaluable to helping know your character and to helping readers know them as well.

Their Past—Our past, however we might revise it in memory, is who we believe we are. It shapes our image of ourselves.

Their Reputation—Characters are also restricted and affected by what others think of and expect of them. How are they known? Who do others think they are?

Their Relationships—Who is important to them? Who do they love? Who do they have relationships with that are good, and who do they have bad relationships with and why? And how does this affect their motives and actions and their self-perception? Not all of these relationships will be used in the story or appear on screen, so to speak, but they are part of who the character is and is becoming and what drives them, so you need to know them.

Their Habits and Patterns—Habits and patterns imply things about a person. From personal tics to emotional patterns, we form our expectations based on these characteristic habits that suggest how they will behave in any given situation; often these traits communicate unspoken things about the character's state of mind, emotions, and more.

Many story possibilities can emerge from these. And they make the character seem more well-rounded and realistic because every real person we know has these aspects if we take time to study them.

Their Talents and Abilities—Talents do not have to be extreme to make them a part of a character's identity or even important to their fate. But what they do well and don't do well does matter to us, to them, and to those around them, and also to how they take action and respond to the world around them throughout the story.

Their Tastes and Preferences—Someone can like all the same things you do and still not be someone you want to spend time with or would trust to care for your pets or kids. Tastes and preferences tell us a lot about someone while also opening story possibilities and potential conflicts that can help drive the story and build characters and relationships.

Their Appearance—What color are their eyes? Do they have any handicaps? What color is their hair? These are not characterization alone, but they add depth and they can affect self-esteem and how characters are perceived by readers and by other characters, so they matter.

In filling out a character profile that identifies all these characteristics, observe people you know. Think about people you have seen and encountered. What stands out about them? What annoyed you? What did you love? And can any of these things be used to make a real, interesting, dimensional character?

There are three questions readers will ask that must always be considered. And they expect good answers at some point to hold their interest. In fact, your honeymoon with readers lasts only a few paragraphs, so you must constantly keep such questions in mind.

1. Why should I care about what's going on in the story?
2. Why should I believe anyone would do that?
3. What's happening?

Fail to answer these questions at your own peril. It may sound harsh, but do your job and it will almost never be an issue. Uncertainties can be part of storytelling, but even intentional uncertainties must be clear, so readers will know you meant it to be that way and continue to trust you to pay it off later. Trust between reader and author is key to any novel's success. As always, you need to know a lot more about your characters than readers may need for understanding the present story. Some of this stuff may never get written directly into your book, but knowing it may profoundly impact how you write your character and will be very useful in keeping clearly in mind who they are and how they move through the world and interact with it.

In *The X-Files*, Agent Fox Mulder is the true believer, whereas his partner Dana Scully is the skeptic. These quirks defined those popular characters. So will the right quirks define yours. Here are some possible quirks to consider using for your characters:

- Twitches while nervous
- Always does things in twos

- Always chewing gum
- Snorts when laughing
- Uses obscure, large words few people know
- Fear of silly objects or animals
- Always quotes pop culture when stressed in lame attempt at humor
- Always hot or cold
- Fear of heights
- Can't swim
- Can't be bothered learning to drive so relies on others or public transport
- Overachiever
- Underachiever
- Can't let go of deceased pet/loved one/friend
- Cosplays in public to hide their true self for safety
- Bites/chews lips
- Scratches behind ears when thinking
- Paces nervously when uncertain/while thinking
- Practices talking into mirrors or to self

Do you get the idea? These are just a few of hundreds of possibilities. Each of them is distinctive and when repeated in a pattern will be memorable to readers and feel unique, not common, which makes the character stand out. They also can be used for humor or sympathy and become part of the character's arc and growth pattern throughout the story, even the very obstacle the character must overcome to succeed and reach his or her goal.

Stereotypes can also be useful at times though less so with the protagonist and antagonist. Just remember that stereotypes come from a reality. Stereotypes are archetypes. They are types of people we see around us commonly. Using them to strictly limit people and characters based solely on assumption is wrong, but using them to quickly point out aspects of characters is shorthand that can be very effective and useful as a writer. Archetypes are important to storytelling, and they are often the stereotypes of storytelling. How you use them and then twist and depart from them determines if they will be accepted and successfully employed or annoy readers. So use them with care.

To work out all the details of the aspects mentioned, it might be helpful to interview your character. Make a list of questions you'd like to ask and start having the character answer them. Add questions as needed. This can help you start filling out your character profile and inspire your character creation. Do you need a formal character profile? Some work fine without it. It is not required, but it is a perfectly valid and potentially valuable tool you can add to your arsenal. Make a character sketch of one page, at least three to five paragraphs, for both your protagonist and your antagonist. Again, they can be as long as you want, but we want to see at least a page before you move on. Fill in the answers to the various questions and details that occur to you both as you write and before you write. Again, these are tools. They can change as the story requires, but having some of them in advance is a resource to draw from and help you write from a place of knowing and confidence, not ignorance and self-doubt. That is the purpose of all these exercises. They should make writing easier for you, not harder.

Once you have your protagonist and antagonist, there may be other major characters as well. For example, you may have a team of heroes or baddies. You may be telling the story of multiple characters. Most of the time these two will be enough, but if your story requires multiple major characters, use the techniques and approaches discussed to develop them. In creating them, you may find the need for supporting characters with whom they have key relationships who will also populate your story. These and other characters who fill the world around your characters are secondary characters. Let's look now at how to approach them.

Secondary Characters

Secondary Characters can range from walk-ons to minor characters to major supporting roles, depending on the needs of the story. But all characters should serve to further plot and/or character development. If they don't play a part in that somehow, they are unnecessary and should be dropped.

For major supporting characters, you should treat them much like the protagonist and antagonist. These are the characters readers remember because they are the ones with the power to make choices that change other characters' lives. These characters do and say things that matter, so readers' expectations are higher, and they need to be more developed and often have their own character arcs, even substories within the larger whole to follow. Character sketches, interrogations, and other tools we discussed earlier will be of use for developing them.

First, we will deal with the walk-ons and minor characters. To be realistic, your world will be populated with all sorts of these. Most will appear once and disappear with only a line or two. Some will interact with your larger characters a bit and play a key role for a scene, then be gone. Either way, these characters tend to be part of the background and matter little to the story once they've served their purpose. For these characters, stereotyping can be a very useful tool. Because stereotypes represent typical members of a group, they do and say exactly what we expect them to do. Readers encounter many like them day in and out, so they will make quick assumptions about who they are that save you time describing and explaining. These characters come on, serve the purpose, and disappear quickly behind us into the scenery. These are characters like butchers, bakers, preachers, blacksmiths, mechanics, and more who walk in and out of the scenes when needed, then never appear again. Many will not even have names or need them. They are utterly ordinary and not unique and don't stand out in any way, which is exactly what we need them to do, so as not to distract from the main characters and storyline into which they cameo and then disappear.

One way to make the slightly larger minor characters unique is to make them quirky—exaggerated, eccentric, or obsessive. Most minor characters won't warrant such effort, but some will serve to add humor, world-building information, and more and thus need to stand out and be remembered rather than just fade into the scenery. Take this example from *In Big Trouble* by Laura Lippman:

> Kleinschmidt lit a cigarette and looked around for an ashtray. A bright orange oval one sat on some bracketed shelves on the wall to his right. He could have reached it if he stretched. Apparently, Kleinschmidt had decided that a man's reach shouldn't exceed his grasp, for he flicked the ashes into a half-empty glass of Coke instead, then dropped the hand holding the cigarette behind the desk, as if fearful Tess might demand a puff. Such stinginess seemed instinctive to him, Darwinian even. He hadn't gotten to his current size by sharing.

Note how many little details we get in just a few sentences. His name, the fact that he is a smoker, his laziness, his stinginess, and his large size—also said with a bit of irony to add to the quirkiness. This is a minor character we'll remember, despite his brief appearance and disappearance from the story.

Since all characters are equal at the beginning of a story, minor characters are usually introduced after the main characters have already appeared. This is because who we meet first will determine who we expect to matter more and stick around longer, but there are exceptions. Over all, the difference between major and minor characters is determined by how much time you spend on them in not only dialogue but number of scenes, amount of description, etc.

Because these secondary characters serve the story, rather than the story serving them—as often happens reciprocally with major characters—there are a number of common character archetypes that will be useful for these types of characters:

> **The Buddy or Confidant**—Sometimes also the comic relief, this character is a sidekick who may or may not stay with the major character throughout the story but who offers advice—good and bad—encouragement, discouragement, etc. and is let in on the major character's plans, desires, and deepest needs, etc. Chewbacca to Han Solo, Huck Finn to Tom Sawyer, Big Jim to Huck Finn, Henry Standing Bear of Vic Moretti to Longmire, Dr. Watson to Sherlock Holmes, Rudy, Top, and Bunny in Joe Ledger, etc.

> **The Mentor or Sage**—Someone who helps train or advise the protagonist for their journey. Can be a family member or a stranger who has developed a special bond. Like Obi-Wan Kenobi to Luke Skywalker, the sages or mentors are key useful secondary characters in many stories. Gandalf in *The Lords of the Rings*, Parson Adams in Fielding's *Joseph Andrews*, and Senex in L'Engle's *A Wind in the Door*, etc.

The Bully—We've all met them. The larger-than-life, my-way-or-the-highway types who push others around and pick on them. Someone who forces others to bend to their will. These may be challenges or obstacles your hero needs to overcome. The antagonist often plays this role, but there can be others as well throughout the story. Orlick from *Great Expectations*, Henry Bowers from *IT*, Heathcliff from *Wuthering Heights*, Biff from *Back to the Future*, Draco and Lucius Malfoy from Harry Potter, etc.

The Lover—This is a supportive character, always. They have to be, because the role of the lover is to be a partner, an enthusiast, to support the one or ones they love most. This is not just about sex or romance. In fact, those feelings can be absent entirely. If combined with another role, this could be a major character, but often they are expendable and short lived, though not always. They can be sacrificed for the good of the story to motivate the protagonist. Or they can be the confidant and trusted sidekick, depending upon the story's needs. Laura in *American Gods*, Samwise Gamgee and Arwen in *Lord of the Rings*, Mina Harker in *Dracula*, Irene Adler in *Sherlock Holmes*, and Edward in *Twilight* are some examples.

The Caregiver—This is a motherly character who isn't necessarily the mother. This is the supporter and sometimes the martyr, the soul who takes care of everyone else first—but first and foremost, the protagonist. They help prepare the protagonist to go out and face the world and whatever life throws at them. Some examples are Lucy and Madame Defarge from Dickens's *A Tale of Two Cities*, Dilsey from Faulkner's *The Sound and the Fury*, Galadriel from *Lord of the Rings*, Glinda from *The Wizard of Oz*, Merlin to King Arthur, Rudy in Joe Ledger, etc.

The Creator or Artist/Inventor—The creator is an artist, or a god. This is the character driven by the need to create what will endure the passage of time. Creators feel that if you can imagine it, you can do it. Nothing is impossible for the creator archetype. They can aid or assist the protagonist or antagonist in their quest, sometimes by creating useful tools, magic, etc., which they will need to succeed. Marquis de Carabas in *Neverwhere*, Aslan in *The Chronicles of Narnia*, Q in the James Bond books and movies, Madam Ping in McCaffrey's Pern books.

The Jester—Provider of comic relief, this character will appear at times when you need to break up the drama or action with a lighter tone, and while they still serve a purpose, they often have very small roles and appear once or only a few times in a story. Their role, while humorous, may also serve to teach lessons or provide answers to the Protagonist or Antagonist somehow despite their silliness or sarcasm. This type can be easily combined with another archetype for a meatier role. The droid K-2SO in *Rogue One*, Merry and

Pippin in *The Lord of the Rings*, Anansi in *American Gods*, Spider in *Anasi's Boys*.

The Ruler—The government official, royal, or other community or world leader, even law officer, is a key and frequent character who can help or hinder the protagonist or antagonist, often both, throughout the course of a story. They can discourage or encourage as well. General Tarkin in *Star Wars*, Cornelius Fudge in *Harry Potter*, Elrond, Denethor, Saruman, and Galadriel in *Lord of the Rings*, Dionysus and Poseidon in Percy Jackson, M in James Bond, Chief Irving in Harry Bosch, and Church in Joe Ledger.

There are other archetypes, of course, but I think these are the most common and useful for our focus on secondary characters. Hopefully they will give you ideas for useful characters you can use to populate your world, interact with protagonist and antagonist, and move the story along.

Remember that with these characters come different voices for their dialogue and attitude, which can help make your world come alive and seem real. Using their different ethnicities, backgrounds, cultures, and even languages to regional dialects and differences, make sure these characters also serve world building as well as pushing forward plot and main character arcs and journeys as you write them.

Growing Your Characters

The most interesting characters always change in the course of a story, overcoming flaws and emotional handicaps, learning and becoming better people, etc. For your main characters and your major supporting characters, you will want to develop character arcs to ensure that like the plots, they follow three-act character growth arcs over the course of your story. One of the best techniques for doing this is the GMC Method: Goal, Motivation, Conflict. Author and editor Claire Ashgrove explains this approach in our next Sidebar.

SIDEBAR: GMC APPROACH by Claire Ashgrove

One of the strongest character development methods is known as GMC – Goal, Motivation, and Conflict. But GMC doesn't just apply to the characters, but to the story as a whole as well. Let's break these down and apply it to a well-known character, Frodo, from *The Lord of the Rings* by J.R.R. Tolkien.

It's important to understand, first, that GMC is both internal and external. While they exist as separate aspects of characterization and plot, they twine and tangle together to create the whole story. But before we delve into how it all comes together, we need some basic definitions.

> **Goal**—Every character has a goal, a secret desire perhaps, something they wish to accomplish. Conversely, they could want to avoid a particular circumstance. This can be simple or complex. It is integral to the character and will define or substantiate every decision he or she makes.

Motivation—Why the character wants to achieve the goal. Why the goal is important to the character. In other words—why the character is driven.

Conflict—What is keeping the character from achieving his or her goal. Whatever the limiting factor is, it will impact the character internally and externally.

Let's look at *External GMC* first, as in many ways it's the simplest, and often where a writer starts when a story idea takes life. External GMC is the overall plot, plain and simple. External GMC defines the story an author wants to tell. For Tolkien in *The Lord of the Rings*, the External GMC is: *This is a book about a young man who embarks on a perilous journey to destroy a ring of immense power in order to save the world from the dark intentions of an ancient evil.* If you look closely you can see the elements of GMC in that simplified statement. Goal—destroy the ring. Motivation—save the world. Conflict—perilous journey and ancient evil. To elaborate further:

A character's *External Goal* is a clearly defined task that establishes the overarching plot. It's something that is black and white, and the character will either fail or succeed. It is not subjective or open to interpretation on whether the character succeeded or failed. When we consider Frodo, his goal is to destroy the ring—there are no ifs, ands, or buts. He must do it, or he must not. No gray areas or half-accomplished deeds.

A character's *External Motivation* is why they are trying to achieve their particular goal. Again, this is a very clear, very objective aspect of the story with no gray areas. There is no emotion tied to external motivation. When it comes to Frodo, his external motivation to save the world is because he is the only one who can resist the ring's effects. No emotion, no justification, just the simple fact that he's the only one capable.

A character's *External Conflict* is the circumstance, or set of circumstances, preventing him from achieving his goal. And as plot is concerned, this usually involves a series of events all related to one, overarching theme. This may take the form of a singular antagonist, or it may be the government, natural circumstances (environment), a group in opposition, etc. Continuing with our example, Frodo's overarching circumstance is the evil trying to prevent his success, which creates the perilous journey through a series of hurdles he must overcome.

To reiterate: External GMC is the basic plot of the book and what the character's role in the book is. It encompasses the desired outcome, the reason the outcome is important, and what is hindering that outcome. External GMC has very limited, if none at all, emotional ties in the vast majority of books.

Now, let's take a look at Internal GMC.

Internal GMC is specific to every character in the story, not just the primary hero or heroine, or even just the secondary characters. It affects tertiary characters, and while it may only skim the surface in situational characters (like a random shopkeeper a primary character interacts with only once), it impacts them as well. So what, exactly, is it?

A character's *Internal Goal* is seldom clearly defined in act or deed. It is more of an emotional aspect, and a good way to consider it is to look at how the character feels about the situation around them. Attempt to answer how he feels about his circumstances or how he wishes to feel by achieving his goal. A common theme is that a character seeks independence. Or a character may desire revenge. Note that both independence and revenge are emotional states of being. This emotional state may or may not relate to the external goal, but in layered stories, it frequently does. In our example character's situation, Frodo's state of being is that of obligation and a desire to remain happy and carefree in the Shire, as he has always been in life. Be conscious of the fact that the goal is emotion-oriented, and it is individual and specific to the character.

Another aspect of a character's *Internal Goal* is that it is seldom voiced aloud. Consider yourself a moment. You have goals you want to achieve because you believe some state of contentment will occur from them. You do not necessarily tell someone, "I want to go on a vacation because I need a break *and it will make me happy*." Often, you will keep the "happy" part to yourself. But you know in your subconscious that the break will provide some happiness to your state of mind or well-being. This works the same in avoidance-plots, where a character does not want to do whatever it is he or she is presented with because he or she fears a negative state of emotional being will occur. Coincidence does not work. The author must take the time to find out *why* or the reader won't connect.

A character's *Internal Motivation* is, very simply, the emotion that drives him or her to act. Almost always, this is tied to some aspect of the character's past, or the character's backstory. In contrast to external motivation, it is subjective, and specific to the character's *opinion* of himself and of the events surrounding him. Part of what drives Frodo to accept the role of Ring-bearer is his secret desire to experience a journey like his uncle Bilbo. Very clearly, this ties into his backstory. However, in a plot where the character resists his calling or the tasks laid before him, it could be because some unpleasant, similar event earlier in life has taught him he will suffer. In a romance, this theme is typically employed with the "eternal bachelor" male hero, the man who never wants to marry. It is his reason for avoiding all entanglements with women that have any sense of permanence.

A character's *Internal Conflicts* are all the elements that come into play to put him in conflict *with himself.* Usually, the plot events, specifically the external conflict, propel the character in a way that opposes his internal goal and motivation, thus creating an internal conflict. In Frodo's case, as the ring begins to affect him, he begins to feel he may not ever succeed in his journey and know the happiness that comes with the Shire. He begins to doubt his ability to succeed. If we return to the romance plot, and the eternal bachelor, the happiness he experiences with the heroine makes him doubt all his convictions about remaining single.

Some points to remember:

1. If the goal can be touched, heard, seen, or otherwise physically interacted with, it is *external.* If the goal is emotion-driven or emotion-based, it is *internal.*
2. Every character begins the book with a predefined goal and reasons for it. It may be as simple as getting to the grocery store for a big dinner that night, when they encounter a beggar who suddenly pulls a gun on them.
3. If a character behaves in a manner that is outside traditionally accepted norms, clearly defined GMC is not only necessary, but mandatory, in order for the reader to relate to the character and his actions.
4. Motivation establishes the reader's connections with the character and makes even morally ambiguous characters people readers can support.
5. Conflict is not a random battle or physical altercation. Internal and external conflicts are designed to test the hero, to push him to, and beyond, his limit and see how he overcomes.

Building on a background of fantasy game design, a fascination with history, and a lifetime love of books, award-winning author Claire Ashgrove brings to life action-filled, passionate journeys of the heart. Her paranormal series, The Curse of the Templars, marries the history of the Knights Templar with the chilling aspirations of the most unholy—a must-read for speculative fiction fans. For romance fans, she also writes as the national bestselling author Tori St. Claire and historical romance as Sophia Garrett. For epic fantasy fans, she writes both middle grade and adult fiction as G.P. Charles.

As I said in Chapter 1, great stories are about characters who are larger than life, who talk, think, and act in ways not everyone does or can. These types of characters have a boldness, drive, and determination to pursue journeys we only dream about and take risks and actions we only wish we had the courage to take ourselves. In the process they undergo growth and changes we admire greatly, that inspire us, embolden us, and leave us breathless with admiration. So, once we know the GMC of the story and characters, it is important to build characters who are relatable but flawed people. Characters we can relate to inspire us. Characters we can't relate to don't. So as larger than life as they may be, your characters must have traits, positive and negative, that are familiar and sympathetic to us to draw us in and hold our interest over the course of a story. Readers want characters who matter.

What makes a character matter? First of all, characters must be memorable and special in some way. Remember the people in your life who keep coming to mind years later, time and again? What is it about them that keeps them in your memory? What makes them indelible parts of your life story? Successful characters will have this aspect to them. Let's take an example from Dean Koontz, the character Odd Thomas. Odd Thomas is not that extraordinary in most ways. He is a short-order cook, young, and really not seemingly ambitious or driven to status or importance in how he lives and the choices he makes for his everyday life. Yet Odd Thomas has one unique, special distinguishing trait: the dead talk to him. And the living are also drawn to him, in that he has a lot of friends—kooky friends, but friends nonetheless.

A wimpy character does not make for an interesting story. You need a character who has found himself or herself enough to take action, to have agency. The character we will admire and follow must do something. That doesn't mean they have to do it perfectly. They just need potential. Give your characters flaws. Make them bad with money, bad with girls or boys, make them moody or even cocky. Maybe they are not good at keeping jobs. Maybe they are not good at being a coworker or partner or spouse. Characters like this have problems to overcome, obstacles that interfere with their competence at accomplishing their goals, no matter how motivated they are, and which create conflict. This we can relate to, because we have flaws, and we stumble over them and find conflict from them in trying to succeed in our lives, too. In fact, the character can be relatively ordinary in most ways, but have one exceptional trait that leads to an interesting journey of growth that draws us in. Strong heroes must also be conflicted between competing emotions, like wanting not to hurt people while fighting bad guys who have no similar compunction, or wanting to keep a simple life and avoid conflict while feeling called to go out and fight for what's right. Without such duality, internal conflicts will never play powerfully in the story. In truth, the characters are often less interesting than their journey. It is the journey that makes the tale compelling. So, make sure your characters, especially the main ones but key supporting ones, too, have somewhere to go, a journey to take, to achieve success and accomplish their goals. That will make them interesting to follow for readers.

There are tons of books on character traits, character emotions, flaws, etc., to explore, so I am only going to talk a bit more here and leave you to it. Characters are so important that I strongly encourage you to study this aspect of your writing in depth, specifically in books focused on writing character. Because they are only one part of a larger picture here, I cannot devote much more than a chapter to them. But there is one pitfall that is so common I must mention it by way of warning, and that has to do with writing villains.

Cardboard villains never work. Villains who have no redeeming qualities, no flaws besides the obvious evilness of their deeds, no struggles or doubts, no obstacles except the protagonist, are flat characters. It is very important to develop your villains as much as your heroes, to imbue them with the same kinds of traits and GMC as everyone else. This will make them more challenging, interesting opponents, and it will make them more interesting and relatable to readers. Sure, we may not relate to them because they are perverted in their twisted decisions and actions, but their motives make sense. We understand that they do what they do for a reason with an internal logic that we can grasp, even if we find it abhorrent. Actually, not all antagonists are bad or worse than our protagonists. Sometimes they are just people with opposing goals. It is challenging to decide what the great good is and who to root for at times. Complex villains can be much more compelling and challenging and make for far more interesting reads than just straight evil bad guys tend to.

Just be careful not to make your antagonist such a larger-than-life obstacle that we can't see how the protagonist can ever win, or so weak and cardboard and obviously bad that we cannot understand how they keep winning. Antagonists whom other characters may like and follow are far more dangerous and far more interesting than those who seem obviously on the wrong side of the tracks. So, put as much thought into developing your antagonist as your protagonist. Your readers will thank you for it.

Key to all of this is describing characters, and we will get to description in the next chapter, but John Grisham is a master of building tension just by describing characters in terms that immediately put them at odds. Pick your aspects carefully when you set up characters. Use the most dramatic points first, and let the rest unfold as opportunity presents itself. This will automatically serve to raise the tension and sense of conflict and drama in your story for readers, even if the real clashing is yet to come. Creating characters rife for conflict is one of the best ways to keep them reading.

The trick is picking the right details that say volumes with few words. Look at how John Grisham introduces one of his most famous characters, Harry Rex Vonner in *A Time to Kill*:

> Harry Rex Vonner was a huge slob of a lawyer who specialized in nasty divorces and perpetually kept some jerk in jail for back child support. He was vile and vicious, and his services were in high demand by divorcing parties in Ford County. He could get the children, the house, the farm, the VCR, and microwave, everything. One wealthy farmer kept him on retainer just so the current wife couldn't hire him for the next divorce.

A whole lot is said with few words, right? And yet, you can immediately tell he's a character rife with conflict, and that makes him immediately interesting. One more example from the same novel:

> The Honorable Omar Noose had not always been so honorable. Before he became the circuit judge for the Twenty-second Judicial District, he was a lawyer with meager talent and few clients, but he was a politician of formidable skills. Five terms in the Mississippi Legislature had corrupted him and taught him the art of political swindling and manipulation. Senator Noose prospered handsomely as chairman of the Senate Finance Committee, and few people in Van Buren County questioned how he and his family lived so affluently on his legislative salary of seven thousand dollars a year.

The beauty of his well-chosen words is that we get an immediate sense of the characters without a whole lot of detail— just enough to make certain assumptions about likeability, moral fiber, and relationship to those around them. It's enough to set expectations that can then be played upon either affirmatively or with surprising twists. Either way, the descriptions make us feel we know the characters' type immediately, and that is what counts.

Finally, remember that supporting characters often have arcs as well, and they should. Especially the major ones. Minor ones may pop in and out as needed, but the ones who reappear time and again have their own stories and their GMC as it conflicts with the protagonist's GMC or the antagonist's GMC, and add nuance, layers, and conflict that make the story more dramatic and compelling to follow.

Although it is closely related to character, we will cover viewpoint in Chapter 6 as we talk about voice and style. First, let's cover another subject key to structuring or outlining your story: setting and description.

CHAPTER 5
SETTING AND DESCRIPTION

It is easy for writers to get so caught up in plot and character that they undervalue the role of time and place in their storytelling. But more than any other element, setting—time and place—is essential to creating a story that captivates readers and transports them to a new world that is exciting and fascinating. The right setting and description can add drama and gravitas to any scene. The right setting lends itself to the theme, emotion, pace, tone, and conflict of a scene. The wrong one can be a scene killer. Because just as the scene is a core building block of the story, setting is a core building block of any scene. And description is the key way to establish setting.

Setting

Settings are important tools for drama. Often, the same setting is used in multiple scenes of the same story. Some settings have many rooms, some are smaller and simpler, but choosing the right setting is key to making any scene work. The proper setting can lend energy and atmosphere, but not all types of stories rely on clearly defined settings. Sometimes unnamed locations are part of the story's impact. That doesn't mean describing details isn't important, however. The trick is to pick the right aspects to describe.

Blue eyes wide, Lady Sandrilene fa Toren watched her near-empty oil lamp. Her small mouth quivered as the flame at the end of the wick danced and shrank, throwing grim shadows on the barrels of food and water that shared her prison. When that flame was gone, she would be without light in this windowless storeroom.

This passage from *Sandry's Book* by Tamora Pierce is a great example of choice details revealing setting. Nowhere in the passage does she mention anything but things relevant to the immediate space, and every detail is vivid enough for the reader to begin picturing the space. She even throws in a bit about the character, too—"her small mouth quivered"—which reveals her emotional state perfectly: fear. The right setting can illuminate so much, and the right description at the right time is essential to its effectiveness.

Settings can say a lot about characters. If they own or occupy or regularly inhabit a setting, it says something about who they are. The details demonstrate things about them—from what they keep on shelves, what they hang on walls, and how they arrange furniture and clean a space to what they don't include as well. Do they hide who they are from people who come there? Do they value the space, or is it more utilitarian? How much have they invested in making it theirs, like a home or second home?

Let's consider an iconic setting: the cantina in *Star Wars: A New Hope*. The cantina represents a very foreign and intimidating environment for Luke Skywalker, the protagonist. Not only is it filled with exotic and even menacing aliens, but the whole unfriendliness of the place creates a sense of danger and hostility. Then, not only does Luke face attack by two hoodlums, from which Ben must rescue him, but they meet with a scoundrel pilot and his giant alien companion, leaving Luke feeling very uncertain and anxious about the journey he has just agreed to embark upon with Kenobi. He's lost everything, and he is about to give up even more—the comfort of the familiar—and this is what he gets? The setting establishes mood and state of mind so much that he doesn't have to really state it. We know how he feels and experience it along with the character. And the whole place became so iconic that filmmakershave tried to re-create it in each sequel, with not always as much success. It's a scene everyone remembers and still talks about. That's a powerful setting.

Another good example is the Beverly Hills hotel in *Pretty Woman*, where the poor hooker, Vivian—played by Julia Roberts—goes to stay with her $3,000 client, Edward (Richard Gere), at the Regent Beverly Wilshire Hotel, which is as ritzy as they come. She is a fish out of water like Luke Skywalker. From elevator attendants to everything else, everything is unfamiliar; she is out of her element and the experience is unsettling, which echoes her own personal doubts about her profession and her desire to find a better life. This setting in every way epitomizes her internal struggle and juxtaposes itself with her usual life in ways that Richard Gere soon does as well. This dashing stranger, Edward Lewis, treats her unexpectedly, as do many hotel staff. Some of Edward's companions, especially his lawyer, treat her as she is used to, and the dichotomy makes her and us realize all the more that she deserves more and better. It's a great use of setting to help tell the story. Like the *Star Wars* cantina, the setting very much becomes a character in the story. That is a perfect choice of setting. And you should aim whenever possible to have your settings be just as effective—especially, as is the case with the hotel in *Pretty Woman*, your main, most oft-used setting.

It's no accident that Middle Earth is like a character in J.R.R. Tolkien's *Lord of the Rings*. In nineteenth-century writing, this was common practice. In speculative fiction—science fiction, fantasy, and horror, all genres I have spent a great deal of time writing in—authors must frequently create entire worlds. And what you quickly learn is that a setting is much more than just a place and time. As Donald Maass puts it in *The Breakout Novel*,

> building breakout time and place starts with the realization that the world of the novel is composed of much more than the landscape and rooms. It is milieu, period, fashion, ideas, human outlook, historical moment, spiritual mood, and more. It is capturing not only place, but people in an environment; not only history, but people changing as the story unfolds. Description is the least of it. Bringing people alive in a place and time is the essence of it.

So what are the key attributes of creating a good setting?

The Psychology of Place—We've all been in settings that evoke certain emotions or feelings: creep us out, comfort us, make us nervous, etc. Places have ambience and atmosphere that affect people, and those impressions can change with time. Maybe a place starts out bland and unthreatening but comes to be terrifying for the character due to events of the story. Examining the active relationship between your characters and the settings they live in during the story is an important part of creating effective settings. Settings they barely notice have one role. Settings that have them noticing every minute detail have another. Using the psychology of places in your story employed as your settings adds drama and tension to your story.

Sense of Time—Both historical time and the passing of days, hours, and minutes are important aspects of the settings in your story. Some settings have historical significance globally for many people in the world around them, while some just mark significant moments in the lives of particular characters. Some are just spots characters pass through and barely notice, where time either flies by or drags on due to the activities that bring them there. Department of Motor Vehicle offices, churches, supermarkets, hospitals, schools, houses, apartments, streets, alleys, parks—all these and more affect different people differently for various reasons. And some of them make time matter more—where every minute or second gets counted off—while in others, time hardly matters. Finding the places and moments that matter or don't and using them for the right action and dialogue scenes allows you to craft a novel enhanced by sense of time.

Social Context—People live in environments filled with social issues, from class to politics to trends and more, that influence their attitudes and thinking toward places and each other. Noting when characters notice their social context and when they don't in your writing will enhance the sense of realism of your world and can magnify your story in fascinating ways.

Cosmology and Religion—What the characters believe and how they regard the universe as affecting them is also a key element of good setting. Unexpected moments of tragedy and grace that reflect these beliefs and demonstrate the context and attitude with which people live and flow through the world of your story add nuance and depth and even excitement and emotional resonance to your story.

Detail—Settings are the sum of their parts. Detail matters. But as I've said, not just any detail—the right details. Different settings tend to inspire people to notice different things about them for various reasons. People visiting hospitals often remember the smells, for example, just as people visiting jails remember the bars and the cold atmosphere and cramped spaces. Figuring out which details matter most to which setting in your story and incorporating them is also key to bringing your settings to life and using them to enhance your story.

So let's take a moment to consider how one might approach describing a setting. Descriptions of setting can be big and sweeping or minute and compact. Do you need the whole forest or just one tree? Determining this depends on what is best for the particular story. Epic fantasies and historical fiction tend to be rich in details about their worlds and settings, whereas sometimes procedurals, mysteries, and romances just give you what you need and focus on character, plot, and language instead. Choose your details carefully. The right amount of detail can make the story richer, stronger, and more dramatic and powerful, but too much or too little can leave the reader confused or bored, or cause them to lose interest. The general rule is to tell us what we need at that moment to understand the characters and story and leave the rest for later. Descriptive paragraphs of more than three sentences should be used sparingly; instead, descriptive details should be sprinkled out in bits throughout the text. Here's an example:

"Beth!" The heavy, oversized wood door slammed behind John with a thump and click of the metal knob as he raced into the room and looked around for his sister. The bright glare of fluorescents overhead filled the space, reflecting off the bare, white, antiseptic walls as he approached the large, railed bed where she lay, the hiss of the breathing machine attached to her face ominous in his ears. "Oh my God! What happened?" he demanded of the nurse as she stepped in his path to stop him from touching Beth.

Notice how I didn't even tell you we were in a medical facility, but you already know that. Did you picture an emergency room or hospital room or something similar? How many details did it take me? Seven in this case, but I'll bet you imagined the location after the first five, right? Accuracy and relevance of details is what matters. Sure, I could take the time to describe the hospital and surroundings, the smell of antiseptic, and more. But it would slow the dramatic impact of the entrance. Those details can come in the scene before as he arrives if needed or later in this scene at appropriate moments, sprinkled in. The trick is to provide the imagery needed while keeping the scene moving forward dramatically with good emotional and dramatic pacing at the same time. Note how the choice of details and setting lend emotional depth and gravitas to the scene. There's a sense of danger, worry, and more added to the scene, which increases dramatic impact. This is how a good setting should work.

Let's look at my choices. Hospital doors are often large enough to permit stretchers, ambulance crews, rolling beds, and other equipment through, so they are oversized and heavy with strong metal knobs to better handle the weight. Hospitals have bare, often white walls that are clean and shiny from antiseptic. The beds often have rails. And rooms are brightly lit with overhead lights, at least in medical treatment areas. All of those choices served to paint the image of a medical facility of some kind. They were accurate and relevant. Sure, wall color may vary at times as well as a few other details, but they are common enough, so you got it. That's what counts.

Just in case my meager efforts aren't enough to impress this upon you, let's conclude this section with a passage from *The Lord of the Rings*, showing Tolkien's mastery of milieu:

> Even from the outside the inn looked a pleasant house to familiar eyes. It had a front on the Road and two wings running back on land partly cut out of the lower slopes of the hill, so that at the rear the second-floor windows were level with the ground. There was a wide arch leading to a courtyard between the two wings, and on the left under the arch there was a large doorway reached by a few broad steps. The door was open and light streamed out of it. Above the arch, there was a lamp, and beneath it swung a large signboard: a fat white pony reared up on its hind legs. Over the door was painted in white letters: the prancing pony by barliman butterbur. Many of the lower windows showed lights behind thick curtains.

Notice how every word evokes imagery that allows the scene to unfold like a picture in your mind as you read. You can picture the inn, your imagination filling in a few details here and there, like perhaps the color of paint or the materials making up the walls or roof, but there are enough details that you almost don't notice this because it seems to unfold so naturally in your mind as if it were all there. As this passage demonstrates well, the trick is not just choosing the right details, but presenting them in a way that is visceral and evokes imagery that brings the story alive rather than just flatly describes them for readers. This is where showing versus telling becomes a major concern.

Description

Description lies at the very essence of prose fiction. It is the creation of mental images that allows readers to fully experience a story. Description relies on details, and a good detail is a word or phrase or image that helps readers "see." Every decision you make in writing a story—from point of view to length of sentences—becomes part of the story's description. Good description takes many forms and does not rely solely on adjectives and adverbs for impact. What makes a story become alive and real is not the number and choice of adjectives or adverbs but the accuracy and relevance of the details you choose to describe.

Showing versus Telling

We've all heard the saying "Show, don't tell." Description and settings are the most common area where this problem arises. Telling is just stating things in passive and direct ways. Showing involves describing key details so they unfold like a movie before our mind, and we get the message without it having to be just stated outright. These key details evoke empathy in us so that we experience what the character experiences in a way that just telling us doesn't accomplish. Visceral descriptions evoke readers' emotions and memories in a unique way. This is why "show, don't tell" is so oft repeated that it almost sounds cliché. The key is to tell as little as possible and show as much as possible. Sometimes, you just need to tell readers a few bits of backstory or facts to get them out of the way quickly. In short bits, this is fine and very effective. But around that, we need you to show us the story so the prose unfolds almost like a movie in our minds as we read, drawing us into the book and connecting us with the world and characters in a way that makes us care and want to read on. That's what showing versus telling is all about.

In essence, it comes down to the difference between scene and narrative. Narrative is the writer telling the tale by providing all the information directly. Scene is a dramatic structure that involves dialogue, action, beginning, middle, and end, characters, and drama. Every scene contains some narrative, but narrative alone does not constitute a scene. Narrative passages tend to use weak verbs, expository language, and nonvisceral point-by-point description of what is going on, what readers need to know. Scene uses visceral cues to show and imply emotions, state of mind, motivations, and more while also playing out actions and dialogue dramatically. The best writing does both, combining them effortlessly into a larger whole.

In her book *Description*, Monica Wood offers two great examples demonstrating the difference:

> **Telling/Narrative:** Alice was a timid young woman who looked like a mouse. She was short and skinny, with brown hair, small eyes, and a pointed face. She always peeked inside a doorway before entering a party, thus giving herself a chance to flee in case she saw no one she knows.

Showing/Scene: Alice hovered at the door of Everett's apartment, chin lifted, tiny feet balanced on their toes. She peered inside, shrinking at the loudness of Everett's new stereo. She breathed quickly, her black eyes darting back and forth, as if keeping her face in motion might prevent her from toppling over. When she finally spotted the wide-grinning Everett approaching, she scurried to the punch bowl, her flat shoes making a scratching sound on the polished wood.

Did you notice how much more information is imparted in the second example and how it interacts with your imagination differently, stimulating your emotions, raising questions that draw you in, and hinting at aspects missing from the flatter narrative approach? Instead of just stating that she looked inside a party to see if she knew anyone, we experience what that is like for her as she does it, sharing her emotions and thoughts, experiencing her approach. The key is to let the characters reveal themselves through their words and deeds as much as possible. Showing too much can overwhelm readers' senses, but telling too much fails to engage them, so the richest prose combines the two seamlessly by choosing carefully what to dramatically play out and what to provide quickly in exposition. In either case, writers should avoid using great gobs of text and instead spread them out a few lines or words at a time. Every time you stop to describe or exposit something, the pace slows or stops, and the dramatic tension drops. Using a combination of internal monologue and external dialogue and action with exposition, the story unfolds naturally and effectively while holding readers' interest, each scene leading to the next, and each page demanding that they keep turning to find out where it goes from here.

How do you know when to use scene and when to use narrative? When action is required, scene is the best approach. You want to evoke empathy by revealing telling (significant and insightful) details about the characters and world as the plot unfolds dramatically. Every story will require a different combination. When you need to quickly impart key information that characters know and readers need to understand the story going forward, then telling comes into play. This can be done in expository description either as direct narrative or internal monologue. Either way, as you will learn in the the next chapter, the goal of viewpoint is to let readers experience the story through the eyes of the characters rather than the eyes of the author. Essential to this are descriptions that regularly employ the impressions of the character's five senses.

Using the Five Senses

Many of us are guilty of falling into the habit of using one or two senses and ignoring the rest. For most of us, sight is the dominant sense—the sense through which we first encounter and examine the world. So how things appear will dominate most narratives naturally, closely followed by sound. But we have five senses, and all have the power to bring useful imagery into your storytelling.

Good description employs all five senses—sight, touch, taste, smell, and hearing—and employs at least one every two pages, sometimes more. A few well-placed details can totally embody a character or place and make them come alive for the reader. And nothing takes us deep inside the character's mind and experience like sensory details. All good settings are rich with detail, so you should have plenty to choose from. From the appearance and smells of a restaurant or grocery store or market to the touch and sounds of the outdoors to the taste of food, there are numerous opportunities to add color and vividness to your prose using these kinds of details.

Here are some suggestions for aspects of each sense to consider:

> **Sight**—Color is usually one of the first things that comes to mind, but studies actually show that spatial dimensions tend to be picked up first by the brain. How large is the area? How high is the ceiling? After dimension, the source of light tends to be noticed next. What is lighting the scene, and what is its source—artificial or natural? Is it bright or white or mixed hues? Then, color impressions form. The dominant color tends to take on significance. Next comes texture, like shadows or rough and smooth surfaces, etc. Finally, there's contrast. Superimposition of colors and other aspects affects how much objects, people, and places draw our attention.

> **Sound**—Sound can be described by the loudness or complexity—simple or multiple sources—tonality (soft or hard, harsh or gentle, etc.), and the location of its source and distance from the hearer. Also, is the sound unknown or familiar?

> **Smell**—While smells can be often overlooked by both writers and in real life, smell can reveal a lot. Is the odor pleasant or unpleasant? What emotions does it evoke—fear like smoke from a fire, or is it the steady everyday scent of vehicles, animals, or

insects in the environment that almost goes unnoticed because it is so common?

Touch—How do things feel—rough or smooth, hot or cold, sharp or dull, etc.?

Taste—Does the character notice sweet or bitter, salty or acidic, pleasant or unpleasant, etc.?

If you're like me, these kinds of details may not come naturally. So, I recommend two key resources that have really helped me up my game on writing sensory content. *The Emotion Thesaurus* by Pugliosi and Ackerman and *Setting* by Jack W. Bingham. These two resources are so invaluable, I often keep them with me on trips and beside me as I write and refer to them often, because writing such visceral descriptions is not first nature to me, and it can be very easy to fall into personal clichés and patterns that repeat the same details and descriptions over and over, which quickly becomes repetitive and glaring to readers. The authors also discuss body language and internal sensations, which can be described to show, not tell, the emotions of characters, the atmosphere of rooms, etc. Additionally, author David Farland describes this as the Kentic, Audio, Visual Cycle and offers useful tips on his website at https://mystorydoctor.com/the-kav-cycle-part-1/.

Sensory experiences and emotions evidence themselves in three ways: internal sensations, external sensations, and body language, and all three are important ways to describe them and help readers experience them too. For example:

Butterflies danced in her stomach as she entered the audition, and she fought to control her face as she took in the other dancers. There were famous faces she'd seen in numerous Broadway shows and performances. What was she doing here? She swallowed and licked her lips, which had suddenly grown parched. Her arm was twitching. She had to make it stop, but it wasn't listening to her internal commands, so she shoved it tight against her side in an attempt to control it.

I don't have to tell you she is nervous and intimidated. The descriptions do the work. This is what you are aiming for. If you are unsure about a particular smell or taste or even sound, Googling can provide impressions others have had of familiar things that can be adapted for your prose. I also recommend practicing by going to a mall or price club or anywhere else and sitting down to take notes of all the things your senses notice as they occur to you. This will give you practice not only at writing visceral (i.e., instinctive and emotional) details but also in noting how they naturally affect you and might also affect your characters.

You've probably deduced by now that description is the art of picking the right details at the right time. Stories are about movement, so be wary of stories where your characters reflect and remember a lot. Instead, action and discovery go hand in hand. As your characters go and do things, they discover sensory cues that provoke memories, emotions, and reactions and inspire further action. People move through life on two levels simultaneously: physical and emotional. Physical movement follows plot and events that unfold A, B, and C, while emotional movement follows character. The physical tends to move with the emotional. So meshing plot and character is the key, and good description is key to your ability to do that well. As Wood writes in *Description*: "A story's pace is controlled by the physical and emotional goings-on in the story, and those goings-on are controlled by description."

Another element where description is especially important is context. Establishing the scope of a story can be vital to making it work, giving characters a scope in which to love and hate each other, to conquer or fall to adversity, discover or lose themselves. Context uses metaphors and symbols to reinforce emerging themes and organize the movement of a story into beginning, middle, and end. Wood writes: "The breadth of the story should dictate the breadth of the context." Contextual details, small or large, reveal character and can serve to contrast with the story itself, adding power. The order in which details are noted can tell us much about a character's values and priorities as well as how they view themselves in relation to those around them. Are they rich or poor? Powerful or weak? Confident or insecure? These details can reveal so much about them.

So, how do you choose which details to use and when? Well, that depends upon what you need the readers to know to understand and connect with the story at any given moment. Let's look at an example from John Connolly's Charlie Parker book *A Song of Shadows*:

> The woman stank of cats and cookies, of piss and mothballs, but Cambion, whose sensory abilities had long been ruined by his disease, and who had grown used to the reek of his own decay, barely noticed it.

How do you not remember that? Ask yourself what you most notice about particular people, places, and things. What do you remember? What stands out about them? What did you notice first? What sticks with you most when you have been away from them awhile and remember? These are the beginnings of finding the most definitive choices to use in describing them because they hint at what stands out when you encounter those people, places, and things. Let's look at another example from Brazilian author Jorge Amado's *Dona Flor and Her Two Husbands*:

> Delicate, pale, with that pallor of romantic poets and gigolos, black hair slicked down with brilliantine and lots of perfume, a smile that was a combination of melancholy and allure, evoking a world of dreams, elegant in bearing and attire, with large, pleading eyes, the Prince would have to be described by very high-flown words: "marmoreal," "wan," "meditative," "pulchritudinous," "brow of alabaster and eyes of onyx."

So much said with just a few words but very colorful, visceral, and intriguing because every word count. This is what good description is all about.

People and places are one thing, but some things can be a challenge to describe with such power—like emotions or animals and food. So, what if you wanted to evoke an emotion like fear in readers? How would you go about describing it? One of the best authors at evoking fear is Stephen King. Here's an example from *The Shining*, in which a young boy holed up in a snowbound Colorado hotel with his parents watches the haunted old place slowly driving them all mad:

> Now, heart thumping loudly in his chest, he came around the corner and looked down the hall past the extinguisher to the stairs. Mommy was down there, sleeping. And if Daddy was back from

his walk, he would probably be sitting down there, eating a sandwich and reading a book. He would just walk right past the old extinguisher and go downstairs.

He started toward it, moving closer to the far wall until his right arm was brushing expensive silk paper. Twenty steps away. Fifteen. A dozen.

When he was ten steps away, the brass nozzle suddenly rolled off the fat

loop it had been lying (sleeping?) on and fell to the hall carpet with a dull thump. It lay there, the dark bore of its muzzle pointing at Danny. He stopped immediately, his shoulders twitching forward with the suddenness of his scare. His blood thumped quickly in his ears and temples. His mouth had gone dry and sour, his hands curled into fists. Yet the nozzle of the hose only lay there, its brass casing glowing mellowly, a loop of fat canvass leading back up to the red-painted frame bolted to the wall …

… His internal temperature plummeted to ten below zero. He stared at the black bore in the center of the nozzle, nearly hypnotized. Maybe it was full of wasps, secret wasps, their brown bodies bloated with poison, so full of autumn poison that it dripped from their stingers in clear drops of fluid.

Suddenly, he knew that he was frozen with terror; if he did not make his feet go now, they would become locked to the carpet and he would stay there, staring at the black hole in the center of the nozzle like a bird staring at a snake, he would stay here until his daddy found him and then what would happen?

With a high moan, he made himself run ... and suddenly he heard it behind him, coming for him, the soft dry wicker of that brass snake's head as it slithered rapidly along the carpet after him like a rattlesnake...

It loses a bit of context if you are unfamiliar with the book, but I think we can all imagine ourselves as children experiencing these kinds of fears when alone in a building at some point. Note the vivid imagery comparing the hose to a snake, making it almost a character in the scene that the boy interacts with. The vividness evokes memories of our own childhood fears and imaginations run wild, allowing us to experience his fear along with him.

Often, your options will be affected by your choice of tone, style, mood, and voice. If a character is uneducated or has a limited vocabulary or is young, the descriptive words you use should reflect that. If you are going for a particular tone, style, or mood, then you need to choose the best aspects to describe and do so in words that amplify the effect you intend. When establishing characters, your best options will be determined by what reveals the most about them. You are crafting a reading experience, not just a story. Choices you make in how to tell a story matter, too.

Let's consider describing an opposite feeling from fear or terror this time, a more pleasant one like love, as demonstrated in the love letter a wife writes to her husband in Nicholas Sparks's *Safe Haven*:

Until you came along, I never knew how much I'd been missing. I never knew that a touch could be so meaningful or an expression so eloquent; I never knew that a kiss could literally take my breath away. You are, and always have been, everything I've always wanted in a husband.

Who wouldn't want to get a letter from a spouse or lover like that? It drips with love and passion. Its simplicity is barely noticeable under the power of the emotion it conveys. You want to write memorable characters, who are larger than life? Make them passionate people—passionate about whatever matters to them, from love to work to justice or family and more.

For food, check out books like *Like Water for Chocolate* by Laura Esquivel or even *The Belly of Paris* by Emile Zola:

Beneath the stall show-table, formed of a slab of red marble veined with grey, baskets of eggs gleamed with a chalky whiteness; while on layers of straw in boxes were Bondons, placed end to end, and Gournays, arranged like medals, forming darker patches tinted with green. But it was upon the table that the cheeses appeared in greatest profusion. Here, by the side of the pound-rolls of butter lying on white-beet leaves, spread a gigantic Cantal cheese, cloven here and there as by an axe; then came a golden-hued Cheshire, and next a Gruyere, resembling a wheel fallen from some barbarian chariot; whilst farther on were some Dutch cheeses, suggesting decapitated heads suffused with dry blood, and having all that hardness of skulls which in France has gained them the name of "death's heads." Amidst the heavy exhalations of these, a Parmesan set a spicy aroma. Then there came three Brie cheeses displayed on round platters, and looking like melancholy extinct moons. Two of them, very dry, were at the full; the third, in its second quarter, was melting away in a white cream, which had spread into a pool and flowed over the little wooden barriers with which an attempt had been made to arrest its course... The Roqueforts under their glass covers also had a princely air, their fat faces marbled with blue and yellow, as though they were suffering from some unpleasant malady such as attacks the wealthy gluttons who eat too many truffles. And on a dish by the side of these, the hard grey goats' milk cheeses, about the size of a child's fist, resembled the pebbles which the billy-goats send rolling down the stony paths as they clamber along ahead of their flocks. Next came the strong smelling cheeses: the Mont d'Ors, of a bright yellow hue, and exhaling a comparatively mild odor; the Troyes, very thick, and bruised at the edges, and of a far more pungent smell, recalling the dampness of a cellar; the Camemberts, suggestive of high game; the square Neufchatels, Limbourgs, Marolles, and Pont l'Eveques, each adding its own particular sharp scent to the malodorous bouquet, till it became perfectly pestilential; the Livarots, ruddy in hue, and as irritating to the throat as sulphur fumes; and, lastly, stronger than all the others, the Olivets, wrapped in walnut leaves, like the carrion which peasants cover with branches as it lies rotting in the hedgerow under the blazing sun.

I don't know about you, but my taste buds are intrigued.

And here's a great example of describing an animal from *The Lion, the Witch, and the Wardrobe* by C.S. Lewis, when the mighty lion king Aslan first appears:

> But as for Aslan himself, the Beavers and the children didn't know what to do or say when they saw him. People who have not been in Narnia sometimes think that a thing cannot be good and terrible at the same time. If the children had ever thought so, they were cured of it now. For when they tried to look at Aslan's face they just caught a glimpse of the golden mane or great, royal, solemn, overwhelming eyes; and then they found they couldn't look at him and went all trembly.

How much description you need at a particular moment depends upon concerns like pacing and how important what's being described is. Minor characters will get less attention than your major ones. The same is true of minor settings. Hopefully these examples give you ideas of how to approach description effectively. Again, I highly suggest you check out a number of books further exploring the subject which are listed in the References and Recommended Reading at the end of this book.

Besides setting and description, the next concern of craft is finding your voice and style and choosing a viewpoint, topics we will explore next in Chapter 6.

CHAPTER 6
VIEWPOINT, VOICE, AND STYLE

A strong narrative voice creates confidence in readers that the narrator and author know what they're talking about. The tone and command of details inspire trust, allowing readers to relax and go along for the ride, enjoying the story. Beginning writers take a while to find their voice or voices, because, in fact, good writers have several to choose from. You can use voices in writing that you'd never use in speaking. You can, in effect, become someone else. So, what is voice? How do you develop it and craft it? How do you find your own?

In *Voice & Style*, Johnny Payne defines voices as "the key element in fiction ... one which contains and shapes all the other elements of the story." Plot, character, dialogue, theme, and setting are all brought together and empowered by voice. And voice is made up of style.

So now that we have defined voice, let's start with the first choice you must make in determining the voice for your story: Point of View, the choice of character through whose senses we experience the story.

Viewpoint

Johnny Payne writes in *Voice & Style*: "The connection between voice and point of view can have profound consequences for the story as a whole, including its plot and structure."

"Bob Barnes says they got a dead body out on BLM land. He's on line one." She might have knocked but I didn't hear it, because I was watching the geese. I watch the geese a lot in the fall, when the days get shorter and the ice traces the rocky edges of Clear Creek.

With these words, Craig Johnson establishes the voice of Sheriff Walt Longmire in his first Longmire mystery, *The Cold Dish*.

She woke in the dark. Through the slats on the window shade, the first murky hint of dawn slipping, slanting shadowy bars over the bed. It was like waking in a cell.

With this, J.D. Robb welcomes us into the mind of Eve Dallas, her famous 2058 police lieutenant, protagonist of her #1 *New York Times* bestselling Death series of novels in *Naked in Death*.

Both are examples of point of view, the character's view of the world.

In *How to Write a Damn Good Novel*, James N. Frey writes of viewpoint: "A character's viewpoint is a combination of his collective opinions, prejudices, tastes, and attitudes. His viewpoint defines how the character views the world." Viewpoint grows out of a character's sociology, psychology, physiology, theology, etc. It is their way of interpreting what and whom they see around them.

There are two key decisions an author must make when choosing viewpoint: locus of narrative and tense. Locus of narrative refers to where the character stands in relation to the world and story he or she is telling. If they are an outside observer, reporting objectively, their locus is an objective viewpoint. The narrator will describe everything happening in the story as if watching it unfolding before his or her eyes.

A subjective viewpoint, on the other hand, can be omniscient or limited. The narrator chooses which viewpoints and thoughts of which characters to reveal and when. While the narrator is inside a particular character's head, he or she is living the story through their eyes, their five senses, sharing what they think, how they interpret the world and people around them, and only what they can observe or know. In other eras, omniscient viewpoints were common, with the narrator seeing and telling all about any moment in the story, reading any character's mind, going to any setting in a moment's notice at any point in the story. In modern writing, subjective viewpoint tends to be limited, using only a limited number of point-of-view characters.

Tense refers to the tense of the prose: past, present, or future. Your voice will have two aspects: first person, second person, or third person and tense—usually designated as first-person past, third-person past, etc. Here's a simple chart demonstrating the basic differences in person of voice:

	Singular	*Plural*
First Person	I go	We go
Second Person	You go	You (all) go
Third Person	He goes, she goes	They go

Figure 6-1

First person is used for the eyewitness, objective account, though it can also be subjective. Because the narrator is interpreting everything they see, hear, taste, touch, and smell for readers, their biases and opinions can slant what they tell and how they report it. Third person is a removed perspective where the narration is an internal voice of a viewpoint character interpreting what they encounter as the story unfolds, also subjective. Which you choose is really narrative strategy.

Tense is another step. Most stories in fiction are told in past tense. It's what most readers expect when they pick up a book. And most are told in either first or third person. Second person is rarely used in fiction. Sometimes, present tense is used for effect, and there is a movement wherein some writers of young adult genres use present tense, but in my experience, many readers and most editors shy away from, and even dislike, present tense as an overall strategy. They are much more comfortable and used to past tense, and so the appearance of present tense can take them out of the story or cause them to stumble. Ultimately, know your audience and know your market when making the choice, and you should be fine.

Keep in mind that writing is about communicating, and to communicate well, you must be clear and concise. Writing a novel is about connecting with readers. It is not a great time to try odd things or experiment oddly with style and prose choices. A few highly skilled, established authors can get away with this, and every once in a while, a newcomer also pulls it off, but only one of extreme talent and intuitive skill. Most of us do better sticking to basics and norms. Strangeness in life draws people's attention, but strangeness in storytelling does the opposite: it distracts people from the story to the craft and the writer. Most of the time, your storytelling will work best in a universal tense that readers hardly notice: and that tends to be first- or third-person past. Rather than a barrier, this universal, expected norm acts as a conduit between writer and reader, channeling the story without distractions. In the examples that began this chapter, Craig Johnson was writing in first-person past, while J.D. Robb was writing in third-person past.

109

Orson Scott Card writes in *Characters and Viewpoint*:

> If your purpose in writing is to transform your audience, to give them a clear memory and understanding of truthful and important tales, your writing will be not an end in itself but a tool … great writers will always be the ones who have passionate, truthful stories to tell, and who do all they can to help their readers receive them.

So, when choosing viewpoint, make the choice that will be the least disruptive and distracting from the story you need to tell. That will always be the best viewpoint in which to tell your story.

The question to ask yourself in choosing viewpoint is which character is the best person to tell this story or scene? In the case of singular viewpoints, everything readers learn will be what one character learns or knows, solely their experience and interpretation of people and events. With multiple narrators, you must choose who has the most to lose. Usually that character is the best one to tell a particular scene because their stakes are the highest. In first-person narratives, there tends to be one character throughout. In third person, multiple viewpoints are more common. In the end, it's all about center of consciousness. Center of consciousness narration comes through a single viewpoint and allows us to look over a character's shoulder and see what they see, hear what they hear, experiencing what they experience.

Quite often genre will be a factor in choosing your viewpoint. I already mentioned the YA first-person-present-tense style, but another example is noir detective novels, which have a long tradition of first-person past tense, such as Raymond Chandler's famous Philip Marlowe novels.

It was about eleven o'clock in the morning, mid October, with the sun not shining and a look of hard wet rain in the clearness of the foothills. I was wearing my powder-blue suit, with dark blue shirt, tie and display handkerchief, black brogues, black wool socks with dark blue clocks on them. I was neat, clean, shaved and sober, and I didn't care who knew it. I was everything the well-dressed private detective ought to be.

— *The Big Sleep*

Megan Abbott, a more contemporary noir writer, also uses this style in her Gloria Denton novels, like *Queenpin*:

I want the legs.

That was the first thing that came into my head. The legs were the legs of a twenty-year-old Vegas showgirl, a hundred feet long and with just enough curve and give and promise. Sure, there was no hiding the slightly worn hands or the beginning tugs of skin framing the bones in her face. But the legs, they lasted, I tell you. They endured. Two decades her junior, my skinny matchsticks were no competition.

You can see how in both cases the narrator's sarcastic tone lends a certain edge to the story. It's the confidence of someone who's seen it all, or a lot anyway, and who speaks with authority in telling us about his or her world. One advantage of first person is establishing empathy and sympathy more readily and directly. In this case, Marlowe describes himself in a way that reflects our stereotypes about detectives, giving us confidence that he is a professional and fits the mold, thus being trustworthy to offer a detective's perspective on the story we are about to be told. For Abbott, Gloria's viewpoint here establishes some humility by showing her envy of traits someone else has that she doesn't. Humility is a great lead into empathy. We tend to like people who are not cocky and arrogant but instead very aware of their own flaws and imperfections, because we can relate to them better.

Charlaine Harris's blockbuster Sookie Stackhouse series, the basis of the HBO TV series, is an urban fantasy that uses first-person past to great effect. Here's the opening passage from *Dead Until Dark*, the first novel in that series:

> I'd been waiting for the vampire for years when he walked into the bar.
>
> Ever since vampires came out of the coffin (as they laughingly put it) two years ago, I'd hoped one would come to Bon Temps. We had all the other minorities in our town—why not the newest, the legally recognized undead? But rural northern Louisiana wasn't too tempting to vampires, apparently; on the other hand, New Orleans was a real center for them—the whole Anne Rice thing, right?

Notice how Harris immediately tells us several things through this opening passage:

1. This is a world with vampires.
2. The setting is northern Louisiana.
3. This is a world in which the vampire fiction of Anne Rice exists.
4. The narrator is excited to meet a vampire and has heard them speak on media about coming out of coffins.

All of this prepares us for the world of the story we're about to read. This is not necessarily a place where people fear vampires. In fact, it is a contemporary modern-day setting, one in which vampires live in the open, not hiding in the shadows. All of these details give important context for the story and, being spoken so confidently and casually by the narrator, help lead readers to accept them more readily as they continue to read. The narrator's casualness prepares us to believe.

Typically, one viewpoint is used per scene, but there are exceptions. In the case of action scenes, a common technique is to break the scenes into segments told by different point-of-view characters to raise tension and increase the pace. The multiple points of view provide diversion and perspective from the protagonist's point of view that can deepen conflict, enlarge scope, and add nuance and texture. At the same time, it is not uncommon for novels to be primarily told from one viewpoint with occasional scenes as needed told from other points of view when the main viewpoint character is not present. Sometimes a scene is needed to further the story but does not involve a viewpoint character. If the information is essential to a reader's understanding, then this may be your only option, so it is perfectly fine to do so. Quite often this may be the only scene in a novel told from that point of view. In other cases, scattered scenes may be told from the same points of view other than the protagonist or narrator throughout the story at various times. It is also common to see stories told from four to six points of view but usually primarily when told in third person, not first. Mixing points of view in first person takes a lot of skill to differentiate the voices and characters so readers don't lose track. Instead, what sometimes happens is the bulk of a novel is told from first-person point of view with a few scenes told in third when they involve another character's viewpoint. Usually the first and third scenes are separated into different chapters to avoid jolting readers.

Another viable method is to switch tense and voice in different novels of the same series. For example, Michael Connelly has used primarily third-person past tense to tell the stories of his Harry Bosch series, except in a couple of books where Bosch left the Los Angeles Police Department to become a private detective. Those were told in first person. The first-person perspective suited the story better, so Connelly wisely chose to switch for those books, and I doubt readers had any complaint. Always do what's best for the particular story you are writing, then your decisions will be the right ones every time.

With any viewpoint character, the trick is to create identification with readers as quickly as possible, and the best way to do this is to use emotional touchpoints. Frey writes: "You can touch your reader best if you introduce a character with problems the reader can sympathize with at the very beginning." Then, once empathy and identification have been established, you plunge the character into an immediate crisis and the ride begins. Frey offers the following examples:

> In Charles Dickens's *A Christmas Carol*, the Scrooge is established as miserly and cruel. Readers loathe him.

> At the beginning of *Lolita*, Humbert Humbert loves Lolita 'til it hurts, so we sympathize with him.

> Mario Puzo's *The Godfather* opens with a father watching the trial of two men who assaulted his daughter. Readers feel for him.

Ernest Hemingway's *The Old Man and the Sea* opens with a fisherman who has not caught a fish in years and is facing hardship.

I'm sure other examples come to mind. Creating empathy or sympathy or any strong emotional reaction in your viewpoint character as soon as possible is always an effective way to spur reader interest in your story. Even in the case of Scrooge, whom we loathe, we want to read to see how he gets his just desserts.

Another technique that is commonly used to add tension and suspense is to have an unreliable narrator. This is a point-of-view character who lies or twists the truth so that readers are misled and uncover various surprises along the way. A prime example of where this might occur is when your viewpoint character is mentally ill or a criminal. In both cases, readers will discover the characters' minds do not always work with the same truth as everyone else's. For this to work, however, it is very important to clue readers in to the unreliability early on. The easiest way is to have the narrator caught in a lie and admit it so we know he or she is not trustworthy. Another way is to use another viewpoint character who is trustworthy to contradict the falsehoods stated by the narrator. Either way, it is essential readers are aware of the deceit to avoid angering them and turning them off. Readers like twists and turns and mystery in their reads, but they don't like feeling misled and toyed with by authors. You must maintain the author–reader contract—the promise that you will pay off whatever happens and deliver on your promises whether using an unreliable or a reliable narrator. Johnny Payne writes in *Voice & Style*:

"For a fiction writer, the advantage of employing an unreliable narrator is to keep the reader off

115

balance in strategic ways, so that character motives can be entered into more deeply and more unexpectedly."

Voice and Style

Once you have determined the correct viewpoint for your narrator, other elements of voice should begin falling into place. Ultimately, the voice is a combination of the character viewpoints and your own. While it is important to avoid jarring readers out of the story by intruding too much as the narrator, inevitably your own unique way of saying things will always come through. And it should. In *Writing the Breakout Novel*, Donald Maass explains that when editors talk of voice, "they mean not only a unique way of putting words together, but a unique sensibility, a distinctive way of looking at the world, an outlook that enriches an author's oeuvre. They want to read an author who is like no other." Voice is your unique writing language and approach, reflecting your own diction and style along with that of the characters. Maass adds: "You can facilitate voice by giving yourself the freedom to say things in your own unique style… To set your voice free, set your words free. Set your characters free. Most important, set your heart free." Voice is indeed the single most unique thing any writer brings to their storytelling.

The best way to develop your voice is to read thoughtfully a lot. Pay attention to and study what other writers are doing that you like and don't like, then imitate it. Practice writing in their various voices, and play around to develop your own. What stands out about a particular voice? What types of details do they tend to use most often, and how do they affect you as a reader? What do they say about the world and characters? If you want to be a good writer, you must read. All too many writers make the excuse that they don't have time to read. I read a book or two a week and still hit 1,300 words a day on average when on a book project. If you make it a priority, it will happen, and consider it part of your work research and author development time. It really is that valuable. Not only can you stay abreast of the latest trends and shifts in genres and subgenres, but you will discover much about what works and doesn't in fiction that will be invaluable to you in developing your own craft—especially voice and style.

Let's look at examples from two classic books which I borrow from Frey's *How to Write a Damn Good Novel II*. First, from *Gone with the Wind* by Margaret Mitchell:

Scarlett O'Hara was not beautiful, but men seldom realized it when caught by her charm as the Tarleton twins were. In her face were too sharply blended the delicate features of her mother, a Coast aristocrat of French descent, and the heavy ones of her florid Irish father. But it was an arresting face, pointed of chin, square of jaw. Her eyes were pale green without a touch of hazel, starred with bristly black lashes and slightly tilted at the ends. Above them, her thick black brows slanted upward, cutting a startling oblique line in her magnolia white skin—the skin so prized by Southern women and so carefully guarded with bonnets, veils, and mittens against hot Georgia suns.

Okay, let's examine what all we learn here. First, we learn what Scarlet looks like in many details and that she is not considered beautiful but is charming. We learn of her French and Irish parentage as well. Additionally, we learn of the Southern attitudes toward pale skin and beauty. So there is appearance, heritage, and cultural context all in a few sentences of very specific details. These are the kinds of details that give the voice authority, and while the voice is neutral and not passing judgments, its melodramatic tone does aid the tone of the larger story.

Next, here's a passage from Stephen King's *Carrie*:

Momma was a very big woman, and she always wore a hat. Lately her legs had begun to swell and her feet always seemed on the point of overflowing her shoes. She wore a black cloth coat with a black fur collar. Her eyes were blue and magnified behind rimless bifocals. She always carried a large black satchel purse and in it was her change purse, her billfold (both black), a large King James Bible (also black) with her name stamped on the front in gold, a stack of tracts secured with a rubber band. The tracts were usually orange, and smearily printed.

Note the feel of sarcastic or ironic tone to this narrative voice. There are rich details, but the tone lends almost a sense of commentary to the descriptions. "Her feet always seemed on the point of overflowing her shoes" is a very specific detail that evokes an immediate image of fat feet crammed into too-small shoes, and the clothing and accessories are big and stand out to match the big woman and make her stand out, intentional or not. We also see she is a Christian or at least a Bible reader, and the public display of this, along with her size, makes her come across as foreboding, even perhaps a bit serious or intimidating. These kinds of subtle details are vivid and memorable and create characters who readily reflect the complex people we meet in the world around us, making the author's voice ring with truth that inspires confidence in its telling of the story.

In his stunning debut Harry Bosch novel, *The Black Echo*, Michael Connelly introduces his main narrative voice and protagonist with a flashback dream that tells us volumes about the character without stating it outright:

> Harry Bosch could hear the helicopter up there, somewhere above the darkness, circling up in the light. Why didn't it land? Why didn't it bring help? Harry was moving through a smoky, dark tunnel and his batteries were dying. The beam of the flashlight grew weaker every yard he covered. He needed help. He needed to move faster. He needed to reach the end of the tunnel before the light was gone and he was alone in the black. He heard the chopper make one more pass. Why didn't it land? Where was the help he needed? When the drone of the blades fluttered away again, he felt the terror build and he moved faster, crawling on scraped and bloody knees, one hand holding the dim light up, the other pawing to keep his balance. He did not look back, for he knew the enemy was behind him in the black mist. Unseen, but there, and closing in.
>
> When the phone rang in the kitchen, Bosch immediately woke...

Note the mixture of narrative description with inner thoughts that provide emotional context for what the character is experiencing. When he thinks, "Why didn't it land? Why didn't it bring help?" we suddenly know he is feeling afraid or in trouble, when all we have been told before this is that he heard the helicopter. This sets the emotional tone and tension for what follows. The "smoky, dark tunnel" as setting lends an air of danger to it that just adds to the tension, and his dying flashlight, which the comment on batteries tells us before the word "flashlight" is even introduced, also ups the stakes. Who hasn't been afraid in the misty dark with a dying flashlight? No mention is made of fear or terror until the helicopter has appeared for the third time and he is then crawling, his knees in pain, desperate to escape the dark. This shows how the right details, ordered carefully, can create a whole atmosphere, tone, and ambience that indicates so much more than actually needs to be said, demonstrating how a character's own experiences and background affect and interplay with what he or she is experiencing in the immediate moment of the story scene.

If this isn't how you read, then you should start, because this is how one reads and studies the craft. It will transform your reading into work at times, for sure, but if you don't pay attention to such details, a good book will catch you up and breeze you away without helping you notice the stylistic choices that make up the voice so you can think about them as you develop your own voice or voices. I say "voices" because most writers have more than one and employ them as needed in different genres and books or stories that they write. Few writers have only one voice, but again, it takes time to develop the voices and write in them with confidence, because none of your narrative voices will ever be completely you at any point as you naturally converse or think in the world. All of them are amalgamations of character and author, affected by considerations of diction, tone, and more. Your fiction will always take on a personality of its own, and it should do so well. That personality is not you nor is it just a character, but a combination of them.

One thing narrators can do that characters and authors cannot is legitimize character and world by showing the characters' emotional reactions to various circumstances and actions they experience. The narrative voice can speak as if it knows them intimately and cares deeply about them or loathes them, depending upon the needs of the situation. It can legitimize their pain and anger or characterize it as unusual or inappropriate in ways that will guide the reader's own opinions and impressions and guide them along in how they connect with the story. Johnny Payne writes: "The narrating voice provides a more sensible and level-headed account than the character's simply because its passions are not engaged in the flow of the action in the same way." Unlike the character, the narrator doesn't have anything to lose or gain. They don't have to worry about the reactions of other characters or consequences for its thoughts or actions. They can merely observe, comment, and hover like a ghost. Of the difference between first- and third-person narration, Payne reminds us: "Third-person narrators tend to offer more range and elicit fewer questions, while first-person narrators, even when they're volatile, offer the advantage of a more immediate and tangible voice." This is because the first-person "I was" lends itself to a feel of being closer to events and actions in the story than the third-person "he was." The first is talking about itself and the third about some stranger, removed from the self.

The voice is key to setting atmosphere and tone by its word choices. It can layer a mood over any scene just by how it describes the events and characters as the scene unfolds. The wellspring here is character emotions grounded objectively in the setting. Authors should not engage in atmospherics or hysterics. That kind of melodrama should instead flow from the characters themselves. Description should never be written for its own sake but should serve the characters and story always, every time. This is how the writer guides the storytelling without inserting himself or herself directly into it. Tone always flows from who is telling the story, whereas point of view flows from character. The author brings the tone, the character brings the point of view, and the two combine and unify into one narrative voice that sets forth the story dramatically, weaving the emotional tone, atmosphere, etc. necessary to engage readers and tell the story with the appropriate gravitas and effect. The impression your story makes, Payne reminds us, "will depend to a large degree on the tone established at the beginning and sustained throughout the performance." This is why sometimes reviews note changes in tone that render novels less effective or troubled. Consistency in tone is very important to readers and their experience of receiving a story.

Ultimately, if you set the proper tone and maintain it, providing the right details to gain confidence from your reader, your main responsibility as a writer is then to ensure you honor the author–reader contract, making all the details and emotions of the story pay off rewardingly for readers.

The Author–Reader Contract

A contract is essentially an exchange of promises. Party A promises X, and Party B promises Y. One leads to the other. Each gets something in return. The reader essentially promises to read your whole story and enjoy it as long as you deliver on your promises. It is an implied contract for sure, but essential to your success as an author. Remember when I talked about plot being a series of questions asked and answered? This is the heart of your author–reader contract. The details and authority of your voice promise various possibilities and raise questions the reader reads on with hopes of getting answers to. They want a satisfying conclusion to your story. They want to see the protagonist conquer his or her flaws and face the antagonist for a final showdown (and hopefully win). They want the story to lead somewhere that both answers their questions and is emotionally fulfilling. As the author, your implied promise is that you will provide that experience. Those who do get good reviews. Those who don't do not. And return readers tend to flock more to authors who fulfill that contract over those who do not. That's the simple gist of the author–reader contract underlying every book you write.

It's not that you can't surprise them or deliver a tragedy. It's not that every book has to end happily to be emotionally satisfying.

It is that the trust your authoritative, informed author voice instills from the beginning proves reliable in the end. If your voice fulfills this promise, readers will follow you anywhere. That is why it is so important to develop a skillful voice and style for each book you write and carry them through to the end. It's why genres have conventions that cannot be ignored by readers, because readers come in with certain built-in expectations that must be fulfilled for them to be satisfied and come back for more. It is why readers come back to the same genres time and again, too, because those conventions and the promises that go with them are what they want out of a good read. So, it's your job to give them one. You learn these conventions by reading books in the genres you hope to write, learning how they are used, how they can be twisted, and what the must-haves are verses the options.

From the start of the story, your readers will be guessing about your premise. And your job is to prove the argument. The only way to do that is to deliver upon its promise. When you hint at a certain type of story in the beginning, even if the full premise has yet to be revealed, readers immediately form expectations about how the book will go, including how it will be written to deliver upon that promise. This is why you must carefully choose what to withhold and what to reveal and when to do so, with the ultimate aim of satisfying your readers and paying off their expectations by delivering that satisfying story and logical conclusion that ties it all together and fulfills the emotional promise, answering their questions. You must at all times play fair, allowing the reader to try to outguess you while still providing surprises and twists that enrich their reading experience. And to do so, you must limit the intrusion of yourself and your beliefs or philosophy and instead deliver upon those of the characters and their world. It's not that your books cannot reflect who you are. They inevitably will. You won't even have to try. But your first and foremost priority is not preaching but telling a good story, and the rest will come out in the craft naturally through theme and voice as long as you do that job well. Every single time.

In the end, it's your plot, characters, settings, and theme as told via your narrative voice, with all the stylistic choices that make up its parts, that enables you to fulfill this contract and deliver a great book to readers, one that fulfills its promise, proves its premise, and keeps them turning pages, making them want to return to you time and again for more great stories. *That* is the power and importance of voice and style.

Now, the next area of craft we should address is the area as closely tied to voice as description is: dialogue. Dialogue and description are the two areas where voice is made manifest. And both are the key building blocks of storytelling that lives, breathes, and comes alive for readers.

CHAPTER 7
DIALOGUE

Chances are, 50 percent or more of your novel will consist of dialogue. Dialogue is the characters' chief method of communicating information to one another (and readers). But remember: conversation isn't dialogue. Dialogue is drama. It is a certain type of dramatic representation of conversation that has conflict and drama and urgency. It may imitate conversation, but there is no chitchat. Dialogue involves imparting key information about plot, emotion, character, setting, and more that drives the story forward. It involves building tension, building pace, and foreshadowing conflict as well as expressing present conflict. Dialogue is one of the essential craft tools of good fiction writing.

Johnny Payne writes in *Voice & Style*:

> Dialogue is the essence of teaching… The role of dialogue within fiction can be defined as not so different from the one it plays in learning. Ideally, it should deepen with progressive readings, leaving the reader with an increased understanding of the story's consequences.

In some ways, dialogue exists in tension with, and separate from, the authorial voice. Characters care nothing about the author's life or concerns, just their own. When two or more characters have a dialogue, they are in a sense "talking back" to the author or narrative voice. They contest it at times, challenge it, add complexity to its views. This tension gives us perspective on the narrative voice while also clarifying the independence of characters in the story from the narrator. By necessity, fiction must be truer than life in order to give us different perspectives on it. Because characters always speak in opposition—conflict lies at the heart of drama, remember—the tension between character voices and author voice is a key element of the storytelling experience, adding tension and drama and upping the stakes. While dialogue is part of overall voice, because characters and narrator can also speak in opposition, they create the kind of multiple meanings and complexity associated with dramatic irony. As narration directs and lays out the story, dialogue detonates and creates explosions that create twists, surprises, turns, and consequences that affect the rest of the story and keep it interesting. This is the essence of narrative drama.

So, how do you develop a skill for good dialogue? Let's look at several aspects, starting with the purpose of dialogue, diction and dialect, dialogue and pacing, and then dialogue and speech tags.

The Purpose of Dialogue

Jack Hart writes in *Storycraft*:

> Dialogue isn't an end in itself; it has to do some real work. It can advance action as characters encounter and struggle with obstacles, such as an antagonist who resists a character's progress in resolving a complication. It can help shape a scene as characters comment on objects in their environment, such as the clothes one of them wears.

Advancing action, imparting information, revealing character, increasing conflict—all of these are the purpose of dialogue, and its every word should serve one or more of these at all times.

According to screenwriter John Howard Lawson, speaking "comes from energy and not inertia." It serves "as it does in life, to broaden the scope of action; it organizes and extends what people do. It also intensifies the action. The emotion which people feel in a situation grows out of their sense of scope and meaning." James Scott Bell writes in *How to Write Dazzling Dialogue*: "Characters talk in fiction because they want to further their own ends... Every word, every phrase that comes out of a character's mouth is uttered because the character hopes it will further a purpose." Because dialogue can foreshadow action, explain it, or set it up, advancing action is a core role of dialogue. Also, dialogue exchanges are laden with conflict and can increase the tension and stakes of action and confrontations, thus advancing action and leading from one action to another. The very act of dialoguing is, in effect, taking an action: to confront, to question, to ask, to discuss, etc. and in all cases, this dialogical action furthers plot, story, and character in some way (or should).

Because, in many ways, we reveal who we are by how we speak, what dialogue does best is reveal or advance character. In the next section we will cover dialect and diction, but it's not just the word choice that is at work here but the interaction with other characters and the world that reveals much, too. Word choice can reveal education level, social stratus, historical background, ethnicity, nationality, etc., but dialogue with others reveals attitudes about society, setting, the world, and relationships. We talk to different people differently for various reasons, and that very act reveals much about who we are and who they are to us.

Because much dialogue involves opposition between characters, conflict is inherent in its nature. Stephen King writes in *On Writing*:

It's dialogue that gives your cast their voices and is crucial in defining their characters—only what people do tells us more about what they're like, and talk is sneaky: what people say often conveys their character to others in ways of which they—the speakers—are completely unaware.

Dialogue is intimately connected to character motivation. It reveals motive constantly, setting and revising the characters' agendas. These agenda checks oppose those of other characters, creating conflict and tension and leading to action, imparting information, and upping the stakes. This is a key difference between conversation and dialogue. Dialogue is always about tension and conflict, whereas conversation is not. Conversation can be casual and consumed with minute details, facts, and experiences that interest the involved parties but are irrelevant to those around them. Dialogue must always function to advance the story by revealing motives, information, character, action, and more, so dialogue and conversation are very different in both purpose and style. In dialogue, characters sometimes say things to inform readers of information they already know in order to advance the story. This exposition is a manufactured trait of narrative dialogue that is not common in real life except with strangers. Many times, there are things we don't have to say, because the party we are speaking to just knows them, but with readers watching, in narrative, these things cannot go unsaid.

Dialogue can also be external and internal. At the same time as characters engage in dialogue with other characters, they may maintain an internal dialogue that can conflict with the external dialogue but performs the same functions. It can impart backstory, history, and details readers need to know and also things characters may not share, for various reasons, with other characters but which they know and hold in reserve—and which readers need to know to further the story, action, and character. These two streams of dialogue go on simultaneously and intertwine with the narrator's voice as the story unfolds.

A couple of examples. Here's an example from romance author Catherine Bybee's *Wife by Wednesday*:

"Kissing me is wrong?"

"Yes," she blurted out. "I mean, no."

He chuckled, "Which is it?"

"Ugh. What if I choke? What if I don't look convincing?" What if she screwed up and gave the camera exactly what they wanted and Blake lost his inheritance?

Blake removed one hand from the steering wheel and placed it over her cold ones. "Samantha?"

"Yes?"

"Relax. Let me take charge here."

She wanted to trust him. But her hands shook as they pulled into her driveway. He removed the key from the ignition and shifted in his seat. "Let's just go inside and start packing."

"Are you going to kiss me the minute we're inside?" God, she had to know ... so she could prepare herself.

Okay, clearly Blake and Samantha are lovers. And they are going somewhere important with potential consequences for Blake that Samantha is worried she'll screw up. Notice also how Samantha's internal and external monologue are both at play here to impart understanding of motives and thought behind her reactions and words. Also note how while she is tense and anxious, Blake's body language and words combine to demonstrate he is not. He is relaxed, at ease. This is a very solid demonstration of effective dialogue.

The next is from *The Cold Dish* by Craig Johnson:

"What are you smiling at?"

"Leave me alone. I'm having a moment of grace."

He stared at me. "Well, we would not want to interrupt that."

I tossed a piece of shale at him, missing by a good two feet. "If you can have multiple lives, I can have moments of grace."

He grunted. "How was your moment of grace last night?"

"Not bad, as moments of grace go." I thought for a while. "More like a moment of truth."

He nodded. "That is good. They are harder to come by." He winced as he stretched the tendons in his right knee; maybe he wasn't indestructible. "So, she left the Jeep?"

"Yep."

"You drive her home?"

"Yep."

He stretched for a minute more, leaned against the mile-marker post I was leaning against, and sighed. "Okay ..."

"Okay, what?"

"We do not have to talk about it."

"We are talking about it."

"No, I am talking about it, and all you are doing is saying, 'Yep.'"

Even without a lot of context, hopefully you can tell these are characters who know each other well. In this case, Sheriff Walt Longmire and Henry Standing Bear are childhood friends, now adults. Henry is an American Indian, Walt white. The sarcasm inherent here shows familiarity, as does the inside reference to "multiple lives." Characters with a history spar as they talk frequently. There is a playfulness and tension to it as they test each other, sometimes in fun, sometimes in anger, but always in shared knowledge. Just four lines of dialogue and two of description, but you see what that can reveal, even out of context. Walt, it appears, had a date or something the night before. Also, notice that Henry uses no contractions in his syntax. He has a unique way of talking that distinguishes him from Walt.

Now let's take a closer look at word choices, accents, etc., in Diction and Dialect.

Diction and Dialect

Diction has to do with tone and style, whereas syntax, which is closely related, has to do with the form of the sentence. The level of diction of a truck driver has a different level than a bishop, but syntax and diction depend on one another. The truck driver may speak more base, slangy language than the elevated diction of the bishop, for example. This is dependent upon levels of diction with which they choose to speak. It is also dependent upon the word order (syntax) they choose to use.

A truck driver might say, "I been having sad thoughts when I'm alone."

A bishop, "Thoughts of grief came to me when alone."

Yoda: "Thoughts of grief, I have."

Just as Henry Standing Bear stands out because he never uses contractions, another character might stand out for going to pains to use "whom" instead of "who" whenever it is grammatically correct or the opposite. Subtle grammatical quirks can be quite effective characterization tools. What if a character says "the killer musta wore gloves" instead of "the killer must have worn gloves"—"must have worn" being grammatically correct? Some of these quirks are quite common in usage and can be observed daily in those around us. Often, they subtly reveal things about people's backgrounds—education, social class, where they come from—that will make your dialogue more realistic.

Stephen King writes: "Well-crafted dialogue will indicate if a character is smart or dumb, honest or dishonest, amusing or an old sobersides." When done well, dialogue can impart several bits of information about your characters just through word choice. Bishops, kings, politicians, professors, and others all speak differently and with more sophistication and less common vernacular than truck drivers, plumbers, mechanics, and farmers. Add in gang members, foreigners, and others and you have a third style of diction as well. Use diction to differentiate between characters and help readers know who is speaking without even requiring a speech tag. You can know the area of the world they come from, their education level, their level of class and refinement, their self-esteem level, their social circles, their religion or lack of religion, and so much more just by how a character speaks. The unique voice of each character will add depth and realness to your world and story like nothing else.

In my novel *Simon Says*, a tough Kansas City police detective is forced to team with a humanoid android to solve his partner's murder. At one point, Simon points out the humanoid's speech patterns:

> "I function ninety percent like a human being in most respects," Lucas said as they continued up the stairs.

> "Yeah, and at least ten percent is how you talk," Simon teased.

> Lucas turned a puzzled look at him. "You think I do not speak like a human?"

> "No normal human uses the cadence you use, no," Simon said.

> Lucas looked disappointed. "Well, I hope you will assist me to do better. I am designed to blend in with humans and wish to learn."

> "You want to blend stop saying things like 'in most respects' or 'I am designed,'" Simon said, shaking his head. "You sound like a machine."

> Lucas harrumphed. "I will remember."

Just listening to them, you can tell the difference. This is a prime example of syntax and diction at work. The same thing can happen with socioeconomic class.

"You, stop!" The detective stepped in front of the vagrant and raised his hand.

"What ya want?" the disheveled woman demanded, her dirty, unkempt hair hanging down off her forehead to obscure most of one eye, her nose brown with dirt and grime from life on the street.

"I have a couple of questions. Did you see what happened down there last night?"

"Huh? I was 'sleep."

"No way you slept through that," the detective countered. "Were you here?"

Her face shriveled as she shook her head and looked away. "I don' know nothin'."

"You're not in trouble. We just need your help. People died."

"Not my pro'lem," she said.

Dialogue can also tell readers about your world. Do characters speak familiarly to present-day people around us or like people from another place or time? Do they speak with familiar vernacular and nuance and pop-culture references, or are the references odd and unusual, even requiring us to work a bit to understand them? All of this is key to world and character building, and creating a sense of place and dialogue is a key tool for accomplishing it.

Here's an example from *Wager of My Heart* by Claire Ashgrove:

> "What seems to be the problem, Thomas?"
>
> "A wreck, sir," the man replied as he bounced the long reins to quiet the agitated horse.
>
> "Easy, girl. Stand now."
>
> "A wreck?"
>
> "Aye. The crowd's thick—I cannot make it all out. But a coach is twisted at such an angle I can clearly see the top of it."
>
> Perfect. Lord only knew how long it would take to right a coach. "Is there a way around?" he asked, his patience rapidly deteriorating. "I would prefer not to linger in this stench."
>
> "No, my lord. Not unless you wish me to drive over the onlookers, sir."

Both the vocabulary and the descriptions clearly indicate a different time, in this case Victorian-era London.

Point-of-view characters engage in two main types of dialogue throughout a fictional work: external dialogue with other characters and internal dialogue with themselves. Internal dialogue is similar to external dialogue, as I described in the last section, but it is rather their inner voice and thoughts taking expression.

Here's an example from my novel *The Worker Prince*, a science fiction space opera:

"I can't tell you what to do, Davi, but it's a big risk."

"Now you sound just like Farien," Davi growled and drowned the words with another gulp from his beer.

Yao's purple eyes softened to violet with sympathy. "Hey, I'm on your side here, okay? One man can't change an entire culture."

Davi wiped his lips on his sleeve and met his friend's eyes again. "This man has to try."

Yao sighed, sinking back into the couch again. "Why?"
Davi stared at him a moment, anger mixed with disgust. But Yao wasn't the bad guy. You've got to tell him. Ignoring his internal voice, he shrugged.

"Have you spoken to Farien since?" Yao asked.

"No. There hasn't been an occasion."

"Maybe we could pay him a visit," Yao said. "Be good to have the three musketeers back together again." Yao loved references to the classics. Along with history, he'd read many novels.

"Sure. Of course …" Davi's voice trailed off as he looked away, lost in thought. Should I tell him? He needed to confide in someone before he burst.

Internal speech is often written in italics to differentiate it. When needed, phrases such as "he thought," etc. are used to indicate the words are unspoken thoughts. In this case, we can see

Davi has two conversations going on at once—one external with Yao and the other internal with himself.

In *The Lord of the Rings*, J.R.R. Tolkien uses elevated diction combined with a formal syntax to suggest an ancient language:

> Gimli shivered. They had brought only one blanket apiece. "Let us light a fire," he said. "I care no longer for the danger. Let the orcs come as thick as summer moths around the candle!"
>
> "If those unhappy hobbits are astray in the woods, it might draw them hither," said Legolas.
>
> "And it might draw other things, neither Orc nor Hobbit," said Aragorn. "We are near the mountain-marshes of the traitor Saruman. Also, we are on the very edge of Fangorn, and it is perilous to touch the trees of that wood, it is said."
>
> —The Two Towers

So, using different dictions is a great technique and device for characterization. If a character is a con artist, they may use different diction externally than they do internally. This tells us about your character. Or they may fake an accent they don't really have, etc. Also, the character's internal dialogue will show what they choose to reveal and hide to various characters, which tells us much about their motives, emotions, etc. Internal dialogue is where characters debate decisions, mourn mistakes, and so much more, and it is necessary for storytelling because we cannot see what we are not shown, so it provides a method of showing what is going on in the inner life of characters that is essential to building good conflict and drama in your story.

Remember that characters may speak differently to one character than to another depending upon their relationship, their motives, etc. If hanging with old friends from the old ghetto, one character may slip into a dialect left behind in childhood for those interactions even if the character usually speaks in a more refined way with characters outside that world and life. Ever have a friend from a foreign country or the US Deep South who talks with one accent with you but goes home and slips back into a native accent? People speak to a lover differently than to a mother or a sister or a boss or a priest. One also speaks differently to a king or ruler than to a fellow citizen and to a teacher differently than to fellow students, and so on. So, remember to establish changes in dialogue appropriate to the circumstances in which the dialogue is occurring and appropriate to who is speaking, and to whom. This will make your world come alive and feel realistic.

Lewis Turco writes in *Dialogue* that characterization "is largely what dialect is about—identifying the persona and his or her traits, including the main personality trait on which much of the story will depend for its plot and the motivations of its characters." Remember that characters who speak with the same diction only recognize the difference when speaking with outsiders. The same is true of dialect or accents. Characters with accents only know they have one when someone points it out or when they talk with another character. Even then, to them they sound normal and the other person has the accent.

Dialect is a particular way of speaking that is represented in a modified written form to reflect its accent or peculiarities. It is particularly common in older novels but frowned upon these days because it is often challenging for readers to read. Use dialect sparingly and only for strategic purposes. Often just a line or two is all you need to remind readers of the character's accent. The rest can be rendered more naturally. Another technique is to render a few key words in dialect. Here's another example from my novel *The Worker Prince*:

As he neared a tent, someone poked his arm—a smiling vendor who looked half-human and half-Lhamor, gesturing with his bottom two arms when he spoke, his forked tongue giving him a strong lisp.

"'ello, Capt'in, my frien', wha'ever you nee', I can ge' for you," he said with the accent of Italis and patted Davi's back like they had been lifelong pals.

There's a reason other of your race use translators. "No thank you, just passing through," Davi said with forced politeness, moving on through quickly.

The Lhamori here is speaking in dialect, and a particularly hard one to understand, which is why I used it sparingly (though not sparingly enough according to some readers. It was my first novel.)

In *How to Write Dazzling Dialogue,* James Scott Bell suggests three guidelines for using dialect:

1. Decide if dialect is absolutely needed in a scene.
2. If so, go ahead and use it in the first spoken line.
3. Use it sparingly after that, only as a reminder to readers of the voice.

Here's another example from James Michener's *Sayonara*:

I started to get up but Makino, the cook, grabbed my arm and translated, "She not angry. Only she say very dangerous Fumiko-san walk with Americans."

"She wasn't walking," I cried. "She was sitting here."

"Please!" Makino protested. "I not speak good. Trouble too much."

Here, Michener is representing the broken English of a nonnative speaker fairly well using dialect to give a realness to the dialogue, another appropriate technique. In this case, rather than odd or modified spellings, it involves missing words or rearranged syntax.

Generally speaking, it is advisable to use standard diction and avoid dialect. Remember, writing is communication and communication is about clarity first and foremost. Anything that might be a stumbling block for readers is to be handled with care.

Similar to dialect are idioms. An idiom is "an expression whose meaning is not predictable from the usual meanings of its constituent elements, as in *kick the bucket* or *hang one's head*, or from the general grammatical rules of a language, as *the table round* for *the round table*, and that is not a constituent of a larger expression of like characteristics; a language, dialect, or style of speaking peculiar to a people" (Dictionary.com). Mark Twain is the US master and Charles Dickens the UK master of idioms. Lewis Turco writes: "An expression may begin as the slang—or 'popular jargon'—of a particular generation, but once it enters the language permanently, it becomes an idiomatic expression." So, for example, where Brits might say "throwing crockery," Americans would say "throwing dishes."

Both Dickens and Twain exploit idiomatic expressions freely in their novels and sometimes develop or perpetuate them into greater popularity by repeating the same phrases over and over again in their works, giving them a stability in the language. Examples from Dickens are "heart and soul," "jog-trot," and "turn and turn about," the last two of which are particularly British. Examples from Twain include "without you" (unless you), "by some stretchers" (lies), "back to the drawing board," and "I lit out." The following passage from Twain's *The Adventures of Huckleberry Finn* contains some more:

The Widow Douglas, she took me for her son, and allowed she would sivilize me; but it was rough living in the house all the time, considering how dismal regular and decent the widow was in all her ways; and so when I couldn't stand it no longer, I lit out.

Twain and Dickens both use colloquialisms to give characters distinctive voices. Huck misspells civilize as "sivilize," which reveals his lack of formal education, and uses "allowed" instead of "said." He also uses adjectives in unusual and informal ways in phrases like "it was rough living" and "dismal regular" (instead of dismally regular). And he uses a lot of double negatives like "I couldn't stand it no longer." These details add authenticity that capture the time and place and bring the characters to life. Idioms can be a great tool for this but must be used skillfully and handled well to avoid confusing or drowning readers.

To write dialogue well, it helps to go out and observe people as well as to read a lot. If you are writing a historical period, find movies, newsreels, and other books and observe carefully, taking notes on how people talk, turns of phrase, idioms, etc. To write teenagers, go to Sam's Club or Costco or Walmart and sit in the food court or to a mall or theater and listen. Note how the teens speak to each other versus adults, how they address strangers versus friends, etc. Do the same with anyone else you need to study in whatever profession: from cops to priests, jewelers to plumbers, and more. Writing down key observations in a notebook will create an invaluable resource to jog your memory when the time comes to write various characters, especially if you want to find turns of phrase, idioms, or other idiosyncrasies you can employ to add authenticity and bring characters to life. You want dialogue to sound believable and real, after all, and that means you have to write it so it sounds natural while still performing all the dramatic functions beyond conversation that it must do to move your story forward.

Dialogue and Pacing (*in Medias Res*)

In Chapter 3, when talking about scenes, I mentioned the technique of *in medias res*—the rule that you should get into a scene as late as possible and get out as soon after as you can to increase the tension and help pacing. This is particularly true in dialogue scenes. Dialogue, as a rule, tends to move faster than action and description, upping your novel's pace. In *How to Write a Damn Good Novel*, James N. Frey writes:

> Plunging into the middle of scenes speeds your novel along and keeps the reader involved in the rising conflict… When critics say a work is fast-paced, it is often because the writer keeps his characters engaged in intense conflicts and cuts directly into scenes with rising conflict.

A lot of time can be saved by starting scenes with the conflict already happening or ending them right as it ends. The results will also make your story feel faster.

For example:

> Johnny opened the door and stepped into his kitchen.

> "Hi, honey," his wife said, singsong as usual, and bounced across the floor to greet him. They embraced and kissed as usual before she asked, "How was your day?"

"Boring. Usual sales calls. Nagging boss. How was yours?"

"It sucked. I got fired," she said, frowning. Johnny hadn't expected it, given her great mood.

Now what if it were written like this?

"Today sucked," Johnny's wife said the minute he opened the door.

"What happened?" he asked as she moped across the floor to greet him.

"My boss is an asshole," she said, then kissed him.

"Well, we kinda knew that."

She smiled. "Well, now we have proof."

Which feels more dramatic and fast paced? In every scene you write, look for the best way to enter dramatically and shape the dialogue for the greatest dramatic effect. In real life, niceties like greetings and chatter might be socially expected, but in dramatic narrative, they kill pacing. Just cut to the drama. In *The Way of the Writer*, Charles Johnson said:

> We should remember that dialogue occurs in a context, in other words, within a specific scene. And every dramatic scene has a structure. If we have two characters, say, each enters a scene motivated by a desire or need (or conflict) that has brought him or her there.

Sometimes establishing a rhythm requires getting the characters into a scene with a greeting or setup, and sometimes they jump right into the conflict or have "a hit," as Johnson calls it, "the heightened moment in the scene where what has brought them there is finally revealed." Whether you jump in or set it up depends on the needs of the story and scene and characters at that moment. It must be natural while at the same time dramatic. Still, finding ways to cut to the chase will make your dramatic narrative more effective every time.

Here's an example of dealing with a phone call, from John Sandford's *Rules of Prey*:

> Lucas looked up at the clock. Eleven-forty. Damn. If the cop who took the gun was planning to call, he should have done it. Lucas looked at the phone, willing it to ring.
>
> It rang. He nearly fell off his drawing stool in surprise.
>
> "Yes?"
>
> "Lucas? This is Jennifer."
>
> "Hey. I'm expecting a call. I need the line open."
>
> "I got a tip from a friend," Jennifer said. "He says there was a survivor. Somebody who fought off the killer. I want to know who it was."
>
> "Who told you this bullshit?"

Two techniques are used to increase the tension of the scene. First, Lucas, a detective, is awaiting an important call. By telling us this, Sandford allows readers to feel the character's tension as he looks at the phone. Second, because the caller is a TV reporter and not the fellow cop he was waiting to hear from, we get more tension, despite the routine nature of the chitchat that opens the call. If you need a bit of social nicety, this is a great way to handle it while still keeping the scene as dramatic as possible. Also, note the varied length in sentences, none of which are especially long. Johnson writes: "Characters usually speak naturally or colloquially in short, crisp sentences." Study the speech patterns of others around you, and you'll see this is true. Varied length of sentences also affects pacing and can add dramatic effect to a scene, in addition to being more natural, particularly in dialogue.

Dialogue is not normal conversation. It is conversation with drama. It is a medium of performance. William Noble writes in *Conflict, Action, & Suspense*:

> The throwaway words of conversation such as "Hello," "How are you," "I'm fine," "Good" should never be thought of as dialogue ... because they don't contain drama. Don't reproduce conversation and call it dialogue; reproduce only that portion of the conversation that has drama... Dialogue must contribute to telling the story. If it doesn't, it's of no use.

Dialogue needs to move in a few short sentences. Take this example from *Skinwalkers* by Tony Hillerman:

> "Where was it?"
>
> "On the floor under the bunk. Maybe it fell out when I changed the
>
> bedding."
>
> "What do you think?" Leaphorn asked.
>
> "I think I never had anything that had beads like that on it or knew
>
> anybody who did. And I wonder how it got here."
>
> "Or why?" Leaphorn asked.

In this scene, Navajo detectives Joe Leaphorn and Jim Chee are at Chee's trailer, which was shot up the night before, looking for evidence. The bead they discover raises ominous questions, upping the tension, and it becomes a major key to the unfolding mystery of the overall story. This is how you write effective, dramatic dialogue. Cut to the chase, the drama, what matters, and skip everything else. Noble writes: "When dialogue disintegrates into dull conversation, it destroys the forward movement of the tale, and once this happens, the conflict falls apart and the action and suspense hold no one's interest." Dialogue must always fulfill two purposes: keeping the story moving and developing characterization. This is why most dialogue inevitably becomes confrontation. "Readers are interested in confrontation because the drama inherent in a face-off carries excitement and uncertainty," Noble writes. The "Yes/No" countering in dialogue carries inherent disagreement that ups the drama every time.

Also, humans are rarely directly responsive to each other when conversing. Oblique or partial responses, especially those that ask or raise questions, are common. And this keeps the pace of the conversation flowing.

"It's cold out tonight."

"I'll get locked out if we don't hurry."

Not, "my fingers are cold," which would be a commentary on the coldness. Instead, the reply is about the agenda of the second character. Since caring about our own agenda is a natural human trait most of us possess due to poor listening skills, it is a great tool to utilize for keeping dialogue dramatic and moving. It avoids bogging down the story in chitchat, while also providing information about the characters: their motives, priorities, what is on their minds.

Varying character emotions is also an effective tool. If one character underplays and responds calmly while the other is tense and emotional, this has the effect of varying pace while also building the story. When we are stressed and talking to someone who isn't, we naturally want them to share our sense of urgent emotion. Tension increases each time they respond calmly to our urgency. The same is true in dramatic scenes. Subtext—implying more than the words say directly—is a great technique for upping the drama via underplay. It makes the impact more devastating, too.

"You're not sleeping," Roger said.

"I'm trying," Julie replied.

"You answered."

"Well, you talked to me," she replied but left her arm laying over her eyes just where it had been.

He rolled over and touched her shoulder. "I can't stop thinking about it."

She groaned. "Damn it."

Subtext is when something is going on beneath the surface that changes the meaning of a scene. Here, the subtext is that Roger has something urgent on his mind, but Julie doesn't want to talk about it. She is annoyed at being bothered. But this is never stated outright. The mystery of it allows the story to build because we are waiting to see what happens, wondering how it will play out. Will they talk or will she go to sleep? Will this lead to more conflict later? It is subtle but very effective, and not unrealistic to life.

Stream of consciousness in interior dialogue can also be used to increase tension, especially in scenes where dialogue with others is impossible because a character is alone:

She was coming toward me. I couldn't get into it again. I glanced around for somewhere to hide.

147

This kind of inner monologue adds tension, even if the "she" is someone we have not seen before, by raising questions we want to know the answers to, thus upping tension and building expectation that it will pay off in a dramatic fashion at some point later.

Another technique to aid pacing with underplayed dialogue is gesturing.

> "Someone's coming," Al said.
>
> "Is it him?" Rick never even looked up from his newspaper.
>
> "Blonde, tall, thin, about twenty or so?"
>
> "That's what the boss said, yeah."
>
> Al watched as Rick reached down and fingered the blade in his pocket. "I think it's him," Al motioned. This time they both looked.

Two mobsters waiting for their victim. Plenty of tension from the implied expectation, but the dialogue itself isn't all that dramatic. It is the subtext that adds the drama. The gesturing adds dimension by having the characters' innocuous dialogue be underscored by what they are doing: waiting for a victim, knife ready. When the body movement happens, it is almost like the start of violence. It is restrained, but we anticipate it, and the physical movement punctuates the anticipation by foreshadowing a physical response to go with the subtext.

These techniques are always effective time and again when keeping dialogue dramatic and well paced, so they keep the story moving and reveal character at the same time.

Dialogue and Speech Tags

Another area of concern related to dialogue is the use of speech tags. The most common of these, of course, is "said." But sometimes people try to get creative and do so badly. Creative speech tags are generally a bad idea. All too often they stand out as forced or awkward and draw attention to the writer and craft, away from the story, rather than just flying by like they are supposed to, allowing readers to stay in the story. All of us can probably think of examples we've encountered in our reading. Here are 10 common tips to avoid frequent pitfalls in writing dialogue and speech tags:

> **1) Use simple tags sparingly.** Fancy tags like "he expostulated" or "she espoused" are less clear and more distracting than anything. So keep the tags simple when you absolutely must use them. Instead, convey the manner in which a character speaks instead. Make it obvious from what is said.
>
> **2) Instead of tags, use actions.** The goal of speech tags is solely to help readers keep track of who is speaking, when. That is their sole purpose. It is not a chance to insert adjectives for emotional effect or to show off fancy word-slinging vocabularies. They are another tool best used as subtly as possible. Since people talk while actively engaging in activities, so should your characters. Giving them business to do during dialogue allows you to identify who's speaking without resorting to overused tags. Some can come in the form of characterizing the speaker: "His eyebrows lifted with menace," for example. "Bob's fist clenched as he spoke." "Tears rolled down her cheek with every word." Business is actions or activities undertaken while conversing that keep the

149

character busy multitasking, such as real people often do.

3) Avoid expositional dialogue when possible. We've all violated this rule, but especially when two characters should already know the information being imparted, it seems unnatural and distracting. In such cases, internal monologue is a better tool and feels more natural. Characters may think about stuff they already know, but they wouldn't tell each other stuff each of them knows.

4) Keep it short. People talk in choppy sentences. Long soliloquies are rare. So, in dialogue, use short sentences to make it flow and feel like real people talking. Let them interrupt each other, too. People do that in real life. It adds to the pace, tension, and drama of it.

5) Avoid phonetic spellings for accents. They are difficult to read. Indications of dialect can be used instead to get the reader to do the rest. Overuse of a dialect becomes distracting to readers and can actually take them out of the story. Keep the words your characters say as unobtrusive as possible so your story flows seamlessly.

6) Dialogue is conflict. Conflict keeps the story moving. People talk like they're playing table tennis—back and forth. This moves the story forward. Lace your dialogue with conflict. It adds dramatic urgency to every line the characters say and keeps the story's pace.

7) Use other characters. Let a character imply who's speaking to them by saying something specific to only that person. If you use business well (see number 2 above), having a character refer to something the other character is doing is a great way to do this.

8) Give each character a distinctive voice. Overdo it, and it's caricature, but we all have our own speech tics. Create some for your characters, and sprinkle them throughout. Readers will learn them and know who's speaking. For example, Captain Jack Sparrow loves the term of affection "love" and uses that a lot. He also says "Savvy?" a great deal as well. He has others you can probably remember, too. Study characterization and see what other writers have done.

9) Speak it aloud. Talk it out. Get inside the heads of your characters and say the lines. Play out the conversation you've written. Does it sound natural? Does it flow? Your ears are often a better judge than your eyes, and hearing it will give you an idea of how readers will hear it.

10) Remember what medium you're writing for. TV and film dialogue and novel dialogue are not necessarily the same. In a novel, there is no third party to use intonation, facial expressions, and/or body language to bring it to life. Your words alone are the conduit between yourself and the reader, and your prose skills and the readers' imaginations make it work.

Stephen King writes:

As with all other aspects of fiction, the key to writing good dialogue is honesty... It is important to tell the truth; so much depends on it... The Legion of Decency may not like the word shit, and you might not like it much either, but sometimes you are stuck with it. ... You must tell the truth if your dialogue is to have resonance and realism... If you substitute "Oh sugar!" for "Oh shit!" because you're thinking about The Legion of Decency, you are breaking the unspoken contract that exists between writer and reader—your promise to express the truth of how people act and talk through the medium of made-up story.

That some readers may not want to hear the truth is not your problem. Your quest is to tell the truth at all times, to keep their trust, and sometimes the truth is uncomfortable for all of us. Because it's how characters talk, dialogue is one of the most important crafts to writing your novel. It must feel authentic and real for readers to believe your characters could be real people.

Now, since we talked about dialogue and pacing, let's move on to pacing and suspense in Chapter 8.

CHAPTER 8
PACING AND SUSPENSE

In *Writing the Breakout Novel*, Donald Maass writes:

> Holding readers' attention every word of the way is a function not of the type of novel you're writing, a good premise, tight writing, quick pace, showing not telling, or any of the other widely understood and frequently taught principles of storytelling. Keeping readers in your grip comes from something else ... the moment-by-moment tension that keeps readers in a constant state of suspense over what will happen—not in the story, but in the next few seconds.

This kind of microtension comes not from story but from emotions, specifically conflicting emotions. So, above all else, creating suspense is about making readers care.

Webster's Dictionary defines suspense as: a. The state of being undecided or undetermined; 2. The state of being uncertain, as in awaiting a decision, usually characterized by some anxiety or apprehension.

What is undecided and undetermined are story questions. First and foremost, suspense is about questions. James N. Frey writes in *How to Write a Damn Good Novel II*: "A story question is a device to make the reader curious. Story questions are usually not put in question form. They are rather statements that require further explanation, problems that require resolution, forecasts of crisis, and the like."

> An hour before sunset, on the evening of a day in the beginning of October, 1815, a man traveling afoot entered the little town of D——. The few persons who were at this time at their windows and doors, regarded this traveler with a sort of distrust.

Thus opens Book 2 of Victor Hugo's classic masterpiece *Les Misérables*. The story questions are, "Who is this man?" and "Is he dangerous?" The first question intrigues, the second raises the suspense, and this is how story questions work.

Other examples:

> "The great fish moved silently through the night water, propelled by great sweeps of its crescent tail." (Jaws, Peter Benchley: Who will be the shark's lunch?)

> "It is a truth universally acknowledged that a single man in possession of a good fortune must be in want of a wife." (Pride and Prejudice, Jane Austen: Who's the single man? And: Who's going to be the lucky girl?)

> "Scarlett O'Hara was not beautiful, but men seldom realized it when caught by her charms as the Tarleton twins were." (Gone with the Wind, Margaret Mitchell: What are the consequences of the twins being charmed? Will they fight over her? Etc.)

Remember in Chapter 3, when we discussed plotting as a series of questions asked and answered and how the rhythm of that keeps readers reading? Unless story questions are powerful, life-and-death questions that are strengthened, reinforced, and elaborated, they will not hold the reader long. When they occur at the beginning of a story, they act as "hooks" that draw readers in. That's why so many classic novels start with hooks, and yours should, too. Ultimately, raising story questions—unanswered questions, characters we care about, and tension—are the keys to suspense in any story.

Creating Tension

Since we just discussed dialogue, let's start with how dialogue creates tension. Dialogue in novels is not realistic. Every word is thought through and constructed to create the utmost tension and steadiest pace. Characters say what they mean, are rarely interrupted, don't stumble over words, and all the same, the words often seem unimportant if taken by themselves. The words are not what holds the power. The power comes from the meaning, the motivations of the speakers, and the underlying conflict. Here's an example from John Sandford's *Rule of Prey*:

> "Daniel's hunting for you." Anderson looked harassed, teasing his thinning blond hair as he stepped through Lucas' office door. Lucas had just arrived and stood rattling his keys in his fist.
>
> "Something break?"
>
> "We might go for a warrant."
>
> "On Smithe?"

"Yeah. Sloan spent the night going through his garbage. Found some wrappers from rubbers that use the same kind of lubricant they found in the women. And they found a bunch of invitations to art shows. The betting is, he knows this Ruiz chick."

"I'll talk to the chief."

Now, tension in this scene comes from two things. One, starting abruptly with dialogue that is a warning or feels urgent in a way before establishing setting and that Lucas has just arrived. Two, the underlying tension of the hunt for the killer and the chief wanting Lucas. The words themselves are fairly innocuous at face value, a bunch of information, really. In another context, they might play very differently, but here they carry urgency, a sense of danger, emotional foreboding. A sex killer is loose, and the cops are racing to find him. Yes, some of this was established in earlier scenes, but just from this little short scene alone, you get a lot of it. This dialogue drips with tension as a result. What makes dialogue gripping is not the information or facts imparted, but the tension, the urgency. The tension comes from the people, not the words.

Let's look at another example from *Every Dead Thing* by John Connolly:

"Nice story, Tommy," said Angel.

"It's just a story, Angel. I didn't mean nothing by it. No offense intended."

"None taken," said Angel. "At least not by me."

Behind him there was a movement in the darkness, and Louis appeared. His bald head gleamed in the dim light, his muscular neck emerging from a black silk shirt within an immaculately cut gray suit. He towered over Angel by more than a foot, and as he did so, he eyed Tommy Q intently for a moment.

"Fruit," he said. "That's a … quaint term, Mr. Q. To what does it refer, exactly?"

The blood had drained from Tommy Q's face and it seemed to take a long time for him to find enough saliva to enable him to gulp. When he did eventually manage, it sounded like he was swallowing a golf ball. He opened his mouth but nothing came out, so he closed it again and looked at the floor in vain hope that it would open up and swallow him.

"It's okay, Mr. Q, it was a good story," said Louis in a voice as silky as his shirt.

"Just be careful how you tell it." Then he smiled a bright smile at Tommy Q, the sort of smile a cat might give a mouse to take to the grave with it. A drop of sweat ran down Tommy Q's nose, hung from the tip a moment, then exploded on the floor. By then, Louis had gone.

The tension here comes from the characters, not the dialogue. Separate the dialogue out and there's nothing particularly tense about it, but the context is that Tommy Q has just laughingly told Angel a story about a gay man's murder. Louis and Angel are gay and they are killers, particularly Louis. Puts a whole new spin on it, doesn't it? That's how tension in dialogue works. I imagine that even not knowing everything beforehand, you felt the tension reading it, but now that I've told you, read it again. Even more tense, right? We keep reading at moments like this not because of what they say. We keep reading to see if they will reconcile or fight. Will the tension explode into a fight or resolve?

Ask yourself where the tension is in your dialogue. Look at every passage, every word. How can it be improved? Does the tension come from the words or the situations—the circumstances and characters? Make sure the emotional friction between the speakers is the driving force.

Tension in action works much the same way. Yes, there can be violence, and that has an inherent tension. But even in scenes with action that is nonviolent, you need tension. Let's look at a scene from Harlan Coben's *Tell No One*:

> I put my hands behind my head and lay back. A cloud passed in front of the moon, turning the blue night into something pallid and gray. The air was still. I could hear Elizabeth getting out of the water and stepping onto the dock. My eyes tried to adjust. I could barely make out her naked silhouette. She was, quite simply, breathtaking. I watched her bend at the waist and wring the water out of her hair. Then she arched her spine and threw back her head.
>
> My raft drifted farther away from shore. I tried to sift through what had happened to me, but even I didn't understand it all. The raft kept moving. I started losing sight of Elizabeth. As she faded in the dark, I made a decision: I would tell her. I would tell her everything.
>
> I nodded to myself and closed my eyes. There was a lightness in my chest now. I listened to the water gently lap against my raft.

Then I heard a car door open.

I sat up.

"Elizabeth?" Pure silence, except for my own breathing.

I looked for her silhouette again. It was hard to make out, but for a moment I saw it. Or thought I saw it. I'm not sure anymore or if it even matters. Either way, Elizabeth was standing perfectly still, and maybe she was facing me.

I might have blinked—I'm really not sure about that either—and when I looked again, Elizabeth was gone.

Lots of description, and fairly benign at that. Only one line of dialogue. But what lends tension to this is the descriptive details that follow what is obviously an important decision by the narrator to confess something to Elizabeth. Is she gone? Did someone else arrive? Who? That the narrator, David, is deeply in love and feels guilt over a secret is obvious. It doesn't need to be stated. And that underscores the tension of otherwise mundane action. We want to see what happens. This is how action, even nonviolent, can drip with tension if written well, and it needs to if your book is to hook readers time and again and keep them reading.

Exposition always risks boring readers. Maass writes: "Many novelists merely write out whatever it is that their characters are thinking or feeling—or, more to the point, whatever happens to occur to the author in a given writing session. That is a mistake." Most commonly, exposition fails because it merely restates what we have already learned from the story or information characters would already know. It becomes uninteresting or false because it feels unnecessary. The key to good exposition is to frame it so it offers new ideas and emotions into the tapestry of the story. Remember when I said you should only give us what we need to know to understand the story at any given moment? That's why choosing placement of your exposition carefully is so important. Save it until we need it, so it brings something useful and important to the story. Don't just dump it all at once to be stored up for later use. Instead, leave it until it will advance the story.

In *Pretties*, Scott Westerfeld manages to offer exposition that creates conflicting feelings in the character at the same time:

> As the message ended, Tally felt the bed spin a little. She closed her eyes and let out a long, slow sigh of relief. Finally, she was full-fledged Crim. Everything she'd ever wanted had come to her at last. She was beautiful, and she lived in New Pretty Town with Peris and Shay and tons of new friends. All the disasters and terrors of the last year—running away to Smoke, living there in pre-Rusty squalor, traveling back to the city through the wilds—somehow all of it had worked out.
>
> It was so wonderful, and Tally was so exhausted, that belief took a while to settle over her. She replayed Peris's message a few times, then pulled off the smelly Smokey sweater with shaking hands and threw it in a corner. Tomorrow, she would make the hole in the wall recycle it.
>
> Tally lay back and stared at the ceiling for a while. A ping from Shay came, but she ignored it, setting her interface ring to sleeptime. With everything so perfect, reality seemed somehow fragile, as if the slightest interruption could imperil her pretty future. The bed beneath her, Komachi

Mansion, and even the city around her—all of it felt as tenuous as a soap bubble, shivering and empty.

It was probably just the knock on her head causing the weird missingness that underlay her joy. She only needed a good night's sleep—and hopefully no hangover tomorrow—and everything would feel solid again, as perfect as it really was.

Tally fell asleep a few minutes later, happy to be a Crim at last.

But her dreams were totally bogus.

So, on the surface, she is happy to have accomplished her goal and become a Crim. But she has to try hard to convince herself of it. Too hard. That life is perfect. So hard that it is obvious she is not convinced it is real, that she fears it may be bogus. This underlying emotional conflict makes the exposition feel important and relevant in a way simple words alone, telling the story, never would have. It advances the story and adds tension, keeping our interest.

The trick to making exposition matter is to dig deeper into your characters at such moments and examine what is going on with them. Why is this information important at this moment? What do they feel in saying it and why does it matter? Find the dilemmas, contradictions, impulses, and conflicting ideas and questions that drive the character, and readers will be fascinated. Maass writes: "True tension in exposition comes not from circular worry or repetitive turmoil; it comes from emotions in conflict and ideas at war."

Descriptive passages have a similar problem, which is why readers sometimes skim them. Maass writes: "Description itself does nothing to create tension; tension only comes from people within the landscape." So, the trick is to use description to reveal the conflict of the observer. How does observing various details affect the character? What makes the details stand out for the character? People tend to focus on details that mean something to them and ignore the rest. So, pick the details that are important to the character and describe them so it's clear why they count. Here's a great example from *Memory Man* by David Baldacci:

> The bar was much like every bar Decker had ever been in.
>
> Dark, cold, musty, smoky, where light fell funny and everyone looked like someone you knew or wanted to know. Or, more likely, wanted to forget. Where everyone was your friend until he was your enemy and cracked a pool stick over your skull. Where things were quiet until they weren't. Where you could drink away anything life threw at you. Where a thousand Billy Joel wannabes would serenade you into the wee hours.

Sounds like most bars I've been in for sure. There are elements of familiarity and elements of foreboding. Decker is both at home and ill at ease here—conflicting emotions. The history in the elements described keeps him on edge and us with him. And as a result, we feel the tension of anticipation that something will happen here. And in fact, it does. A confrontation follows moments later.

Maass writes: "Tension can be made out of nothing at all—or, at least, that's how it can appear. In reality, it is feelings—specifically, feelings in conflict with each other—that fill up an otherwise dead span of story and bring it to life." Finding ways to bring out those conflicting emotions through description is the key to keeping tension in every word.

Techniques for Creating Suspense

So, in addition to ratcheting up the tension every chance you get, what are some techniques to use to build suspense? The description of the bar in *Memory Man* is a form of subtlety and misdirection known as foreshadowing. And foreshadowing is a technique all writers should use. Foreshadowing is presenting hints that will pay off in a bigger way later in a story by subtly setting them up earlier so that they are in the reader's mind and will resonate when they pop up again with more dramatic relevance.

For example, in Andy Weir's smash hit novel, *The Martian*, he sets up the background of his protagonist, Mark Watney, as a botanist to foreshadow later events:

> In other news, I'm starting to come up with an idea for food. My botany background may come in useful after all. Why bring a botanist to Mars? After all, it's famous for not having anything growing here. Well, the idea was to figure out how well things grow in Martian gravity, and see what, if anything, we can do with Martian soil. The short answer is: quite a lot ... almost. Martian soil has the basic building blocks needed for plant growth, but there's a lot of stuff going on in Earth soil that Mars soil doesn't have, even when it's placed in an Earth atmosphere and given plenty of water. Bacterial activity, certain nutrients provided by animal life, etc. None of that is happening on Mars. One of my tasks for the mission was to see how

plants grow here, in various combinations of Earth and Mars soil and atmosphere.

That's why I have a small amount of Earth soil and a bunch of plant seeds with me.

I can't get too excited, however. It's about the amount of soil you'd put in a window box, and the only seeds I have are a few species of grass and ferns. They're the most rugged and easily grown plants on earth, so NASA picked them as the test subjects.

So I have two problems: not enough dirt, and nothing edible to plant in it.

Later on, Watney uses materials on the ship and in the environment to grow food and extend his life on the planet while he waits for rescue. In fact, his scientific calculations and knowledge become key to making rescue possible, but the timing for the mission becomes vitally important and dramatic. He has one shot at it, and complications, of course, put the timing in jeopardy. What at first may seem like backstory on the character becomes an essential plot element. This is foreshadowing. A seemingly innocuous mention of science that might otherwise seem boring or useless foreshadows an important skill that will later save his life and be a hinge on which the story's outcome depends.

In my epic fantasy novel *Duneman*, I was creating a world where parts of the lands lived in medieval-like conditions, while others had started industrial development, with steam-powered airships, cranes, and more. Because the story starts in the medieval-like area, at one point, I had the protagonist pass airship landing zones on his journey, hinting that this land may seem medieval and standard fantasy but somewhere there are airships. It was subtle but later became important and set up the contrast between different areas of the lands, which in itself becomes an important source of conflict between various people groups—one that soon puts them on the brink of war. Always look for ways to hint at details early on that will play a key part later. If you don't, readers will feel like you are inventing character skills and abilities or objects just when you need them for the story, which is manufactured and doesn't ring true, and will shake their confidence and trust in you as a storyteller.

What if your characters hear a gunshot out on the street … discover a missing letter in the couch cushions … or smell an out-of-place odor in an unusual place? In *Conflict, Action & Suspense*, William Noble describes this technique as "plot-hypers." Plot-hypers involve "injecting an unexplained event or circumstance" to add uncertainty or raise tension. Some are accomplished via misdirection and others through subtlety. He offers two classic examples:

In Arthur Conan Doyle's Sherlock Holmes book *The Hound of the Baskervilles*, Sherlock discovers that a watchdog did not bark at a crucial moment, an odd coincidence. But at the end of the story, it becomes a significant clue that helps solve the case. This is subtlety.

In Edgar Allan Poe's "The Purloined Letter," a thief places an inoffensive letter next to a crucial one and then slyly slips away with the important one in front of witnesses. Police begin suspecting the thief because of his history and assume a search will turn up the letter, but the thief tricks them and hides it in plain sight. It almost works. This is misdirection.

Both involve one little fact that leads to an assumption. The authors don't hit readers over the heads. Yet the assumptions both take the story in surprising directions.

Another technique for setting up suspense is through flashbacks. Now, some people hate flashbacks. Flashbacks are scenes that take place earlier in a character's history and reveal important information about the character, his or her relationships, or his or her conflict and flaws, which advance the story in their reveal. Admittedly, some authors overuse flashbacks, which can be annoying and also risk killing the pace of storytelling. Like any other scenes, flashbacks should be kept short and begin *in medias res*. Enter and exit the scene as close to the key action as possible. Also, be sure you introduce flashbacks only as vitally needed to further the story. Timing is key, and when used well, flashbacks are an invaluable and quite effective tool for building tension and suspense in storytelling. The catch is that flashbacks can often slow the pace because they take us away from the main tension of the story and out of the present, pressing conflict to another time. For that reason, we will discuss them again briefly under pacing. Here's an example from *Memory Man* by David Baldacci, where a flashback actually continues the suspense and tension, despite interrupting a scene. Decker has just posed as a lawyer in an attempt to get in to see a suspect at a police precinct—a suspect in the murder of his wife and child. As the woman at the counter asks him to sit and wait while she calls for approval, this happens:

Realizing he might have just blown a bunch of money he didn't have on lawyer-looking attire, Decker sat down in a chair bolted to the wall and waited. The old woman picked up her phone and slowly, ever so slowly, punched in numbers.

Numbers. Always numbers.

They had a hypnotic effect on him, sending him to places he didn't always want to go.

Decker closed his eyes and his mind began to whir back … back to the day, no, the exact moment when his life changed forever.

The crowd went berserk every time the hit was replayed on the megatron, and that was often, I was told later. My helmet flew five feet and rolled another six, ending at the feet of a zebra who picked it up and maybe checked inside to see if my head was still in there.

I think my brain bounced against my skull multiple times like a bird trying to introduce itself to a window until its neck breaks.

Yep, the crowd cheered and whooped whenever the megatron belched out the replay.

Then I was told that they stopped cheering. Because I didn't get up. Because I didn't move a muscle. And then someone noticed I had stopped breathing and had also turned blue. They told me the head training was alternating pounding my chest like a punch press attacking metal slabs and blowing air into my mouth. Later, they told me I died on the field twice but he brought me back both times from the hereafter. They told me he was screaming in my ear, "Hang on, ninety-five. Hang the hell on." I was such a nobody that he knew my jersey number but not my name. My professional football player identity was a nine and a five printed on my chest. Nine and five. Violet and brown in my counting colors mind. I never consciously assigned colors to numbers. My brain did it for me without my permission.

The collision changed everything about me, because it essentially rewired my brain. So I died, twice, and then came back, essentially as someone else. And for the longest time I thought that would be the most awful thing that would ever happen to me. And then came that night and those three bodies in neon blue, and the gridiron blindside dropped to number two on the list of my personal devastations.

"Excuse me, sir? Sir?"

Decker opened his eyes to see the woman staring down at him.

Now that is a well-constructed flashback. Not only does he use telling language because Decker is recalling things that happened along with things others told him about them, but it interrupts the moment he has waited for for four long years—a chance to confront his family's killer—yet still manages to maintain tension and suspense. That's because every word drips with the character's emotions and because Baldacci chooses the flashback placement well. It has everything to do with who Decker is and his intensity as a person, and it even ties into the moment at the police station at the end. Planned and written well, flashbacks too can be a device for upping suspense. We'll talk about them more later. First, here's yet another technique.

A fourth technique is reversing the rules. This technique uses contrariness to create excitement and defy expectations. It's about having things go against the established expectations to twist plot and characters from what readers would normally expect. Noble writes: "A reader expects something to be a certain way, but suddenly it's not. The misdirection is in the expectation, the subtlety is in the surprise."

For example, what if a handsome man is cruel, a real jerk, or an evil character happens to have a soft heart for kids, who love and flock to him whenever he's around? A church is corrupt and hides a criminal enterprise. A school teacher is engaged in selling students into sex slavery. All of these are twists on normal expectations that first occur to us, twists that surprise us by defying our natural assumptions. This is reversing the rules.

These four techniques are the most common tools for building suspense, but no doubt some of you—and other authors—can think of others I didn't mention. The general rule is to use whatever works for you and improves your story, and ignore what doesn't. Closely related to suspense is pacing—the flow of your story. It's the combination of tension and suspense—keeping readers wondering, guessing, wanting to know what happens— that sets the pace of your story. We'll examine that next.

Pacing

When people hear the word "pacing," they typically think of "slow" or "fast," or perhaps "action," but in novels, pacing needs both to be successful. Dictionary.com defines pace as "a rate of movement, especially in stepping, walking, etc.; a rate of activity, progress, growth, performance, etc.; tempo." In regard to your novel, the pacing is a combination of steady, fast, and slow passages creating a rhythm that flows for readers, engaging and holding their interest, while still pausing to let them catch their breath and regroup from time to time.

Experienced novelists tend to get a natural sense of pacing as they write. Newer writers, however, will have to learn this.

Imagine yourself on a treadmill, the speed slowly increasing. Your pulse begins pounding, your breathing increases, the rhythm of the humming tread and your footfalls accelerating to combine into a steady beat. Then imagine keeping that speed for 10 hours straight. Do you think you'd last? Probably not. The same is true of readers reading a novel.

While it is true that readers like stories where "something happens," and action is a big part of that, readers also need stories that stop for reflective moments, too, allowing them to catch their breath, take a sip of water, grab a snack, and regroup. In constructing your plot, you should learn to plan for such a rhythm. Two or three high points of tense, fast pace should be followed by a slower, thoughtful point before the next two or three fast, tense points begin. There are various ways to accomplish this, which we will look at next.

Since action is the driving force of drama, let's start with action.

Writing Action

I don't know about you, but I've always been a fan of action. Movies like the *Lethal Weapon* and *Die-Hard* series always entertained me. I like action in my reading, too. Space opera is my favorite science fiction genre, and sword & sorcery tops my fantasy favorites, but I also spend a great deal of my time reading thrillers and police procedurals. Is it any wonder that I find myself often writing action in my stories?

One of the best action writers I know is Jonathan Maberry, the *New York Times* bestselling author of the Joe Ledger thrillers and several other series. Let's look at an action scene from one of his novels, *Assassin's Code*:

170

I struggled to get to my feet.

A minute ago I had thought that the whole world was sliding into the mouth of hell, but now a different kind of hell had come to this place of shadows. There were screams and Upierczi running everywhere. Flares popped in the air, painting everything in bright white light.

I took a step toward Grigor and my foot kicked something. I looked down and saw the code scrambler.

I bent and picked it up.

"Cowboy—on your six!"

It was Khalid's voice, and I turned to see one of the vampires four feet away.

I had no time to run. I didn't want to run. As he slammed into me I buried the pistol under his chin and blew off the top of his head. We hit the ground and I lay there, Upierczi blood all over me. In my face, my eyes, my mouth.

I rolled over and threw up.

Grigor was still screaming. Then I heard a sharp yelp of pain and looked up to see the Upierczi fling Ghost aside. Ghost hit the side of a packing crate and collapsed, spitting blood onto the floor. I saw a couple of teeth, too.

That made me mad. Maybe I needed that to shake off the damage and the pain.

I came out of my daze and finally the situation gelled in my mind. The Upierczi were rushing

171

outward from me, some were seeking cover, most were rushing at Echo Team.

Bunny and Top were at the foot of the metal stairs. Bunny had a combat shotgun with a drum magazine and he was firing, firing, firing. Everything that came at him died. The heavy buckshot soaked with garlic oil poisoned every Upier that wasn't instantly killed by his blasts. The ones who took a few pellets staggered away, gagging and twitching with the onset of allergic shock.

Top was watching his back, firing a big Navy Colt automatic, the hollow points doing terrible work in the tightly packed crowd.

On the other side of the chamber, Khalid and Lydia were behind a packing crate, using it as a shooting blind to create a cross fire.

"Frag out!" Lydia yelled and lobbed grenades into the heart of the vampires.

The fragmentation grenades weren't filled with garlic, but the blasts tore the monsters to pieces.

I saw three Upierczi running along the wall toward them, well out of Lydia's line of sight. I raised my pistol but before I could fire the monsters went down, one, two, three, their heads burst apart by sniper rounds. John Smith, firing from somewhere I couldn't see.

My knife was on the floor too, and I grabbed it as well. I shoved knife and scrambler into my pocket and tapped my earbud. "Echo, Echo, this is

Cowboy. I have the football and I need a doorway out of here."

"I have your back," came the reply, but it wasn't in my earbud. I whirled, and there she was. Dressed all in black, splashed with blood, a wickedly curved blade in each hand.

"Violin," I began, but she shook her head.

"No time."

She lunged past me as several Upierczi rushed my blind side. Until that moment I didn't understand what "gifts" the dhampyri had gotten from the cauldron of their birth.

Violin was not as physically powerful, but my God, she was fast. She met the rushing vampires, and even though I am trained to observe and understand combat at any level, I could not follow what happened. Her arms moved so fast, her body spun and danced as she threaded her way through the pack, the silver blades whipped with such frenzy that the monsters seemed to disintegrate around her. It was so fast that their blood hung in the air like mist. It was hypnotic and beautiful in the most awful way that perfect violence can be beautiful; and it was horrible because there was nothing natural about what I was seeing.

Violin was a thing born from rape, torn from a tortured mother by a monster of a father, raised in a culture of rage and humiliation. If it was possible for the concept of vengeance to be embodied in one form, then that's what I was seeing.

The Upierczi did not understand the nature of their death. I could see that on their faces. They saw a woman—something that to them represented a thing to be taken and used and discarded—and they attacked her with the arrogance of habitual users. They expected her to fall. They expected her to be weak.

They did not expect the precise and unstoppable fury of this daughter of Lilith.

She killed and killed and killed.

And yet, with all of that, I knew it wasn't going to be enough. There were at least a hundred of the Upierczi in the chamber. More of them were seeded through the staff of the refinery. There were a handful of us.

We were going to lose this fight.

In my earbud I heard John Smith say, "Mother of God."

And then I heard him scream.

I wrenched myself away from Violin and raised my gun, searching the catwalks for Smith. I saw him.

I saw what was left of him fall.

Grigor, bloody, torn, perhaps dying, stood on the catwalk fifty yards away. His mouth was bright with fresh blood.

John Smith struck the hard stone floor in a broken sprawl. His throat was completely torn away.

"No!"

I heard that scream of denial fill the air. From Bunny's throat, from Lydia's and Khalid's. From my own.

Before I knew what I was doing I was running with my gun held in both hands, firing, firing. Bullets pinged and whanged off the steel pipes of the catwalk, but Grigor ducked away and fled out through an open doorway.

I raced toward the stairway, but Khalid was closer and he bolted up the metal steps in hot pursuit. Seven Upierczi saw what was happening and they leapt like apes onto the pipes and climbed upward. I emptied my magazine at them. One fell away.

By the time I reached the foot of the stairs I had the magazines swapped out and I ran upward. I was still hurt, still bleeding. Maybe inside, too. My chest was a furnace and it felt like it was consuming me, but I didn't care.

As I reached the top deck, the last of the Upierczi turned and blocked my way.

I put three rounds through his face and kicked his body out of my way.

Behind me there was another massive explosion, and I lingered at the doorway, knowing that the blast signature didn't match our fragmentation grenades. I was right.

Smoke and fire billowed out of one of the tunnels and Upierczi bodies were flung backward. Then a wave of new figures flooded in. Thirty of them. Women.

Arklight. The Mothers of the Fallen come for justice of a kind.

The battle below became a bloodbath.

I turned away and ran after Khalid, the Upierczi, and Grigor.

Note the short sentences and paragraphs, as well as short spurts of dialogue. The description, action, and dialogue are all short and spaced so that readers' eyes will flow down the page at a quick pace as they take it in. Also, note the lack of exposition or great detail. This is not the time for it. As a trained martial artist and experienced bodyguard, Maberry has an innate sense of how action really works and makes his fight scenes as realistic as possible. For those of us lacking such background, writing action scenes can be a challenge. In movies, you have visual and other clues to use to inspire the tension and pacing in the audience, but when writing prose, this can be more difficult. So here are a few key tips I've learned:

1) Write in short snippets as much as possible. Action scenes are not the time for long internal dialogues by characters. Think about a time you were involved in a high-adrenaline situation. You didn't have time to take long pauses for deep thinking. You had to react and do so quickly, and so must your characters. The same is true of long speeches. People tend to be interrupted in speaking by the need to act or react. So dialogue and even action should be described in short spurts. If you have more than four sentences to it, think twice about whether it should be split up.

2) Use action to break up dialogue and dialogue to break up action. Intersperse the two components in short segments to add a sense of pacing and tension. Writing long sections of dialogue and long sections of action will tend to read slowly and thus stall the pacing. This is especially true of dialogue, as I've already noted. Alternating them adds a sense of realism and keeps things moving.

3) Get to the point. Long descriptions of weapons and scenery don't belong here. If things need to be set up, do it before the sequence occurs so you don't have to interrupt the action to do it. You want to focus on sensory details—what the characters see, feel, touch, etc. Are they sweating? Are they hurting? You don't want to focus on what the building behind them looks like or even the street itself. You don't want to spend pages like Tom Clancy does describing their weapons here. We need to know what it is and how it works and their skill level so we cannot be surprised by their actions, but set that up elsewhere. During the action, we should already know.

4) Don't make it too easy. Yes, the hero will likely win. But make it a challenge. Be sure to make the opponents threatening enough that the hero is in real jeopardy; otherwise the dramatic impact will be greatly lessened. No matter how skilled your hero is, he or she must have to face obstacles. In action sequences the odds should seem stacked against them. Let them bleed from a wound. Let them misfire or miss with the sword. Let them sweat and even have to run, barely escaping.

Sometimes it's even good to let them lose one time only to have them win later on. Force them to stretch themselves in some way to succeed. Make them human, or the reader will struggle to care.

5) Keep it believable. This goes hand in hand with number

4) Real people are imperfect. They make mistakes. They fail. Make sure your action sequences are well researched and realistic. Besides humanizing the hero, don't have vehicles or weapons performing beyond their capabilities. You may assume readers won't know the difference, but some will. And writing without limits rings hollow. Make sure you respect the limits and use them to up the tension. A man stuck with a sword fighting men with guns will face tense moments. A man against incredible odds is a man we root for.

6) Keep it tight. Anything absolutely not necessary should be cut. This includes long descriptions and dialogue as mentioned in number 1 but also the scene openings and closings. Nothing hurts pacing more than disobeying this rule. Be sure you start the action as fast as possible and end it the same. Don't drag it out unnecessarily in your desire to make it more dramatic or a "cooler" sequence. Make it exactly as long as it really needs to be to serve the story and no longer.

7) Give the readers breathing space. Be careful about putting too many action sequences too close together. Movies build to a climax that may have 20 minutes of action, but before that action, scenes are interspersed with slower moments. Make sure

178

you intersperse your action sequences with moments of character building and reflection, dialogue and discovery—slower sequences that allow readers to breathe a bit before the next intense action scene. In between scenes are where you make action sequences matter. Action is not just about a character we care about surviving but about stakes he or she has in that victory. What is the character's driving need or goal? This gets set up in other scenes and provides driving undercurrent to the action, which makes us care.

8) Pick your moments. Action stories tend to have several sequences spread throughout. In choosing which sequence to include where, be sure you consider the overall dramatic level of them. You want the biggest action sequence in the entire piece to be at the climactic moments. Those in between should leave room for a buildup to the major action sequence to come. Ideally, each scene builds up to those that follow, but this can be accomplished in ways besides increasing the stakes and tension or odds. With proper character arcs, characters' emotional stakes can be developed in such a way that each later sequence matters that much more, making the readers care more as well.

9) Make it matter. Action scenes do not exist solely to entertain readers and add tension. They have a greater purpose to serve the story. Something must happen that ups the stakes or increases the challenges with each scene in your story, and action scenes are no exception. Don't write action for the sake of action. Write action because it serves the story. Every action sequence should move the story and characters forward in their journey. If not, they don't belong in the story.

10) Incorporate humor. Humor is a great tool for not only breaking the tension but building character during action sequences. It's no accident characters like Lethal Weapon's Riggs and Die Hard's McClane engage in witty banter during such moments, and your characters can as well. From funny actions to funny dialogue snippets, this makes the action both more enjoyable and less tense when done at the right moments, and it can add a lot to reader enjoyment. Don't be afraid to incorporate it when you can. It doesn't have to be cheesy catchphrases, either. It's all in the wording.

Now, thinking about these tips, go back and read the Maberry passage again and see how they are applied. He uses every technique mentioned in his action scenes, and in between, he gives us breathing space. So, what are some techniques for doing that?

Slower Moments

In between the more action-driven scenes, you will need moments that build characters, set up conflict, and even show confrontations and events leading up to the action. Some of these may be quiet, reflective moments, some will have a different intensity. But the trick is to create a flow that lets us breathe, gather our thoughts, and regroup a bit before more action.

Earlier, we talked about flashbacks for building suspense, but as I said, they can also slow things down. If a character breaks the current tension and timeline to go back and recall a key moment from their past, it can ease the pace a bit. The important thing is to make the flashbacks matter by providing key information about characters and their motives or relationships or both, while still not making the scenes too long or slow. You don't want to stop the story dead, you just want to let up on the adrenaline a bit while still moving the story forward. Flashback scenes still need to be written *in medias res* so they are as tight and focused around conflict as any other scene, but when used to break the pace, they can be less action and more conversational, with characters arguing or discussing points of disagreement or even replaying key moments from their past that have stayed with them, motivating the action and decisions they are making in the present timeline. I'm sure we can all think of examples, so I'll skip that here and move on to other options.

Love scenes, planning scenes where the characters compare notes or discuss strategy, meal gatherings, evidence gathering, interrogations, searches, even expositional moments can all can serve the purpose of slowing down the pace in your story. They still need conflict, and they still need to provide information that advances the story, but not every moment has to be high drama. Write these scenes using the tension methods discussed earlier in the chapter and insert them in between your high-action scenes, and you will create a nice flow and rhythm that builds into an ascending arc through the midpoint and then allows for the descent to the climax in the second half, just the right structure. It takes practice, as they say, but you can see how this works in your reading if you pay attention. Then imitate it in your own work. That's how we all learn.

Another trick is to use humor. An anecdote or humorous banter or even a slightly comedic scene can break up the tension and pace just right to allow readers to regroup for more.

Narrative Pacing

Most writers learn to look at writing scenes and stories like planning a race. And to win a race, you need the right pace and rhythm. There are ups and downs, sprints and jogs, and slow scenes are your downs and jogs—not sprints, but that doesn't mean they don't have to move. The key, of course, as already discussed, is maintaining tension. As long as the story is moving forward and story questions are coming up, even slower scenes will feel like they move. Much of this comes down to narrative pacing.

Keeping excitement high doesn't just mean action. What it means is keeping it relevant and interesting. As discussed before, as long as descriptive passages, exposition, and character moments are still providing information that readers want to know and feel advances the story, the pace continues to move. Narrative takes up a lot of space in any novel, and many novels have action unfolding at a steady climb throughout until big crises of action occur. William Noble defines narrative pacing as "pacing without dialogue shifts or quick scene cuts or sharp point-of-view changes." It won't work over the long haul, but in short sections, as long as we know the action and suspense are leading somewhere, narrative pacing keeps your story moving while still giving readers breathers in between tense moments of crisis.

Noble writes:

> Narrative pacing works because we show what is happening; we are moving the story forward using description, anecdotes, and character development. As we depict what happens, we keep our readers involved because the story continues to unfold and the action and suspense grow taut, until we reach that crisis or turning point.

A slow build can be very satisfying—often far more satisfying than a breathless race. The trick is to create flow of movement. Narrative pacing works best, Noble suggests, when it opens a story or chapter, lasts several pages, builds to a crisis, keeps the story moving, and develops conflict early and keeps it pulsing.

Mixing It Up

As mentioned in Chapter 7, dialogue tends to move more quickly than description and exposition, so when constructing a story, writers learn to pay attention to the impact dialogue has on pace. Sometimes you need some background information to understand characters' motives and decisions. And other times you need a conversation as characters gather information, debate options, and confront others. Then they must take action. This pattern will repeat time and again in your novel and should. Well-paced novels have pages with a mix of sentence and paragraph lengths on most pages. You can just look at them and tell where the slow spots and fast spots are. Much of this is intuitive, but when you are learning, paying attention to varying sentence and paragraph lengths is important training. Keep those descriptive and expository passages broken into shorter chunks and multiple paragraphs, so the story feels like it moves. Every paragraph break and turn of the page feels like progress to a reader, so constructing your story with such movement in mind is essential to a well-paced experience.

As you write, description, action, exposition, and dialogue will become intermixed. Sometimes you will have a page or half page of description before a single line of dialogue, then some exposition and action before the next line of dialogue. Other times, dialogue will move quickly, only occasionally interrupted by bits of exposition or description or action. As long as all of these parts have tension and conflict flowing beneath the surface to drive them, all will be well. This is why I spent so much time talking about creating tension at the beginning of this chapter. If you find a scene feeling static, with characters repeating themselves or chitchatting and saying nothing that moves the story forward, trim, trim, trim. Every word must count. Every moment must move. If it doesn't, your novel will be filled with bog-like potholes that stop it dead and force readers to slog onward, risking their loss of interest.

Transitions and scene breaks can also help pacing because both cut away from the action and crisis long enough to allow a shift. Noble writes: "The scene change can cause a variation in the level of action and suspense and generate a continuing interest in what's happening. Without the change of pace, the reader will grow weary and turn away." Cliffhangers are a great way to build suspense. They leave us wanting more, anxious to find out what happens next. But cliffhangers make bad transitions and scene changes if used too often. They are most effective when used for effect, especially when breaking up action scenes to intersperse with other important moments—such as when two sets of characters are involved in different confrontations or actions at the same time—or to end chapters and keep us reading. Otherwise, transitions and scene changes should feel natural and make sense. We need to feel one scene or chapter coming to a natural close before we switch to a new one. This doesn't have to involve long, drawn-out narrative passages. It can be a few sentences or a line of dialogue or action or two. What we need is that sense of conclusion to the present scene or chapter.

A lot of what we are talking about here is learning on instinct. You read and absorb how it plays out in other books, then learn to imitate and apply it to your own. It is not easy to teach, and for some, it will not be easy to learn. But it really becomes instinctive with time, or needs to. Your mind will create the right combinations as you go, and you will hone them in editing and revision to get just the right flow. For most authors, that is how pacing works, and that's probably how it will work for you.

The next area of craft we need to discuss is world building, and that is the subject of Chapter 9.

CHAPTER 9
WORLD BUILDING

World building is something that every author has to do, no matter what the genre or setting. For example, here's a passage from Laura Lippman's *In Big Trouble*:

> A sign hangs next to the cradle of Texas liberty, reminding visitors that concealed firearms are not permitted on the grounds...

> Within the walls, it's like being in a shallow dish—azure sky above, the taller buildings crowded around, dwarfing the Spanish mission, which isn't very big to begin with. She walks through the gardens, noting the placement of each plant, each bench, each sign. Change is not to be tolerated. She picks up a cup with a little electric blue raspa juice inside and drops it in the trash, as fastidious in her own way as the Alamo's keepers, the Daughters of the Republic of Texas. It is a shrine, and not only to Texas liberty. A shrine to her, to them.

And here's another one from Robert Silverberg's *Lord Valentine's Castle*:

> And then after walking all day through a golden haze of humid warmth that gathered around him like fine wet fleece, Valentine came to a great ridge of outcropping white stone overlooking the city of Pidruid. It was the provincial capital, sprawling and

splendid, the biggest city he had come upon since—since?—the biggest in a long while of wandering in any case.

There he halted, finding a seat at the edge of the soft, crumbling white ridge, digging his booted feet into the flaking ragged stone, and he sat there staring down at Pidruid, blinking as though newly out of sleep. On this summer day, twilight was still some hours away, and the sun hung high to the southwest beyond Pidruid, out over the Great Sea. I will rest here for a while, Valentine thought, and then I will go down into Pidruid and find lodging for the night.

The Lippman passage establishes the setting as contemporary San Antonio, downtown to be specific. The Silverberg passage describes a science fiction secondary world, but both have the same effect: introducing and drawing us into a living, breathing setting we can picture in our minds. *This* is world building.

No matter what your genre or setting, the basic concerns tend to be the same. In some genres—science fiction and fantasy especially—extra concerns are important for world building, like space travel, alien cultures, other planets, etc., but all genres still call for thoughtful consideration of the same categories of details. For instance, space travel for a science fiction writer poses essentially the same question that must be answered if a literary fiction writer must move a character from the US to Puerto Rico. Bug-eyed monsters are no more alien in some cases than people from cultures just across the ocean; just read the Mark Twain classic *Innocents Abroad*, and you can see just how different even someone who speaks the same language can be. This chapter is meant to inspire a way of thinking and demonstrate questions and a pattern of logic that will be useful to you in effective world building. Individual application may vary, so as always, use what you need and skip the rest until you need it.

To help get us started, in her chapbook *Checking on Culture*, Lee Killough offers a great checklist that lists many relevant concerns. Here's my adaptation of it:

Habitat_	Cosmetics_	Humor_	Religion_
Anatomy_	Cosmology_	Hygiene_	Science/Magic_
Psychology_	Death_	Knowledge Preservation_	Sex_
Agriculture_	Education_	Labor_	Sports/Games_
Animals: Domestic_	Etiquette_	Laws_	Superstitions_
Animals: Wild_	Elders_	Machines/Tools_	Taboos_
Architecture_	Families_	Marriage_	Timekeeping_
Arts_	Food/Cooking_	Math/Counting_	Towns_
Calendar_	Gestures_	Medicine_	Travel_
Childhood_	Government_	Modesty_	Transport_
Class_	History/Heroes_	Mythos_	Infrastructure_
Clothing_	Hospitality_	Pregnancy_	Warfare/Weapons_
Commerce_	Horticulture_	Professions_	Weights/Measures_
Communication_	Housing_	Property_	

Figure 9-1

Use this table by checking off the items as you go through them and think through that aspect of your world. But first things first. Before you start world building, you must already know your time frame. Far past, near past, current day, near future, or far future? When does your story take place and where? This will determine everything else. Then your research and planning can center on things relevant to that time period. Once we know the time frame, we proceed with the list. The order depends on your priorities, but for me, it usually goes something like the order that follows.

Existing or Secondary World

He returned his attention to Barbirike Sea, which stretched, long and slender as a spear, for fifty miles or so through the valley below the gray cliff on which Kasinibon's fortress-like retreat was perched. Long rows of tall sharp-tipped crescent dunes, soft as clouds from this distance, bordered its shores. They too were red. Even the air here had a red reflected shimmer. The sun itself seemed to have taken on a tinge of it. Kasinibon had explained yesterday, though Furvain had not been particularly interested in hearing it at the time, that the Sea of Barbirike was home to untold billions of tiny crustaceans whose fragile brightcolored shells, decomposing over the millennia, had imparted that bloody hue to the sea's waters and given rise also to the red sands of the adjacent dunes. Furvain wondered whether his royal father, who had such an obsessive interest in intense color effects, had ever made the journey out here to see this place. Surely, he had. Surely.

— Robert Silverberg, The Book of Changes

Existing worlds are Earth or known planets in our solar system or even a few beyond that we know a lot about. Secondary worlds are inventions of the author. Are you inventing everything or building on what already exists and what we already know in the contemporary world of planet Earth? Regardless, you need to know geography, gravity, culture of life-forms, etc. How many suns or moons are there? How many other planets? And so on. If you keep your story on Earth, then many of the concerns having to do with secondary worlds won't apply. You will just have to concern yourself with the science of our planet.

Specifically, in science fiction and fantasy, if you are creating a secondary world, do not put your planet around a famous celestial body just because it is well known. Many of these are highly unlikely to have habitable planets around them, and it requires careful thought about viability before placing planets there, particularly earthlike, human-inhabited ones. You should carefully consider the scientific realities of planetary location and solar-system building before deciding upon such a course, even if writing a soft science story instead of hard science fiction, because believability for readers is paramount. Remember: you should create the questions readers ask carefully and guide them toward questions you can answer satisfactorily and away from ones you cannot. No one covers everything. There will always be gaps. But try to avoid awkwardly obvious, glaring ones. Also, constellations will appear differently from various points around the galaxy, so don't describe them as they appear on Earth when viewed from elsewhere.

About any world you create, ask yourself what the key geographic features are and how they affect population density, location of settlements, travel around and across the surface, economics, weather, etc. Avoid oversimplifying by just saying a planet is all jungle, all ice, etc. because based on location from sun, rotation, geography, and other factors, this is not scientifically plausible and will tend to seem unrealistic and poorly considered. Frank Herbert put a lot of thought into his desert *Dune* planet, but too often, in many novels, the results of oversimplifying come across as lazy thinking. Planets are big places and will have a lot of variety. For example, civilizations will form cities around bodies of drinking water and food supplies, and their diets will vary depending upon the area in which they live and the wildlife, plants, etc. that also reside there. Living creatures also choose habitats based upon location of resources and so on and so forth. There is a circle and a chain of logic to the choices of habitat made by plants and animals that determines much of it and should be considered. You can see these patterns readily in studying Earth, for example. Secondary worlds should follow a similar logic.

On any world, geography always determines travel options. Heavily mountainous areas may not have room for landing zones for starships or local air travel. Large bodies of water may need to be traversed via boats, ships, or other craft in order to avoid long delays in supply, commerce, shipping, etc. So, consider these things in determining where your cities are located and how people get between them.

Gravity levels affect quality of life, from retention of water and atmosphere to breathing to ability to run and jump, etc. But this can also affect the magnetic field and exposure to radiation from solar flares, cosmic rays, and more. High-gravity worlds would have shorter mountains and produce people who have thicker, stronger muscles, and are shorter and flatter like turtles. Air would be denser and tension on body parts might lead to premature aging, sagging faces, etc. Also, accidents might multiply as objects are thrown about or pulled loose by stronger gravity and strike people, vehicles, buildings, life-forms, etc. In high-gravity worlds, rain and rivers would erode land much more quickly as well, smoothing rough edges. Oceans would be calmer and bigger, more extensive, and evaporation would be slower, leaving the air and atmosphere drier with water taking longer to boil and clouds hanging lower. Planes would need bigger wings as well. Reverse these factors for lower-gravity worlds, with larger land masses and smaller bodies of water, etc.

If your world has an earthlike atmosphere, a very slow day will result in extremes of temperature from day to night. Wind speeds will be affected by rotation as well. Oblation will tend to occur for planets with shorter days and rotations versus those with longer ones. It will be thicker or thinner at the equator accordingly. Axial tilt will determine the seasons. Slants greater than Earth will create more extreme seasons. Weather conditions will be affected. The amount of exposure to the sun's heat determines extremes. Wind and ocean currents will moderate the effects. Higher-rotation planets will have more hurricanes and dangerous winds. Ice caps form because poles receive less heat and water freezes. Planets with ice caps will generally be cooler than those without. The skin color of people can be affected by location, with desert peoples generally tending toward darker tones due to sun exposure, while people living in shadows or colder climates who spend much time underground, indoors, etc. may have lighter skin. All of these are interesting factors to take into account.

As you can see, there are many factors to consider, and I can only scratch the surface here. You may not use all the details, but knowing them gives you the option to write the story you need to tell, without being boxed in or slowed down by ignorance.

Solar System and Galaxy Relations

The thirteen planets in the star system all varied in size and shape, the outermost and innermost planets being the smallest. Three of the larger planets had several moons. Vertullis had two. While Vertullis, Tertullis, and Legallis alone had atmospheres suitable for human life, due to Borali scientists' determination and skill with terraforming, all but one of the system's planets had been inhabited, though some with populations consisting only of a few workers and military personnel. The planets revolved around the two suns, Boralis and Charlis, in an unusual orbital pattern due to the effect of the twin gravities. Because of the limitations in terraforming science, the four planets nearest to the suns had been surrendered as viable habitats for humans. Of the thirteen planets, Vertullis was the sole planet which had a surface containing fifty percent forest, and it had one other distinction. It remained the only planet in the solar system whose native citizens weren't free.

— Bryan Thomas Schmidt, *The Worker Prince*

Interplanetary relations and intercultural relations are parallel concerns. They deal with a lot of the same issues. If you are dealing with interplanetary relations, is more than one planet involved? If so, what are their relationships physically and spatially, and do people travel between them? Are there unique transports like space elevators or quantum tunnels or something? Do they use FTL, Faster Than Light tech? Or do they travel for days and weeks as our current limitations would allow? If you are dealing with cultures, what are their preferred modes of travel? What limitations does culture set—like Amish not using technology—if there are any? Does one culture regard certain modes as the provinces of the other due to wealth or status? What concerns arise?

As most of us know, one of the key tropes of science fiction is starships. They come in all shapes and sizes, from planet-sized like the Death Star to slightly smaller like Imperial Destroyers down to shuttlecraft and tiny fighters like X-Wings or Vipers. Some ships are meant for short-term travel to and from one locale to another. Others are actually living spaces like cities where hundreds or thousands of people reside and work for years on end. Obviously, the size and scope of usage determines the facilities required. And one should take into account the various needs for sleeping, recreation and entertainment, food, medical facilities, waste disposal and personal hygiene, storage, and more. The longer the ships must function as homes and the larger the number of inhabitants, the more concern for supplies, storage, etc. becomes an issue. For every inhabitant, a certain amount of food, water, and other necessities will need to be regularly used and thus available and stored between ports and stops, with extra reserves for periods of battle, long-distance travel, etc. Haircuts, clothing, shoes, grooming, and more are also concerns, as well as psychology and counseling, law enforcement and regulations—even criminal detainment and disposal of deceased—sex, and much more. Are the ships warships or peaceful? Do they have weapons and defenses? What are they? How secure are they? How does this vary according to uses and needs? How does having such items affect the crew compliment and training and roles? All of this must be considered and weighed carefully in designing your starships according to their purposes and uses.

Solar systems can be big. Pluto is 4.5 billion miles from the sun at its farthest, while Earth is 92.96 million miles away. Light can traverse 4.5 billion miles in 5.5 hours, but at current rates, spacecraft would take years, even in our own solar system. So, to expedite things and make interaction between planets possible, science fiction writers created Faster Than Light travel, or FTL for short. This tends to be a minimally defined variant that allows ships to travel between planets in days or hours rather than years. It is a cheat that even some hard science fiction writers employ because the practical reality of space travel deals with numbers so high it is hard for writers, let alone readers, to fathom. Not to mention the loss of dramatic tension one experiences when ships must fly toward each other for years before engaging in battle. Woo-hoo, how tense and exciting that is! For creating dramatic tension alone, FTL is really useful. There have been many forms and explanations for it, from hyperdrives to warp drives, but all generally come down to the same thing: faster travel between celestial bodies and galaxies.

Hyperspace, in use since the 1940s, is often depicted as an alternate reality or universe or some sort of subspace existence. Since the science involved is imaginary, you can make assumptions, design mechanisms, and assign limits any way you choose as long as you are consistent and plausible. Are there preexisting gates used to enter hyperspace, or is it created through some kind of physics or scientific displacement using the special hyperdrive? Are the gravity wells of planets and stars necessary for its success, or can it be done anywhere? What role do gravitational fields play? How do you calculate and carry enough fuel and resources to get there and back? Where do you acquire them along the way if needed? Then, what about communications? At such high speeds, sound waves are affected. Can they keep up, or do you need special communications methods and devices?

And of course, if you can travel between planets, you must address the issue: How are they related to each other? Are they familiar with established relationships that are good or bad? Are they strangers and unknown? Do they share a government or treaties or other common agreements and rules, or is it a free-for-all? Who are their primary populations, and what species are they? What is their primary language and currency? How do any differences get bridged when two different planets interact? How are conflicts resolved and what incompatibilities must be overcome? What is the ongoing history of relations, if any, and what are the issues and obstacles that have arisen and continue to affect ongoing relations?

You must consider separate geography, resources, etc. for each planet and culture. What do they trade? Why? How do their resources, tools, etc. differ? Do they travel across the planet differently? Do they need life-support domes? Is gravity modification required? How can different species interact in spaces that support different life-forms?

If your story takes place on Earth or a single planet, on what part of the planet is the story focused? Does the story take your characters to many places, or is it concentrated in one area? Knowing this will define the amount and type of research you will need to do on geography, politics, sociology, etc. and where you need to focus attention for world-building details included in your story. Obviously, knowing one or a few areas really well will be simpler than having to research many and answer all of these questions about them.

Society and Cultures

> Doubled, I walk the street. Though we are no longer in the Commander's compound, there are large houses here also. In front of one of them, a Guardian is mowing the lawn. The lawns are tidy, the facades are gracious, in good repair; they're like the beautiful pictures they used to print in the magazines about homes and gardens and interior decoration. There is the same absence of people, the same air of being asleep. The street is almost like a museum, or a street in a model town constructed to show the way people used to live. As in those pictures, those museums, those model towns, there are no children.
>
> — Margaret Atwood, The Handmaid's Tale

The next concern is what kind of society and cultures will be present in the setting of your story? If the cultures are cultures of Earth, then research their language, lifestyle, economic circumstances, religion, etc. in detail and do your best to represent them in a way that members of the culture itself, if reading your work, will recognize themselves and compliment it. If you create extraterrestrial aliens or nonhumans, you must first determine how humanoid they are going to be or how different from us. Why are they different? And how did they come to be that way? These questions can be decided by a number of factors: factors about the world on which they will live; practical concerns for language and communication; the relationship they will have with humans, etc.; biological and geographic factors; and more. Since aliens are often what draws many readers to science fiction, they are important, as is the distinction from mythological creatures. Unlike these folkloric beings, aliens are grounded in scientific possibility, so such factors must be careful considered and employed in designing and presenting them. Luckily, the research can be fun. There are substances other than oxygen that can release energy from sugar and serve biological function, for example. Hydrogen sulfide can replace water in photosynthesis as well. And silicon serves just as well as carbon as a basic building block of life. Your imagination can take you to fun but scientifically plausible places if you do the research.

Besides having scientific plausibility, however, your aliens must also serve narrative interest by being able to interact with native characters and sometimes even communicate with them, and by being intriguing enough to engage reader interest, pique their curiosity, or even inspire fear. Most of the time, this will require sentient beings, but on occasion, when the aliens are meant to serve only as obstacles and antagonists to native characters' goals and interests, nonsentient alien monsters will do. Don't forget to consider the evolutionary advantages of the aliens' unique features. If they don't need hands, what do they have for limbs? If they can float and don't need legs, what other features might they need instead? Is genetic engineering involved, or is it entirely organic? All of these concerns can lead you in interesting and intriguing directions. Remember also that alien encounters don't necessarily occur strictly between humans and beings from other planets. James Clavell's Shōgun is one of the all-time great first-encounter stories of alien cultures—between Western sailors and the Japanese samurai. Aliens are all around us—basically anyone whose culture and experience, and thus common frame of reference, significantly differs from our own.

If dealing solely with humans on Earth, what races are involved, and what are their relationships to each other? What social classes, attitudes, and history do they share, and how does that affect their interactions and determine their relationships, etc.? What are the societal roles for each gender? How are LGBT people regarded and treated, and what place can they have in society? Are there any limitations placed on people for reasons of class, sexual preference, race, religion, or something else? What reasons lie behind any restrictions, and what is their history? Instead of making things up yourself, use research materials from the library, the internet, and even interviews with live persons to get the details right and find the right details to add nuance and depth to your characters and story.

There are also environmental factors. If elements other than oxygen and carbon are key elements in your world, what the inhabitants value, what they eat, and what resources they need will all be affected. Their priorities will be influenced accordingly and so will trade, economics, sociocultural interactions, etc. Their goals and values will also reflect this. Food chain, ecology, economy, and the implications of each are key factors as well. Each alien culture will have something distinctive to offer the larger whole toward economy, etc. What that is, how it developed, and what it says about them are important factors to consider as well. Additionally, their evolutionary makeup affects their emotions and memory and learning styles. What if they have a group brain and can share information? How does this group mind affect individuation or emotions or relationships? Is there privacy or none at all? How does this interconnectedness affect their attitude toward and trust of strangers and outsiders?

If you have extraterrestrial aliens, can they communicate directly, or is some form of mind-to-mind communication used rather than vocal speech? Are universal translators or interpreters required for people of different worlds, cultures, or languages? Behavioral and physiological traits can both serve as barriers and increase bonding in relationships with native characters, depending upon how you design them. Thinking these through carefully is key. Also the societal mores, roles, statuses, and laws are factors that will play a role in how aliens and natives think of and about each other and how they interact, and will often be key to their relationships and interactions on many levels. What are mating and childbearing and -rearing rituals? Are they monogamous or polygamous? Do they love? Do they form attachments for life or short term or at all? Do they have philosophy or religion? Do they have science or industry? What are the various roles, and how are these affected by geography, physiology, beliefs, and more?

And did I mention the arts? Do they have fine arts? What about music, drama, painting, sculpting, etc.? What forms do they take, and what value do the inhabitants place on them? What instruments and mediums are used? What languages? Where are they performed or displayed? What do they look and sound like? How valued are they and by whom in the culture, etc.? A realistic culture will always have such things interwoven into daily life. Loved or hated, characters will take note of them.

> "Remember this, son, if you forget everything else. A poet is a musician who can't sing. Words have to find a man's mind before they can touch his heart, and some men's minds are woeful small targets. Music touches their hearts directly no

matter how small or stubborn the mind of the man who listens."

— Patrick Rothfuss, The Name of the Wind

Science and Industrial Development

The battery was a lithium thionyl chloride non-rechargeable. I figured that out from some subtle clues: the shape of the connection points, the thickness of the insulation, and the fact that it had "LiSOCl2 NON-RCHRG" written on it.

— Andy Weir, *The Martian*

The planet's famous red colour is from iron oxide coating everything. So, it's not just a desert. It's a desert so old it's literally rusting.

— Andy Weir, *The Martian*

Another key area of world building is always science and industry. In science fiction, the futuristic and scientific aspects of this take on special importance and significance for both narrative plausibility and practical reasons—science and development are key elements readers expect. Science fiction readers love cool tech and science that makes sense or even the hint of such. Even if it is not real, if you make it sound plausible, they will often find this fascinating and engaging.

What kind of transportation methods exist? Horses and wagons or buggies? Cars and trucks? Planes or spaceships? Hovercraft? Each type of transportation requires the industrial and scientific development to make it possible. Given that we barely have anything of the sort ourselves, a lot of thought will need to go into these aspects. Where do they get the fuel? How did they devise it? What materials are starships and their various parts made of? Do the ships have laser or projectile weapons (not just guns but rocket launchers or catapults or spear guns, etc.)? What kind of defensive armaments do people and ships have, and what are they made of? Are they physical or digital? And what kinds of hand weapons exist and why? There have to be practical and reasoned explanations. Armaments are not just devised for no reason; and at the same time, are limits like gun control, carry permits, concealed carry, etc. necessary and why? What are the restrictions for buying, selling, and carrying?

Then there are questions of military practices. What type of military do they have—formal or informal? Private or government? Do they have armor? What type? What is the structure and ranking system? Where are the bases and training facilities? How do they recruit—volunteers or conscription? Do they use animals or vehicles or both? What kinds of duties and missions are they usually called upon to undertake? What is their history? What is their relationship with larger society—respected or hated? Feared or loved?

Technological dependence also says a lot about a culture and affects it in many ways and has many meanings. For stories on Earth, all this will depend on the time frame in which your story is set. For example, Twain talks in *Innocents Abroad* about how cost concerns affect travel and opportunities for cultural interaction between Europeans and Americans as well as any other cultures. These kinds of concerns need to be considered thoughtfully. For secondary worlds, ask yourself, How advanced are they? How did they get there? If there is tech and science, there must be engineers and scientists. How did they develop these abilities and create or acquire the tools required to perform the tasks? Do they make them themselves or trade for them? How do various cultural approaches differ in performing, understanding, and approaching various tasks? Here's an aspect where time frame, as mentioned earlier, plays a key role. If they are a very advanced society, time frame matters. For humans especially, believable time must have passed for certain technologies to be possible. If you are writing Earth history but modifying the science or inventions of the period, you will need to explain these changes logically for readers. Some technologies require science and engineering feats we have yet to develop, so time must be allowed for those to occur as well. For alien cultures, it is possible to have societies that are advanced over our own, but again, they must have science and tech and engineering knowledge and skills that they acquired earlier which surpasses our own. Not all of this always has to be explained in detail, but the writer should think it through and be fully aware of the implications of it and write the story accordingly so it adds credence to the world building for readers.

Are there robots or androids in your story? Are human cyborgs or modified humans part of it? What about animals? Are there hybrids? Is there nanotechnology? What is the state of computers and media? Is there virtual reality? What problems from our own world and times have been solved to make such things possible or to advance society? What modifications to laws, mores, etc. have been required to permit the developments, if any? What sciences are used and understood by alien cultures, and how does this compare to human knowledge? What ability to exchange such information exists? Writers must consider all of this and more as they create.

I realize that at this point in the chapter, you may be feeling overwhelmed by all that we've covered. But I hope you are beginning to see the complexity of world building and how one set of questions leads to many others on many different topics. There's a reason so many authors choose to work with our existing world and its history rather than make up their own. It's complicated to create a well-rounded world, and as I have said, you don't always know what you'll need until you need it, but it is also easy to overlook things that may stand out to readers as omissions that were important to questions they are asking.

In the rest of this chapter, we're going to cover some areas that get overlooked a lot in world building but may be just as important as the rest. Let's start with agriculture, horticulture, and diet.

Agriculture, Horticulture, Diet, and Medicine

On the bare forest floor, in the open space between the trees, grew stemless plants of colossal size. Their leaves, four or five inches broad and eight or nine feet in length, sharp-toothed along their sides and metallic of texture, were arranged in loose rosettes. At the center of each gaped a deep cup a foot in diameter, half filled with a noxious-looking greenish fluid, out of which a complex array of stubby organs projected. It seemed to Valentine that there were things like knifeblades in there, and paired grinders, that could come together nastily, and still other things that might have been delicate flowers partly submerged.

— Robert Silverberg, Lord Valentine's Castle

Agricultural development is very much determined by geography and technological and scientific development. The types of crops and animals used for food and clothing depend upon the resources available, like location of water supply, crops, grass and plant life, landscape, and more. You won't grow much in a desert, for example, but if there are oases with water, some sheep herding can occur, like in the Middle East. There can also be camels, horses, and other desert animals. In mountains, it is hard to farm the land, but animals like bears, deer, various birds, and other mammals can live there, which could be hunted for food.

Plains are great for farming but limited as home for much beyond domestic animals, though coyotes, wild birds, rabbits, and other animals may thrive. And with each decision about animals, it is important to consider predators and prey—the circle of life. For anywhere one group of prey lives, predators will arise to feed on them, and not just human predators, but other animals. Additionally, landscape determines what kinds of bushes, shrubs, grasses, trees, etc. will be available and natural to the region for animals to live in and eat from, etc.

What type of crops and natural resources you have, of course, determines the diet of local natives and other inhabitants, and so plant life, crops, and water all determine what people will eat in various parts of your world and how much, as well as what they may trade to other areas for goods they cannot get. At the same time, what clothing they wear is determined by land and weather conditions and resources as well. Do they have technology to manufacture clothing or make it by hand? And so on. Sartorial concerns are easy to overlook. I remember one of the first editor comments on *The Worker Prince*, my first novel, was, "You've written 90k words without mention of what anyone is wearing. It seems odd." Oops. So, I had to go back and work that in and think it through. I know of other authors who have had similar experiences.

Along with crops, animal husbandry, and resources comes the issue of medicine. What kind of medicinal resources do they have? Formal or informal? Do they make drugs from natural processes or manufacture them synthetically? Do they use home remedies or chemically devised cures? Do they have trained medical personnel or just village experts? And so on. Who treats the animals? What kind of training do those people have? Is it science or magic? And if magic exists, how does that work and what are the costs of performing the spells or using magic? There is always a cost for everything. Sometimes casting spells can only be done once every few days, sometimes it costs blood or energy that wipes out the magician, etc. These and more concerns become very relevant.

If there is agricultural technology, do they use machines to farm or just animals and primitive equipment? How industrial is agriculture? How regional is it? What about fishing or hunting or trapping? Can they make hybrid plants somehow by cross-pollinating, or do they just have to plant whatever seeds they can find?

As we think about landscape and natural resources like plants and trees, we must also consider architecture and design. Do they have formal architecture, or is it regional and informal? Are there whole industries for construction and design, or is it done on the fly? Are quarries and mining involved? How do they gather materials? What varied styles and approaches to architecture exist, and which are prominent in the region of your story? What issues and regional concerns come into play to determine locations of towns and types of housing, etc.? Are there formal schools, or are people educated at home? What kind of educational system and higher learning is available? Are there apprenticeships? Are there internships? Trade guilds? What kinds of tools and equipment do they have available, and how are those manufactured? And then, where do they get the money to buy land and build? How is land and wealth allotted? What role does it play in society?

Beyond that, what about energy production? Nuclear, solar, wind, fusion—what kind of power will there be? What of war? What of peace? What about nuclear and chemical weapons? What will medicine look like? Will we have cured diseases, genetic defects, cancer? What new answers and treatments will have been devised? Which communication devices and methods are common? Which have faded away?

Money and Business

Coins of the Four Corners

Cealdish		Common Wealth	
11 Shim	= 1 Iron Drab	5 Iron Penny	= 1 Copper Penny
10 Iron Drab	= 1 Copper Jott	2 Ha'Penny	= 1 Copper Penny
10 Copper Jot	= 1 Silver Talent	10 Copper Penny	= 1 Silver Penny
10 Silver Talent	= 1 Gold Mark	12 Silver Penny	= 1 Common

Vintish		Aturan	
2 Halfpenny	= 1 Penny	3 Rasteur	= 1 Iron Link
2½ Penny	= 1 Bit	3 Iron Link	= 1 Soft Penny
2 Bit	= 1 Quarter Bit	3 Soft Penny	= 1 Hard Penny
4 Quarter Bit	= 1 Round	7 Hard Penny	= 1 Bellum
10 Round	= 1 Royal	12 Bellum	= 1 Lord Rose

10 Bit	= 1 Haft
2 Haft	= 1 Noble
5 Haft	= 1 Reel
5 Reel	= 1 Five Reel Piece

Rates of Exchange

Vintish	1 Half Penny	= 6½ Shim
Common Wealth	1 Iron Penny	= 3 Shim
Aturan	1 Iron Link	= 4½ Shim

Figure 9-2. Monetary exchange rates in *The Name of the Wind*, Patrick Rothfuss, cited on http://www.brinkofcreation.com/KKC-CurrencyExchange/CurrencyExchange.html.

Money and economy are one of the most overlooked of worldbuilding concerns. In his Kingkiller Chronicles, beginning with *The Name of the Wind*, Patrick Rothfuss is an author noted for having created a sophisticated economy for his world, including different monetary systems for various people groups and conversion and even commonwealth currency for use in trade between them. The system is sophisticated enough that fans on Reddit have figured out approximate conversions to US dollars, and Rothfuss himself has created the widget in Figure 9-2 and can lecture on the system for an hour or more (see Figure 9-1). That is a well-thought-out system. And of course, along with money comes the entire business system and how it functions related to currency and trade and what types of businesses thrive and arise according to resources available, as well as needs of the world. Various service industries like money changers and trade posts will arise if needed, along with banks, law enforcement, security, and more, but then there are various other businesses as well, taking on roles in making food, clothing, and materials, etc., and sometimes even vendors who then sell their products to the public.

The key element is what they value—what their economy is based on. In much of the Western world and the wider world today, that would be minerals like gold, silver, bronze, diamonds, etc. In ancient Africa, however, many tribes placed much value on conch shells. They used conch shells to make everything from jewelry to clothing to even tools, weapons, and more. Once Europeans discovered this, they began trading conch shells for things they valued far more, like gold, diamonds, etc., which were abundant in Africa. The Europeans found many sources for obtaining conch shells, and since the African tribesmen valued them so much, convincing them to trade something the Europeans considered worthless for things they coveted was easy. It also gave the Europeans immense power over the Africans, particularly because conch shells were cheap and easily obtained and not valued greatly by anyone else around the world. In part, the colonization of Africa came about at least economically because of this dichotomy. The Europeans used it to establish inroads they exploited to take over mining and other industries to extract minerals and eventually conquer the tribes and their land. So, what do people in your worlds and cultures value? How does that affect their trade relationships and subsequent power relationships with others? These major concerns are related to the economic system of your world and should be carefully considered.

Economic systems can get immensely complicated very quickly, of course, but careful thought should at least be given to basics needed for the story. And economic realities can have fascinating repercussions and nuances for your story and characters. You should be prepared to address the various issues and needs these concerns raise as you go, if you want to create a believable system that doesn't leave readers confused, frustrated, or scratching their heads.

Designing a Past and Future

I remember a television program I once saw; a rerun, made years before. I must have been seven or eight, too young to understand it. It was the sort of thing my mother liked to watch: historical, educational... The program was a documentary, about one of those wars. They interviewed people and showed clips from films of the time, black and white, and still photos... The interviews with people still alive then were in color. The one I remember best was with a woman who had been the mistress of a man who had supervised one of the camps where they put the Jews, before they killed them. In ovens, my mother said; but there weren't any pictures of the ovens, so I got some confused notion that these deaths had taken place in kitchens. There is something especially terrifying to a child in that idea. Ovens mean cooking, and cooking comes before eating. I thought these people had been eaten. Which in a way I suppose they had been.

— Margaret Atwood, The Handmaid's Tale

Last, but far from least, you will need to give thought to the past and future of your world, accounting for how the inhabitants got where they are and anticipating where they are going and what future issues may arise as the result of present events. In addition, what issues in the present can be traced to events in the past? How do people in the present interact with this history? How knowledgeable are they of it? How misinformed? As you imagine a future and past, you must consider what advances have been made and how they have been made, what people are still seeking to do, what problems remain unsolved, etc. The implications of such choices always affect your story and world in key ways. If your world is being made up from scratch (secondary), then you will have to invent all this. If it is on Earth, then you can do the research to get the facts and details correct.

It is important not to get so focused on technology and science that you forget social issues. These, more than anything, will be key to creating a realistic possible future. Technological and scientific advances are great, but they have costs and implications. What if these technologies empower only a few and are unavailable to the many? What if they bring wealth to the few and leave the many poorer? How will your future deal with issues of racism, equal rights, poverty, hunger, education, and income equality? How will your world be better than or a better version of ours, and how will it be worse? Regardless of what you choose, these must be addressed and presented in believable ways.

It is important to think of both what is gained and what is left behind or lost, what is erased and what is invented. And also, where do these ideas, concepts, and possibilities lead—new dangers, new crimes, new threats? Or all positives? Rarely are there all positives and no negatives, remember. Are there ecological nightmares? Totalitarian governments? What of population growth? What of unemployment? And so on. New pitfalls will arise as old ones are erased. Which will stay erased forever and which will come back and how? No future is perfect, and to be believable, yours cannot be either. So, with every advancement, there will be setbacks or problems. And you should deal with both and allow them to drive your story, to inspire conflict on which drama thrives.

It would be impossible for me or anyone else to cover everything or anything in any kind of depth in a book like this, but I hope I have provided a decent guide and overview for how to think through world building, how one set of concerns is connected to others, and many of the types of things you will need to consider as you create worlds. I didn't even cover everything on Lee Killough's checklist, but that, and this chapter, should act as decent guides in creating your world.

Closely connected to world building is research to not only find these things but make them function logically and workably, as well as to learn the terminology and more that you need to describe them intelligently, convincing readers you actually did your homework. All of that, as well as various research approaches and resources, will be covered in Chapter 10.

CHAPTER 10
RESEARCH

I know what you're thinking: "Research is a dirty word. I hate research." A lot of writers seem to have that attitude. I had it myself for years. After four years of college and three of grad school, I thought I was done with all that, and happily so. I wrote five novels and barely did any research, but then I had a project I couldn't do right without it, and my attitude changed. Research can be extremely rewarding if you are able to employ it to make your manuscript better and your story more authentic. And there are many options and sources to choose from that will allow most of you to find a path of least resistance—or at least, with the least discomfort and frustration.

In *On Writing*, Stephen King says of research:

> Research is back story, and the key word in back story is back... What I'm looking for is nothing but a touch of verisimilitude, like the handful of spices you chuck into a good spaghetti sauce to really finish her off. That sense of reality is particularly important in any work of fiction, but ... particularly important in a story dealing with the abnormal or paranormal. Also, enough details— always assuming they are the correct ones—can stem the tide of letters from picky-ass readers who apparently live to tell writers they messed up... When you step away from the "write what you know" rule, research becomes inevitable, and it can

add a lot to your story… [Just remember] the story always comes first.

Certainly, one of the things that makes research so daunting is that to use it well, some must be done before you write. Many of us have a tendency to want to put it off and get to the fun part, pausing only to research when we absolutely have to. After all, you never know how much you'll need until you start writing. The problem with this is that underlying thought processes uninformed by research will lead to writing that is ignorant of key elements and unprepared to ask key questions that research brings out, which will inform your work—how you construct characters, world, and story. With research in your head, you begin employing its implications from word one. Without it, you can't possible do so. If you wait until you need it, not only will your work be weaker, but you will also set yourself up for more rewriting and reworking than you would have had to do if you had completed at least some research before your writing.

So how do you know where to begin and when you've done enough research to write? This is a question only you can answer and one that depends on many factors: the needs of your world building, characterization, plot, settings, etc. Some of those needs arise as you write, especially if you are a discovery writer who does not plan much out in advance. Writers who start with an outline will have an easier time identifying key areas of ignorance in advance, so they can focus their research and bone up their knowledge on those topics. Some writers also assume that if you are making up a secondary world, you can do less research. But readers expect your secondary worlds to follow the same logic as Earth and the existing worlds we know of: the laws of science, reason, logic, etc. There are things that just *are*, and if you break those expectations without really knowing what you are doing and justifying it well, then readers will lose confidence in you as a truthteller and narrator, and that will hurt their opinion of your story.

And as you saw in Chapter 9, world building is filled with questions to answer, and in most cases, the only way to answer them is to do research. Fortunately, all of us live in the age of the internet. The internet will undoubtedly be your greatest research friend. True, there are a lot of lies on the internet and articles lacking good fact-checking. You will have to be discerning about your sources. But for quick, basic information on almost any topic, the internet is a quick, easy solution, and often what you learn there will lay the groundwork that informs the rest of your research—pointing you to sources and topics, helping define what questions you need to address, etc. So, no matter what else your research involves, expect to start with the internet.

There are two other ways you can research that will come in handy for various stories: library research and real-world experience. Libraries are available everywhere, so I probably don't have to explain those. Most offer free or cheap memberships to locals and have research librarians on staff who can help you locate materials, borrow books on interlibrary loan, etc. Make use of them. That is what they are there for, and they enjoy helping people like you. It is their calling. Real-life experience can happen several ways: conducting interviews, scouting (going to locations and talking to people and taking pictures and notes), and consulting experts. One of the most fun and helpful research tools I employed on my police procedural series were ride-along with police. These are free and require only some paperwork and a background check. They are amazingly fascinating and eye opening. Many government agencies have liaisons assigned specifically to help people doing research about their agencies. The FBI (Federal Bureau of Investigation) is one example. Police departments and many others have media people. Often, private businesses and industries have them as well. If you are polite, and patient, you may well get their assistance. You have only to ask. Interviews, of course, are a bit more complex but also can be arranged. You can often observe without permission in public places. Just take a notebook and your eyes and get to work.

Some of you will be able to do the bulk of your research online or in books and never need to go out and make time for real-world experience. This is okay, of course. Do what your stories require. But real-world experience is indeed an option and can be very fulfilling, as I said. Most of you will need to do some combination of the three, especially when it comes to vocabulary and technical knowledge on various topics like medicine, criminal justice, law, science, technology, etc. Talking the talk authentically will be necessary for the credibility of your story. So learning the terminology will be a necessary part of research. You can't wing it, sorry. Not if you want to write a book that feels true and realistic. Fortunately, there are plenty of books on most topics providing such knowledge, and most are widely available. But how do you find sources? That's the topic of the last section of this chapter. First, let's discuss research strategies.

Research Strategies

How you research will ultimately come to be as individualistic as how you write, so what I will do is propose a logical approach, similar to what I use. You can adapt and evolve it from there to suit your needs.

First, start with your key settings, protagonist, and antagonist. Go to as many settings as you can get to. Stop, take them in, and write down the first seven to ten things you notice about them. These can later form the basis of your description. I usually use the voice recorder on my phone for this rather than taking notes. It makes it easier to first note seven to ten things, then compose a more detailed description of various features that can be pulled from to expand later as needed. With settings I cannot get to, I start with Google Maps, pulling up images and doing the same thing: write down the first seven to ten observations, then do a fuller description. Sometimes Wikipedia also describes architectural features, so I paste those descriptions in my notes for later reference. I try to ask people who have been there about sounds and smells common to the location because those are things that can be key details but that cannot be captured online.

For characters, I start with their professions. I talk to real people with those jobs, if possible, but also do lots of internet and book research, particularly looking for vocabulary they would use as well as basic routines they would follow in their daily work lives. These daily life things will be referred to often in your story to make it authentic. Then I research whatever other details occur to me, including what they wear, gathering spots, social habits, hobbies, etc. that seem appropriate as they come up.

I keep either a spreadsheet or a Word file with all the notes to be referred to later. Or, if writing in Scrivener, a great, inexpensive software option for novelists, I paste notes in tabs there for reference. These are easily updated and cut and pasted from as needed. Then you can modify and adjust for voice, length, etc. as needed in using them for your book.

The next things I research are any scientific or technological details that will be key to my story, and then I do the same with businesses or industries or agriculture if any are involved. After that, I pretty much have enough to get started and then research as I go. It's a fairly simple approach, but logical, and it prioritizes the stuff you will probably use the most in your writing. Getting the major research out of the way will allow you to write more and interrupt less for later research. Because once I get into the flow of writing, I hate interrupting that for research, I am quite comfortable with this approach. It may be different for you. Adjust as needed. This example is just to give you an idea of one logical approach you might take.

I am sure writers' research strategies are as abundant as writing styles and approaches to craft, so don't be afraid to ask around. Writers are often more than happy to share tips and ideas on social media about such things. I find it very helpful to learn from others' approaches and incorporate anything that seems useful into my own approach.

One Writer's Approach: Andy Weir

I thought it would be interesting to talk with my friend and famous client, Andy Weir, about how he approaches research, since he is known for using a lot of it in his writing. His first novel, *The Martian*, on which I was the first editor, is a hard science fiction bestseller that became a hit movie and has sold in the millions and continues to sell today. His follow-up, *Artemis*, is less hard science fiction, but still uses as much real science as possible. What follows is an interview with Andy about how he approaches research.

INTERVIEW: ANDY WEIR ON RESEARCH

Bryan Thomas Schmidt: So your books tend to be research heavy as you are very literate on science, mathematics, technology, and such. Which comes first—the story idea or the research?

Andy J. Weir: The research. I usually start with the setting— usually a science-based situation—then work out a story and characters.

217

Yes, of course duct tape works in a near-vacuum. Duct tape works anywhere. Duct tape is magic and should be worshiped.

—Andy Weir, The Martian

BTS: Once you start writing, how do you approach research—do you try and gather as much as possible and create research bibles or spreadsheets or just research what you need when you need it?

AJW: I usually just research what I need to know. But sometimes that's quite a lot.

BTS: I know you've said you always start with the internet. What are some favorite sites you like to start with for your research?

AJW: I always start with a Google search. About half the time, that leads to a Wikipedia page. But the other half of the time I end up all over the place. Oftentimes it'll be at school assignments that have been posted online. Like when I looked into thermal conductivity, I found myself basically doing thermodynamics class homework to try to understand it.

There's an international treaty saying no country can lay claim to anything that's not on Earth. And by another treaty, if you're not in any country's territory, maritime law applies.

So Mars is "international waters."

NASA is an American nonmilitary organization, and it owns the Hab. So, while I'm in the Hab, American law applies. As soon as I step outside, I'm in international waters. Then when I get in the rover, I'm back to American law.

Here's the cool part: I will eventually go to Schiaparelli and commandeer the Ares 4 lander. Nobody explicitly gave me permission to do this, and they can't until I'm aboard Ares 4 and operating the comm system. After I board Ares 4, before talking to NASA, I will take control of a craft in international waters without permission.

That makes me a pirate!

A space pirate!

—Andy Weir, The Martian

BTS: Do you use libraries and books a lot? How do you decide what to research online and what to use books for and how much care and attention goes into verifying the legitimacy of sources?

AJW: I don't do paper research. I'm just too lazy to leave my chair. I try to make sure the sources are solid, but there are no guarantees in life. In the end, my job is to *sound* right. I don't have to actually be right. The goal is to entertain.

BTS: What is the biggest challenge of making all the science, math, etc. accessible for the broader readership, and how do you go about it?

AJW: The hardest part is figuring out where to draw the line and not tell them something. I have to make sure they understand enough science to know why something is a problem and to also understand the solution the characters come up with. But I have to stick to just that—telling them more, no matter how interesting it is to me, is just needless exposition.

BTS: Do you use real-life consultants, and how do you recruit them or find them if you do?

AJW: Not often, no. I've found that internet searches are just so much faster.

> *Problem is (follow me closely here, the science is pretty complicated), if I cut a hole in the Hab, the air won't stay inside anymore.*
>
> —*Andy Weir,* The Martian

BTS: Do real-life consultants require a salary or donate their time generally?

AJW: On the rare occasions when I use real-life sources, they're happy to just chat with me about stuff. No pay.

BTS: What's your favorite bit learned from research? One that stays with you and comes in handy time and again?

AJW: I guess it's just the overarching lesson I learned from *The Martian*, which is that the deeper you research something, the more science will help drive the plot.

BTS: Do you have any tips on research for our readers?

AJW: Don't be afraid to do a deep dive. Try to fully understand the thing you're researching. You'll often discover things you didn't know that can lead to awesome plot events in your story.

ANDY WEIR built a career as a software engineer until the success of his first published novel, *The Martian*, allowed him to live out his dream of writing full time. He is a lifelong space nerd and a devoted hobbyist of subjects such as relativistic physics, orbital mechanics, and the history of manned spaceflight. He also mixes a mean cocktail. He lives in California.

So that's one successful author's approach and it works for him, in large part, because he is immensely smart and knowledgeable about math and science and technology generally. His base knowledge makes it easy for him to convincingly write about such topics and apply his research. Not everyone can do that. And some facts matter more than others. Yes, it is fiction. It is entertainment. But if you are writing about Chicago, you'd better get it right mostly or you will run into readers who are both offended and highly critical of you for it. If you sell three million copies, you might be able to withstand that; if not, you might want to be more careful. The degree to which you can just rely on internet research and eschew fact-checking depends upon a number of factors but chiefly the subject matter, type of story, and likely audience as well as publisher's expectations. In fiction, it is far easier to eschew such things than in nonfiction, of course, where getting it right is demanded and expected. But I would not interpret the interview as implying it's okay to be casual about facts or research.

Also, keep in mind that Wikipedia is filled with inaccuracies, lies, and opinions presented as facts as much as anywhere else on the internet, so corroborating anything found there with other sources is your best bet to ensure accuracy. This applies as well to scientific articles and anything else whose veracity needs verification. It is not that hard to do, if you just ask around or do more searching. Numerous resources are available. Check the source list at the end of this book for great places to start.

Another Approach: Jonathan Maberry

My friend and collaborator Jonathan Maberry is the *New York Times* bestselling author of multiple series, including the Rot and Ruin series for young adults, and the Joe Ledger and Pine Deep series for adults. His approach to research is to try to get as much of the science correct as he can. Here's how he approaches it:

Bryan Thomas Schmidt: So, your books tend to be research heavy as you are very literate on science, mathematics, technology, and such. Which comes first—the story idea or the research?

Jonathan Maberry: I am a bit of a research junkie, or perhaps it's fairer to say that I'm addicted to information. A great deal of what I read for pleasure is nonfiction—books on science, history, folklore, politics—or trade journals from various fields. I subscribe to an absurd number of periodicals dealing with everything from archaeology to true crime to astrophysics. In part this is to feed that hunger to know new things, or to deepen my understanding on a variety of subjects. However, I'm always on the prowl for something that might form the seed of a story. And there are times I'll already have a story in mind and am reading deeply into the subject matter to gain a more informed and less pedestrian set of opinions.

Here are some examples …

My first novel, *Ghost Road Blues*, which is in the genre of contemporary American gothic, may be on the surface a horror thriller, but it didn't start that way. In 2000, I wrote a nonfiction book (using a one-time pen name of Shane MacDougall) on the folklore of supernatural predators—vampires, werewolves, etc. That book was exhaustively researched in terms of folklore, anthropology, history, religion, and related topics. During the phase of research and writing I thought that it would be interesting to try my hand at fiction—something I'd never done at that point—to pit ordinary human protagonists against the versions of these monsters as they appeared in various cultural beliefs. None of the vampires of folklore bear any resemblance at all to the vampires in popular fiction and Hollywood.

> *When Tony lost it, it would be up to Ruger to take Lady Death by the tits and give her a good tweak. That's how he saw it. Give Lady Death's tits a good tweak.*
>
> —*Jonathan Maberry,* Ghost Road Blues

Writing the novel was an experiment, which actually sparked a new addiction: writing fiction. Along the way, though, I had to research all kinds of topics, including rural Pennsylvania police procedure, forensic evidence collection, digital photography, the operation of cellular towers, high explosives, firearms, the treatment of gunshot wounds, the procedures involved in an autopsy, the security systems used in hospitals, and so on. I wanted to get the details right so that the story could be as solidly grounded in reality as possible so that the elements of fantasy and supernatural horror would be more easily hidden and therefore (hopefully) more emotionally powerful.

This kind of detailed on-the-fly research happens in every novel I write. However, not every novel starts with the research. My Joe Ledger thriller series, of which *Deep Silence* is the tenth, began with the story: something big and bad was going to happen that would destabilize the infrastructure of the United States and fracture the government's response to an even greater terrorist threat. That was the broad story idea. Once I had that, I began doing research into a variety of areas, with a bias toward things that might disrupt everything from first responders to administrative oversight and guidance. Usually natural disasters such as hurricanes and superstorms do that, as we saw with Hurricane Katrina, but terrorists conjuring a hurricane was not something for which I could find support in actual science.

So, I started thinking about earthquakes. I read about how fracking increased the frequency of earthquakes in Oklahoma. I knew I didn't want to do a fracking story per se, but that phenomenon proved that humans could induce earthquakes. From there I expanded outward, looking for experts and building the body of research to support the story.

BTS: Once you start writing, how do you approach research—do you try and gather as much as possible and create research bibles or spreadsheets or just research what you need when you need it?

JM: I always start with what I "think" I know. We all have some level of idea, a few details, in our heads, whether that's about diseases, nuclear power, etc. These are things we've picked up from movies, TV, books, conversation, the news, and so on. These are largely assumptions and often greatly oversimplified. However, they're useful for framing research and building a list of "what if?" questions. That's step one for me.

Step two involves my logging some hours doing research, starting with Google searches, often with the word "expert" in the mix. I look for articles or interviews with experts. Then I track those experts back to whatever organization they belong to—a government agency, a university, an R&D group, or something similar. Every company has a contact page and email address. I then reach out to a handful of experts on a given topic, explain in brief that I'm a writer doing research on a certain topic, and ask if I can interview that expert via email. If I need, say, three experts, I'll reach out to eight or ten. That way I usually get at least as many as I need.

Once I have a network of experts established and have sent them some preliminary questions, I begin mapping out who they are, what their field is, what their specialty within that field is (very important!), and how their specialty might deepen my understanding of the topic in order to help me drill down into the subject so my novel's nonfiction backstory isn't obvious or typical.

I'm not sure I could trust a man who would bypass an Oreo in favor of vanilla wafers. It's a fundamental character flaw, possibly a sign of true evil.

—Jonathan Maberry, Patient Zero

BTS: On the internet, what are some favorite sites you like to start with for your research?

JM: Google is a great starting place. Online journals related to each field are key, even when the substance of the articles is so arcane as to be beyond an outsider like me. In those articles, the experts often cite significant works, the names of colleagues, and so on. That allows me to expand out. When in doubt, I can Google a key word or phrase. Granted, Google isn't 100 percent accurate, but it's right more often than it's wrong, and really, I need to have a general understanding of something from it in order to best frame my questions to the experts. If my info from Google is wrong, and the expert has to correct me, that's actually golden, because it means that somehow the "public" info is wrong … which means I can have a character go on assumptions and have either another character or hard-won experience reveal the truth.

BTS: Do you use libraries and books a lot? How do you decide what to research online and what to use books for, and how much care and attention goes into verifying the legitimacy of sources?

JM: I don't visit libraries for research all that often. Certainly, less so than in the pre-internet days. If I need to go somewhere for research it will often be directly to my experts. I might do a ride-along with the police; attend an autopsy; visit a defense contractor (after passing the appropriate FBI background checks!); go to a museum to speak with curators and department heads; sit down with soldiers who have real field experience; tag along with a forensic evidence collection team; visit a crime lab; and so on. Experts often invite writers to do this. It's a great learning experience, and often seeing these experts in their real jobs, interacting with their peers, being "real," allows you to write about characters of those same professions in a way that is realistic and surprising to the reader. For me, this is the surest way to ensure that the information is accurate, fair, and interesting.

BTS: What is the biggest challenge of making all the science, math, etc. accessible for the broader readership, and how do you go about it?

JM: We writers are hoarders of information, and one of our most dangerous flaws is thinking that the readers will be as obsessed with deep detail as we are. This is almost never true. So, in first draft we can indulge our desire to tell-tell-tell by cramming it all in. Then, once the draft is down, it's incumbent on us—indeed *fair* to the reader—to go in with a chainsaw and cut away anything that absolutely does not need to be there. That's hard. It's heartbreaking when you've done weeks of research on, say, transgenic science, and it distills down to a few scant paragraphs spaced out through a novel. So much gets left on the cutting-room floor. But it's important. The book needs to be lean and fast, not bloated and ponderous.

That's one point. The other is making sure that we, as writers, understand what the heck our experts are telling us. I'm pretty literate when it comes to science, but I've had experts turn my brain to cheese dip by going so deep into detail where we've left common understanding far, far behind. Remember, they are even more obsessed with their topic or they wouldn't have devoted their entire lives to it. It's an important tip for writers to have the courage to admit that they don't understand and ask for a layman's explanation. There is *always* a layman's explanation. Always. On every topic.

> *Benny Imura couldn't hold a job so he took to killing. It was the family business. He barely liked his family—and by family he meant his older brother, Tom—and he definitely didn't like the idea of "business." Or work. The only part of the deal that sounded like it might be fun was the actual killing.*
>
> —*Jonathan Maberry,* Rot and Ruin

BTS: Do you use real-life consultants, and how do you recruit them or find them if you do?

JM: I like doing email interviews whenever possible. Real people tend to ramble, they interrupt themselves, they don't always speak in complete thoughts. They are often far more lucid and coherent when writing their answers in an email. And you get the right spelling for technical terms. Sometimes they will include links to sites they trust that have more information, email addresses of colleagues, or PDFs of articles or chapters they've written.

When I approach the experts, I find that a short email explaining things helps. For example, this is the content of an email I sent to forensic odontologists (bite mark experts) for my novel *Dead of Night*:

> Dear Dr. ___, I'm a novelist working on a book that combines two of the most popular themes in current entertainment: crime scene investigation and zombies. I know that a lot of zombie movies and TV shows get it wrong when it comes to bites, bite strength, and so on … but I don't know how wrong they get it. Kind of guessing you do. If you're game, I'd like to hit you with a few questions via email so that I get the science dead on. And, of course, you'd be thanked in the book's acknowledgments page.

I use some variation on that opener. Most experts say yes, even to newbie writers. They *want* us to get the facts right. Now, to deepen that, I ask two key questions once they've agreed to have me interview them. I ask: "What don't I know enough about your field to even ask?" and "What's the weirdest thing happening in your field right now?" And I often ask: "What are some of the most annoying misconceptions about your field that occur in movies, TV, and books?"

The experts love those questions, and that really opens the dialogue up. I often get my best stuff there rather than in the more technical questions I prepare.

One thing to be aware of, though, is that the information the experts give will often substantially change what you're writing. I found this out after I'd cooked up an idea about a directed energy weapon that could act like a portable EMP (electromagnetic pulse) gun. I wanted to have terrorists use those to cause power failures resulting in meltdowns at nuclear power plants. The first experts I talked to pretty much spanked me for that because all American power plants have failsafe devices designed to shut down the reactors in case of power failure. All of them. Killed my whole plot. So, in a lemonade out of lemons move, I had my protagonist discover this after he fell in love with the theory that this was the terrorist's endgame. He was quite abashed to learn how wrong his assumptions were ... as was his chronicler. And so I had to change the central plot of the book ... but I came up with something else based on that "what's the weirdest thing" question I asked of those same experts. The power of research.

BTS: Do real-life consultants require a salary or donate their time generally?

JM: I have never had to pay an expert, and have never been asked. In all cases, however, if an expert's information influences my novel in any way, they are indeed thanked in the acknowledgments page. And those guys really dig that. A win-win. So much so, that experts I used eight or ten novels back keep reaching out to me with cool new bits of information in hopes that it's something I can use for another novel. I've learned, however, to be very careful opening attachments that come with those emails, especially if the expert is a mortician, a pathologist, or an infectious disease doctor. Before I knew what necrotizing fasciitis was I opened a file of high-def photos. As I was eating pizza with my wife at the time, this was a very unfortunate moment. (Google it, you'll see what I mean.)

A select few of my experts become go-to gunslingers for me, and some of those may actually get written into my books. Infectious disease expert Dr. John Cmar has been so overwhelmingly generous with time and information that he is now a semiregular character in my Joe Ledger thrillers. UFO expert George Noory got a walk-on in another book. All by permission, of course, but they loved it.

BTS: What's your favorite bit learned from research? One that stays with you and comes in handy time and again?

JM: My favorite bit of research came when I was delving into transgenic science and asked the "what's the weirdest thing going on in your field?" question. A geneticist asked me if I knew about the "spider goats." I did not, and he proceeded to tell me that the silk-producing gene from orb weaver spiders had been transgenically given to female goats. Of course I had an immediate hope that there would be eight-legged goats crawling on the ceiling. Alas, no ... the goats did not become hybrid monsters. Instead they look quite ordinary, but they are able to produce great quantities of spider silk in their milk. Spider silk is proportionally 10 times stronger than steel, and a great deal more flexible. It's now being used in new generations of protective body armor and elsewhere. But ... c'mon ... spider goats? Pretty damn cool.

BTS: Do you have any tips on research for our readers?

JM: Never be afraid to ask the tough questions. Never be afraid to ask the weird questions. I've found that experts in any given field have *already* thought about the weirdest things that could happen with what they know. When I was writing *Patient Zero* and later

Dead of Night, I interviewed hundreds of experts in all sorts of fields: military, police, the press, the clergy, EMTs, emergency room staff, etc., about how people of their profession would react and respond to something like a zombie outbreak. Every single one of them had already thought it through. Every single one. So … go ahead, ask. Always ask.

JONATHAN MABERRY is a *New York Times* bestselling suspense novelist, five-time Bram Stoker Award winner, and comic book writer. His books include the Joe Ledger thrillers, *The Nightsiders, Dead of Night*, and *The X-Files Origins: Devil's Advocate*, as well as standalone novels in multiple genres. His V-Wars shared-world vampire apocalypse series is now a Netflix TV series. He is the editor of many anthologies including *The X-Files, Aliens: Bug Hunt*, and *Nights of the Living Dead* (coedited with zombie genre creator George A. Romero). His comics include *Captain America*, the Bram Stoker Award-winning *Bad Blood, Black Panther, Punisher, Marvel Zombies Return*, and more. He is one-third of the very popular and mildly weird *Three Guys with Beards* podcast. Jonathan lives in Del Mar, California, with his wife, Sara Jo. Visit his website at www.jonathanmaberry.com

Finding Good Sources

There's no way I could provide information on everything you would need to research well. But for a list of helpful books, see the References and Recommended Reading section at the end of the book. Asking other writers is a key part of finding sources, by the way, and Google and other search engines are a writer's best friend. There's lots of information out there on the internet.

Finding what's legit takes some effort, but you'll learn a lot along the way. And exploring is half the fun, isn't it? Maybe it's just me.

The next chapter explores the topic of how to brighten your characters and world with humor and also use humor to break tension and pacing so readers can breathe. It is an underappreciated skill that is not the same as writing straight comedy but thus far more relevant for the everyday writer.

CHAPTER 11
HUMOR

Writing humor is one of the hardest skills to master, because humor is very subjective. Not all humor is laugh-out-loud funny. There are varying levels, but using humor can be one of the most rewarding and useful tools of the craft to learn. Nothing endears an author to readers like making them feel good through laughter, and knowing when to use humor and using it well can make a good novel great—breaking up the dramatic tension at just the right moments to allow readers to regroup and keep them grounded in the balance of tragedy and joy. So, let's discuss some techniques you can use for inserting humor into your storytelling.

Right off the bat, I'll say that if you're looking to learn comedy writing, that's not what this chapter is about. Instead, this chapter is about techniques for employing various levels of humor in your storytelling to balance tension and pacing. There's a big difference between writing comedy and inserting humor in drama. Writing comedy is something that takes a ton of time and skill to master, but I believe all of us—or most of us at least—can learn to use humorous moments through dialogue and light comedic action that reflects real life and real people in ways that enrich our fiction, and that's the kind of humor this chapter will focus on. This type of humor in many cases will come out of ordinary occurrences. Quirkiness and sarcasm will be key. Most of us use humor in interacting with family and friends daily, from teasing to sarcasm, to eccentric behavior we mock or are mocked for. Humor happens, and it is these moments, however small they may seem, which should inspire you when you need to break tension and give readers a chance to come up for air.

Humor typically comes from two places: characters and situations. Characters banter, joke, tease, etc. Situations can be both naturally and inadvertently humorous. The best humor combines both. Carl Hiaasen is an author who seems to find ways to always build natural humor into his stories. Like *Bad Monkey*:

> On the hottest day of July, trolling in dead-calm waters near Key West, a tourist named James Mayberry reeled up a human arm. His wife flew to the bow of the boat and tossed her breakfast burritos.
>
> "What are you waiting for?" James Mayberry barked at the mate. "Get that thing off my line!"
>
> The kid tugged and twisted, but the barb of the hook was imbedded in bone. Finally the captain came down from the bridge and used bent-nose pliers to free the decomposing limb, which he placed on shaved ice in a deck box.
>
> James Mayberry said, "For Christ's sake, now where are we supposed to put our fish?"

Dark, but funny. And the story gets better—because the arm has an extended middle finger, frozen in place during rigor mortis. And eventually, after catching no fish, Mayberry poses with his catch alongside his wife and her blackfin tuna. Hiaasen's stories tend to be suspenseful dark comedies, with over-the-top characters and situations that often make readers chuckle out loud. They are satires, of course, but just realistic enough that in odd circumstances, you could imagine them happening, and as such, they are highly entertaining. In this case, an ordinarily boring situation becomes amusing through a twist: a decaying arm caught instead of a fish, and the character's reactions just add to the humor. Both characters and situations combine for humorous effect.

Characters with certain relationships are ideal for humor. The emotions and conflict inherent to such relationships as those between parents and children, spouses, lovers, coworkers, business partners, and more create reactions and interactions that lend themselves easily to humor. Here's an example from *Dirty Job* by Christopher Moore about a father fretting over his newborn first child:

> Charlie had held baby Sophie for a few seconds earlier in the day, and had handed her quickly to a nurse insisting that someone more qualified than he do some finger and toe counting. He'd done it twice and kept coming up with twenty-one.
>
> "They act like that's all there is to it. Like if the kid has the minimum ten fingers and ten toes it's all going to be fine. What if there are extra? Extra-credit fingers? Huh? What if the kid had a tail?" Charlie was sure he'd spotted a tail in the six-month sonogram. Umbilical indeed! He'd kept a hard copy.
>
> "She doesn't have a tail, Mr. Asher," the nurse explained. "And it's ten and ten, we've all checked. Perhaps you should go home and get some rest."
>
> "I still love her, even with her extra finger."
>
> "She's perfectly normal."
>
> "Or toe."
>
> "We really do know what we're doing, Mr. Asher. She's a beautiful, healthy baby girl."

"Or a tail."

The nurse sighed. She was short, wide, and had a tattoo of a snake up her right calf that showed through her white nurse stockings. She spent four hours of every workday massaging preemie babies, her hands threaded through ports in a Lucie incubator, like she was handling a radioactive spark in there. She talked to them, coaxed them, told them how special they were, and felt their hearts fluttering in chests no bigger than a balled-up pair of sweat socks. She cried over every one, and believed that her tears and touch poured a bit of her own life into the tiny bodies, which was just fine with her. She could spare it. She had been a neonatal nurse for twenty years, and had never so much as raised her voice to a new father.

"There's no goddamn tail, you doofus! Look!" She pulled down the blanket and aimed baby Sophie's bottom at him like she might unleash a fusillade of weapons-grade poopage, such as guileless Beta Male had never seen.

Panicked new fathers are familiar, but this one's exaggerated reaction makes it funny and charming at the same time because we know this baby will be loved by anyone who'd fret so much. We also know her father has an eccentric, quirky mind. Remember in Chapter 4 when we talked about how character quirks make characters stand out but also reflect the nature of real people around us? Such quicks can also be rife with humor.

Humor between characters can also manifest in banter. Pop-culture references, or even references to earlier moments in your story, can become conduits for amusing dialogue. This is from my novel *Simon Says*, in which a tough detective, a luddite, is forced to team with a humanoid android—the first of his kind—to solve his partner's murder. In the story, the android is told he doesn't sound like a real human, so Simon's daughter helps him learn catchphrases from cop shows and movies to beef up his cop speak and he starts using them, but not appropriately:

"You know, I'd like to be a Police Officer, I think," Lucas said from the passenger's seat as Simon cruised down Ward Parkway, headed east.

"Oh yeah?" Simon smiled.

"You think I could be?"

Simon patted his partner on the back. "This is America. That's what it's all about—possibilities."

Lucas smiled now, his eyes almost sparkling. "No shit?"

Simon laughed. He'd been a bad influence on the poor android. "Yeah, no shit. I might have use for a good sideman."

… Lucas looked satisfied, his eyes scanning off in the distance for a bit as he thought about something. "I was wrong about you, John."

"About what?"

"You're not too old for this shit."

Simon chuckled and punched Lucas in the arm. "Shut the—"

"—fuck up." They finished together, and this time they both laughed.

"But you really should let me drive," Lucas added.

"It's my car, pal," Simon answered.

Lucas shrugged. "Some of us just have more skills."

"Oh! Is that right? Don't worry, I was driving before you were itching in your daddy's pants," Simon said.

Lucas grinned. "Lethal Weapon, nice. But I don't have a daddy."

"I figured it was some old toaster or something," Simon replied, smugly.

"Please, toasters are far too simple."

Simon laughed and rolled his eyes, thinking up another comeback as he squeaked through an intersection just as the light changed and continued on. He might actually like it if Lucas became a cop. Sometimes, it was good to have a partner.

Especially one with a decent skill for banter.

It plays a bit funnier in context of the whole story, because though Lucas studies cop movies and starts quoting them, it's not always in the right context. So the pop-culture movie references are used throughout for comic relief, often in inappropriate contexts. Because we understand the popular references, hearing them used awkwardly or in ways that are wrong or even cause discomfort for characters makes us laugh. We've all probably known a kid or even an adult who overuses such quotes and lacks the skill. The familiarity of the references and the situations in which they are used add to the humorous effect.

Speaking of inside references from your story, a good thing to know when writing humor is the "Rule of Threes." The Rule of Threes, or rule of three, as some call it, is a technique where you set up gags or bits so that they recur three times in a story, each time successively bigger and funnier. Wikipedia defines it as follows:

> The rule of three is a writing principle that suggests that a trio of events or characters is more humorous, satisfying, or effective than other numbers in execution of the story and engaging the reader. The reader or audience of this form of text is also thereby more likely to remember the information conveyed. This is because having three entities combines both brevity and rhythm with having the smallest amount of information to create a pattern.

The repetition makes the payoff greater. The first occurrence tends to be a smaller laugh. The second, medium. The third is hopefully a real guffaw. The actual events of the joke don't recur each time. For example, if a banana peel were the joke, you might start by having someone fall on one. The second time they might dodge a banana peel because they expected to fall and someone else falls instead. The third time they find banana peels falling from a truck and everyone is slipping and sliding. A lame, silly example and a cliché, but it illustrates the point. Each successive recurrence gets bigger with a twist, until the third recurrence is much bigger and much funnier. The payoff breaks the pattern enough that it surprises us but not so much that it is a non sequitur. It is about something unexpected that breaks the pattern yet is connected to it enough so that we recognize it. Hence, the first two times, someone drops a banana peel. The third time, a truck full of banana peels breaks the pattern.

Using the rule of threes is a great way to plant humor in stories and pay them off over time for bigger laughs. The catch is that it must be familiar enough for the audience to understand, and it must be specific. The more specific, the better for comedy. As comedian Simon Taylor explains:

The rule of three creates an assumption by listing two similar items, then a third one that differs in a fundamental way: *I like red wine, classical music, and committing brutal homicides.* They then become more elaborate by having introductions to the items: *I didn't have time to pack much for the weekend, just: socks, undies ... my ninja sword.* To add to these, you can reiterate the assumption at the end of the joke by using what comedians call a "tag": *Man, I love the horse races: the big winnings, the fashion, the woman collapsing in a pool of their own vomit. It's all fun.*

(https://mrsimontaylor.wordpress.com/2010/12/03/the -psychology-of-comedy-rule-of-threes/)

The extra elements of introductions and tags act to reinforce the assumptions created by the first two items in the list. To take the second joke as an example, we hear the word "socks" and subconsciously associate it with categories such as "clothing," "basic," and "essential." When we hear that "undies" is the next item, those categories are reinforced. In comes the "ninja sword" to contradict those categories, which is what causes some nice little chuckles.

In comedy movies and sitcoms, we see this rule applied time and again. Sometimes it occurs so often that audiences can see it coming and have come to expect it. The rule of threes can also be used dramatically because audiences pick up on the pattern and remember. Take "The Three Little Pigs," the three ghosts of *A Christmas Carol*, or "Three Billy Goats Gruff," even Goldilocks and her three bears. The three encounters each play out differently with different emotional and dramatic effects to raise the stakes and challenge the character, each adding to the one(s) before and forcing the character to confront something. In the end, they leave the character changed—usually for the better.

I mentioned earlier, in Chapter 8 on Pacing and Suspense, that sometimes using humor to lighten up between dramatic moments is the best way to pace your book so readers have room to catch their breath. But sometimes, dramatic moments can also be lightened a bit with humorous banter that is natural to the situation but that also helps soften the blow of the emotional scene as it plays out. Here's another example from my novel *Simon Says*:

> Nowlin Middle School was located near 31st Street and South Hardy Avenue in Independence. Simon took I-70 on the loop East out of downtown then took exit 7A to 31st Street and followed it over. Emma stood waiting for him in front of the school, her purple backpack slung over one shoulder, on the driveway that led past the East side of the connected buildings. The area where students came out of the building and north was all red brick, but in the south half, the outer wall had brick on the bottom and white cement making up the top half. The line of parents' cars turned in at the north end of the drive and circled back south.
>
> Simon leaned over and flipped open the door for his daughter as she made a show of glancing at her watch.
>
> "Forget about me as usual?" she said, feigning irritation that Simon easily saw through.
>
> "Nope. You know how it goes. Had to leave a scene to come here," Simon replied. "Sorry, I'm late."

Emma shrugged then pulled the passenger seat forward and casually tossed her backpack on the backseat before shoving the seat top back and sliding in. "What kinda scene? Something exciting?"

She closed the door and slid her seatbelt in place as she waited for him to answer. Simon just sat in silence wondering how to break it to her. Emma loved Blanca Santorios. They had hit it off from the moment they met. She always told him, "She's good for you, Dad. Making you less macho and misogynistic."

Simon hadn't considered himself anti-women at all. He was maybe a little old-fashioned about opening doors and carrying in groceries and lawn work and stuff, but he'd grown up respecting strong women in his life, like his two grandmothers and his mother. They would not have tolerated any misogyny. They'd kept his father in line too.

Finally, as he eased the car back away from the curve and headed south toward the street, Emma looked at him. "What?"

She looked right at him, but Simon couldn't bring himself to lock his eyes on hers. Instead, he made a show of being the ever-conscientious driver as he turned right onto South Hardy and headed back toward 31st.

Emma frowned. "Dad, come on. You're scaring me now."

This time he did look and saw the worry on her face. She bit her lip and looped several hairs around a finger, gently tugging at them as she watched him. Then her eyes widened and she stiffened. "Oh God. It's not Mom, is it? Is Mom okay?!"

Simon swallowed and nodded. "I'm sorry, honey. Yes, your mother's fine. This isn't about her."

Emma released her hair and rubbed her hands on her jeans. "Okay, then tell me."

Simon cleared his throat. "Blanca was murdered today."

"Oh no!" Emma looked away as tears welled in her eyes and began pouring down her cheeks. "Why? Why would someone do that?"

Tears bunched in Simon's eyes now, too, and he hurriedly wiped them away, wanting to be strong for her. "I don't know, honey. I've been asking myself that since I found out."

"How long ago?" she asked.

"They found her an hour ago, at the Admiral," Simon said. He actually had no idea about the time of death yet.

"Ewwww, the Admiral Motel? What a horrid place to go!"

"How would you know? We've never taken you there." Simon looked at her, brow raised in question.

"I've driven by. Kids at school talk about it. I just hear bad things."

Simon tipped a head to one side as he fought off another question.

Emma scowled. "God, Dad. It's not like that. Ewww."

Simon chuckled. "Like what? I didn't say anything."

"You have a dirty mind," she scolded, clearly thinking he'd been wondering if she'd gone there with a boy. The thought had crossed his mind, but he had already dismissed it. Her horrified reaction amused him.

The more realistic the conversation plays, the funnier, actually. The familiar truth of it makes the lighter banter more amusing. As I said before, not all humor has to be laugh-out-loud funny. If you are writing a comedy, you want it to be more so. But in dramatic pieces, where humor is used to ease tension and slow the pace, it doesn't have to be. Even mild amusement can go a long way. And in this case, where a father and daughter are having normal, familiar banter that often happens when parents pick up a daughter from school, and the father shares heartbreaking news, it is heavy, a downer—the kind of moment that tends to stop pacing cold. So, I followed it up with a bit of humor, natural to the situation, to help ease the blow and also get us back into the familiar banter this father and daughter regularly engage in. We still have the emotional power of the reveal of the death of someone they both cared about while having a bit of natural humor in the banter to ease us through it.

With humor, characters may deal with tragedy in even more quirky, humorous ways. Such as this scene from Tawna Fenske's *Making Waves*, when the protagonist learns her deceased uncle wants her to take his ashes to the Virgin Islands:

"You didn't happen to tell Uncle Frank that I'm—"

"Terrified of the ocean? No, I didn't have the heart to mention that."

Juli nodded and watched her mother consult her handwritten recipe before reaching for the Worcestershire sauce.

"Did Uncle Frank say when I need to complete this mission?" Juli asked, grabbing three packets of orange Jell-O and her mother's fish-shaped Jell-O mold. "Do cremated remains have—um—a shelf life or anything?"

"He didn't really say. He was choking on his tongue a lot there at the end, so it was hard to understand him. Could you hand me the feta cheese?"

Juli gave her the container and scooted a knife out of the way, aware of her mother's tendency to drop sharp objects on her bare feet.

"So maybe you didn't understand him right?" Juli asked hopefully. "Maybe instead of 'throw my ashes off a fishing boat,' he said, 'roll my ass over, you stupid whore'?"

"Those bedsores were sure something! Hand me those Junior Mints?"

Notice how the juxtaposition of the ordinary business of a mother and daughter cooking together plays against the tragedy they're discussing and the resistance of the protagonist to the deceased's wishes. What could be a somber moment instead becomes amusing and revealing of the relationship of all three characters—including the dead one who isn't even there. This allows us to process the tragedy in a different light while moving the story and characters forward on multiple levels, using humor in the process. The fact that such common life moments as cooking together often lead to friendly family banter just lends itself to the realism, despite the quirky reactions and sarcasm at play.

Description can also be humorous. In fact, humor lends itself to memorability, such as in Christopher Moore's *Dirty Jobs*:

> The house was an Italianate Victorian on the hill just below the Coit Tower, the great granite column built in honor of the San Francisco firemen who had lost their lives in the line of duty. Although it's said to have been designed with a fire-hose nozzle in mind, almost no one who sees the tower can resist the urge to comment on its resemblance to a giant penis. Madeline Alby's house, a flat-roofed rectangle with ornate scrolling trim and a crowning cornice of carved cherubs, looked like a wedding cake balanced on the tower's scrotum.

Vivid and easy to picture, but hard to forget, right? But what if the place being described is so bland it is startling in its boring unimpressiveness?

> We reached what I assumed was headquarters, possibly the most unexciting building I've seen in a long time. Corrugated steel, which I figured made the place like an oven inside, painted in good old Navajo White, the most boring of paint choices. It was trimmed in taupe. Nothing could have said "industrial boredom" better.

> "Wow. If a building's importance is directly proportional to how dull, dingy, and unassuming it looks, you guys must work for the most important agency in the world."

246

"We do," White said quietly as he opened the thick metal door marked "Employees." He ushered me inside and I was treated to a spectacle of—not very much. Boxes and crates of all different sizes, mostly. It was a warehouse, and I had guessed the interior temperatures correctly.

"Color me totally unimpressed. What is this, prank week at the mental institution? Or is this the Armani outlet, and you're just letting me in on some super deals early?"

"She can tell the designer," Martini said under his breath. "Amazing."

That's from *Touched by an Alien* by Gini Koch, and I'd call it almost equally memorable in its own way, the dialogue commentary just adding to the description and humor. You can do the same with action, of course, even without going into slapstick silliness. The point being that humor employed in your prose can add both wit and bite to your story, easing heavy pacing and breaking tension and also making your book fun and more memorable at the same time.

In learning how to write more comedically, I asked Gini Koch, the bestselling successful novelist of the *Alien* series (just quoted in *Touched by an Alien*) and more, to offer us some humor writing tips.

SIDEBAR: HOW TO PUT HUMOR IN YOUR WRITING by Gini Koch

Humor is subjective. The old saying, "Dying is easy, comedy is hard," is true. Truer words were never spoken is sort of true. Not saying that writing straight is a walk in the park, but by comparison to writing funny, actually funny, it kind of is.

To understand what I'm saying, here are some quick definitions:

Build—the "story" part of a joke that leads to the punchline

Punch line—the "end" line, action, etc., that elicits the hearty laughs, the chuckles, the titters, the giggles (and not all punch lines are created equal, nor are all created to get that big belly laugh; all forms of laughter should be sprinkled in there somewhere)

Opener—the portion that sets up the build

Zinger—also known as a witty comeback or a one-liner, something tossed out that may or may not be a part of the overall joke, but still elicits laughter

Pump Up—the act of going back and crafting your joke to make it funnier

Work—as in, "this joke works"; it makes you laugh months after you wrote it (not all jokes work, ergo, not all jokes remain); also to work the joke to make it better

Timing—an essential skill all good stand-ups and humor writers have; knowing when to toss in the punch line, when to do the pratfall, when to honk the horn to elicit the laughs, both expected and unexpected

Kill—to succeed in standup ("I killed at the improv last night"), and also in other humor forms

There are many more terms, but if you want them, you'll need to ask Chris Rock or Jerry Seinfeld, 'cause I have a space limit. (Which we all know I'll go over. But I digress…)

There are lots of categories of humor, from slapstick to gentle, parody, satire, stand-up, situational, and more besides. Everyone likes some of these, most don't like all. And that's the first lesson—no one is funny enough to consistently make *everyone* laugh. You just want to make enough people laugh often enough so that you can honestly say you killed.

I'm not going to go into detail on each of the many categories, but let's discuss what humor is not.

It's NOT: a joke that only you, or a couple of your buddies, think is funny. It's really not. Most situational humor has to be experienced *by the audience* in order to be enjoyed. If you're telling a story that was hilarious at the time but has no relatability to your audience in the now, it's not funny and it's likely never going to be.

It's NOT: something that takes hours to set up. There are some jokes worth waiting hours for in order to get to the punch line. Most jokes won't work, though, if you're boring your audience on the way to the punch line. Many jokes and much humor fails because the build takes too long.

It's NOT: something made so inaccessible that only you and a couple of high-level rocket scientists locked in a basement at MIT will "get" it. (BTW, those jokes tend to actually be something only you and a couple of lifelong stoners will "get." But I'm a nice girl, so I'll let you keep the MIT illusion.)

It's NOT: something no one laughs at. Seriously. I really mean it. Yes, I'm talking to all of you who told me—someone who writes humor and also edits humor for an online 'zine—that if I didn't "get" your joke it was because I had no sense of humor. I have a helluva sense of humor, but I won't laugh if you're not funny.

Bottom line on humor: it's just like porn, you know it when you see it.

Other bottom line on humor: if they ain't laughin', you ain't funny.

When trying to explain how to be funny, there are honestly only a few things I can tell you that I've found are helpful, necessary ingredients. What you do with them is your own business.

1. It really and truly helps to have a sense of humor naturally.

I know, I know. So many people think they're funny. But pay attention to the laughter. Is it real or forced? Are you introduced by people as the funny friend? Do people ask you to tell your funny story again? Are you fast with a quip, a pun, a witty comeback? (A vital trait in order to write humorous dialogue.) Do people with actual senses of humor laugh at your jokes? Do they encourage you to write them? Do you find the funny in many more things than other people do?

If your jokes are a little too zen, as in, you tell them and there's only the sound of one voice laughing—yours—you're not actually funny to anyone other than yourself.

While I'm sure the humor-impaired are capable of learning to write funny, I have to be honest: it's not going to be worth it. I've read a lot of "I think this is the funniest thing I've ever written" pieces from folks who haven't cracked a joke since they were born, and every single one failed to elicit even a chuckle. And to *make* them funny would have required so much rewriting that it wasn't ever going to happen. Head back to drama—that's where all the respect is, anyway. (And if you don't believe me, I refer you to the late Rodney Dangerfield.)

2. Test out your humor before you start writing it.

My first sales were in short humor, and they were stories I'd been telling for years. I had them honed to perfection. For an oral medium.

When I wrote them down, I first wrote them exactly as I told them, with several funny side trips during the build that led, in a roundabout way, to the ultimate punch line. Which didn't work on paper, because, zingers or no zingers, they made the build too long when someone else was reading it versus me telling it.

So, I worked the jokes. I killed many darlings. Until the pieces were streamlined, the build was the right length, and all the remaining jokes were pumped up enough to keep someone chuckling or guffawing the whole way through.

And then I had everyone who'd heard the oral stories read them, to see if they still laughed. They did. And they sold.

3. Be prepared to work harder at being funny than you've ever worked at something serious.

I'm not joking when I say that in order to ensure that your stuff really is funny, you're going to have to go back, over and over again, and pump up your jokes. You'll have to add catchphrases, zingers, and witty banter. You'll have to ensure that you've added enough funny to all the places it should be—but have not overdone it to the point where the joke runs on too long. It's a delicate balance, and having a good editor helps a lot in determining it, but you still need to learn how, when, what, where, and why to pump up a joke or let it lie.

When I'm writing humor, I'm constantly looking for ways to make a joke or a situation funnier, whether that means witty or sarcastic comments from the characters, or situations that are both ridiculous and yet utterly believable for the characters and the storyline. It's work, and work I take very seriously.

4. Study stand-up comedians, the good ones and the bad ones.

There's a lot to be learned from stand-up because it's hard, and because writing humor is very much like a good stand-up routine. The Henny Youngmans, Jeff Foxworthys, and Stephen Wrights of the world aren't the best people to learn from—setup/joke, setup/joke is funny when you're in the audience but gets tiresome when you're reading.

Concentrate on good comedians who tell stories. Chris Rock, George Carlin, Steve Martin, Kevin Hart, Ron White. These guys tell stories that seem extemporaneous, but they're not off the cuff at all. They've worked for weeks or months to get their stories down just so, so that the build is right, and the ending punch line relates to something they brought up somewhere in the first half of their act.

Honing humorous writing is very much like honing a stand-up act, so put in the effort.

5. Understand that punctuation is your friend.

Because humor has a build, and timing—including the all-important "pause for effect"—are required to make funny work, utilize your punctuation. Commas slow a reader down. Dashes and ellipses do, too. Exclamation points can be too overused, but one at the right time can make a bit work.

Read your humorous piece or section aloud. Note how you have to alter the rhythm of the words to get the most out of the bit. Go back to the standup acts that made you laugh the most and study them. When does the comedian pause to take a drink, take a drag off their cigar, wave their arms around, pace, glare at the audience, etc.? All of those things can be written, but it takes practice to get them right. And it also takes punctuation—the little marks that use their influence to help your comedy make more sense. (Points to whoever knows where I stole that line from.)

So, after all of this, if you still want to write funny, remember this pertinent fact: court jesters held a great deal of power ... right up until the time they ceased to entertain their sovereigns, and then they had their heads chopped off.

In the humor biz, we call that fair warning, and it's all the warning you're going to get. Because when it comes to humor, it really *is* kill or be killed.

GINI KOCH writes the fast, fresh, and funny Alien/Katherine "Kitty" Katt series for DAW Books, the Necropolis Enforcement Files, and the Martian Alliance Chronicles. She also has a humor collection, Random Musings from the Funny Girl. As G.J. Koch she writes the Alexander Outland series, and she's made the most of multiple personality disorder by writing under a variety of other pen names as well, including Anita Ensal, Jemma Chase, A.E. Stanton, and J.C. Koch. She has stories featured in a variety of excellent anthologies, available now and upcoming, writing as all her various personalities. Reach her via www.ginikoch.com

One of the more unique novelists I know of writing humor has rather carved her own niche in the romance market writing romantic comedies. Tawna Fenske has over a dozen novels to her name since 2011, when her debut, *Making Waves*, was released from Sourcebooks Casablanca. You might have noticed a quote from it excerpted earlier in this chapter. A city tourism commission marketer by day, she has also been a journalist and taught English as a second language. Here's what she had to say about writing funny romantic comedies:

INTERVIEW: TAWNA FENSKE

Bryan Thomas Schmidt: What led you to write not just romance but romantic comedy?

Tawna Fenske: After years of writing for my supper as a journalist and marketing geek, I decided to try my hand at fiction in 2002. I've always loved reading romance, and Harlequin was launching a new action/adventure/romance line (Bombshell) that sounded fun. After a few tries, I sold a book to Bombshell and had already written two follow-ups when I got the call that Harlequin was canceling the line one month before my scheduled debut. Did I mention this was my thirtieth birthday? Also the day my cat died? Oh, and that my employer at the time informed me the same day that if I continued violating the company's hosiery policy, they would fire me. (I did. They didn't.)

I remember walking out on my back deck that night with a glass of wine and thinking, "This is actually kinda funny." The fact that I could find humor on what was arguably one of the worst days of my life is part of what set me on the path to writing comedy. Since then, I've found comedic inspiration in things like divorce, death, infidelity, alcoholism, and grief. Mix that up with some heart and some heat, and you've got my career in a nutshell.

> *Her eyes met his, and he tried to remember if*
> *he'd ever seen such a deep shade of blue anywhere*
> *else. What was the word for it? Azure? Cobalt?*
> *Cerulean? Where was the fucking Crayola box*
> *when he needed it?*
>
> —*Tawna Fenske,* About That Fling

BTS: Romance tends to have a pretty specific set of tropes and beats readers expect in its various forms. Does the humor allow you to play with those more easily, or are you still working fairly rigidly within the established, expected genre structures?

TF: The thing I love about tropes is finding ways to push the edges and turn them on their heads. *Marine for Hire* (the first book in my bestselling Front & Center series) is a twist on the old "falling for the nanny" trope. Instead of a billionaire single dad who falls in love with his pretty, young nanny, I have a jaded single mom who has sworn off military men and doesn't know the new manny hired by her brothers is secretly a Marine sniper.

And of course, not all romance is trope-driven. My series books tend to be that way, but I've had a lot more freedom in the longer, meatier rom-coms I've written for Montlake (which tend to straddle the line between women's fiction and romance).

BTS: Did you study any to learn to write humor, or is it just a natural personality trait?

TF: I come from a family of very funny people, so I was raised to find humor in everything.

When people ask why I write comedy, I always suggest they spend a few days looking at my Facebook feed. I'm a magnet for all forms of absurdity, and I post about my awkward moments almost daily. Like the time I tugged a loose thread on my sweater and gave myself a mutant turquoise nipple. Or the time I waxed off my own eyebrow by mistake and accidentally picked the green eyeliner to draw it back on. Or the time I dropped gristle in a stranger's purse at a fancy luncheon and got caught trying to fish it out. Or the time I grabbed a cleaning cloth out of my purse, then realized I was polishing my eyeglasses with a pair of thong panties (don't ask). These kinds of things happen to me on a daily basis, so I really had no choice but to write comedy.

"You're right, we should keep things professional between us. Please—let's give it a shot." She looked down into her lap and fiddled with the tie on the front of the cashmere pants. "No more fooling around?"

"Scout's honor," he said, raising his hand with his palm toward her, thumb extended, fingers parted between his middle and ring finger.

Holly stared at his hand and frowned. "What the hell kind of Boy Scout were you?"

"I wasn't. That's a Vulcan salute."

"Star Trek?"

"Yep. Much more meaningful to a geek than any Boy Scout pledge. As Spock is my witness, I'll do my very best to keep my hands off you."

—Tawna Fenske, The Fix Up

BTS: What are some techniques you use to add humor value to your storytelling?

TF: I borrow as much as humanly possible from my own life, and when I run out of my own embarrassing tidbits, I borrow from other people's lives. This is one of the biggest reasons I'll never give up my day job (I work three days a week as the PR and marketing manager for my city's tourism bureau). I need human interaction to provide fodder for my stories.

BTS: How much rewriting do you do to punch up the funny, if any?

TF: Sometimes, scenes just flow out funny on the first try. That's not usually the case, though. Very often I'll write a boring-as-hell scene with two people sitting around a table having a conversation so dull I want to stab myself in the eyeball with a grapefruit spoon. It usually takes three or four passes for me to layer in snippets of witty dialogue, and before I know it, I've got one of the characters casually decorating cookies to look like genitalia (an actual scene from my newest rom-com, *Chef Sugarlips*). That book also had a scene with the heroine having a very ho-hum phone conversation with the hero, but it eventually became a scene wherein the heroine smells something odd in a client meeting and begins to suspect it's her own bra (when did she last wash it, anyway?). The second the client leaves, she wriggles the bra out of her shirt sleeve, and naturally, that's when the hero walks in. They still have the conversation they would have had on the phone, but now it's laced with awkward humor, sexual tension, and some relatable moments (no one really tells women how often they should wash bras, and does anyone tell guys how to jumpstart a car, or are they just expected to know?).

> "Spank Me," *she muttered, glaring at the receipt in her hand. "That's a stupid name for a boat."*
>
> —*Tawna Fenske,* Making Waves

BTS: Do you find your writing criticized or taken less seriously because of the humor, or does it just appeal to a different audience?

257

TF: Since I write humor, the last thing I want is to be taken seriously.

My publishers have experimented with a lot of different approaches to marketing my 25+ romantic comedies. Sometimes my books get marketed as comedy with some romance woven in. Sometimes they get marketed as romances that happen to be funny. Sometimes I'm marketed as super-sexy romance and the comedy aspect ends up being a surprise to the reader. I can't say I've seen a huge difference in how those approaches work in terms of sales, but I haven't encountered many readers who pick up a romance novel and feel disappointed there's humor in it. Most see it as a happy bonus.

BTS: Who are some authors you read for inspiration in regards to humorous prose?

TF: Kristan Higgins, Jennifer Crusie, Jonathan Tropper, Carl Hiaasen, Tina Fey, Susan Elizabeth Phillips, Jenny Lawson.

BTS: What are some tips you might have for writers wanting to use more humor in their storytelling?

TF: Read as much comedy as you can get your hands on to get a feel for timing and setup. And maybe put yourself in a lot of awkward situations.

BTS: Anything else you'd like to add?

TF: Nope! Thanks for having me! Did that sound porny?

When Tawna Fenske finished her English lit degree at 22, she celebrated by filling a giant trash bag full of romance novels and dragging it everywhere until she'd read them all. Now she's a RITA Award finalist and *USA Today* bestselling author who writes humorous fiction, risqué romance, and heartwarming love stories with a quirky twist. *Publishers Weekly* has praised Tawna's offbeat romances with multiple starred reviews and noted, "There's something wonderfully relaxing about being immersed in a story filled with over-the-top characters in undeniably relatable situations. Heartache and humor go hand in hand."

Tawna lives in Bend, Oregon, with her husband, stepkids, and a menagerie of ill-behaved pets. She loves hiking, snowshoeing, stand-up paddleboarding, and inventing excuses to sip wine on her back porch. She can peel a banana with her toes and loses an average of 20 pairs of eyeglasses per year. To find out more about Tawna and her books, visit www.tawnafenske.com.

CHAPTER 12
BEGINNINGS, MIDDLES, AND ENDS

A long time ago, when all the grandfathers and grandmothers of today were little boys and little girls or very small babies, or perhaps not even born, Pa and Ma and Mary and Laura and Baby Carrie left their little house in the Big Woods of Wisconsin. They drove away and left it lonely and empty in the clearing among the big trees, and they never saw the little house again.

— Laura Ingalls Wilder, Little House on the Prairie

Now that we've covered the basics of craft, you're ready to write. And as you write your novel, there are three areas you'll need to pay particularly close attention to: the beginning—particularly the first two scenes—the middle—particularly the midpoint—and the end—particularly the climax. This chapter will examine them each in turn. All three will work together in a great novel. Nancy Kress writes in *Beginnings, Middles, and Ends*:

> By the time she's read your opening, your reader knows what you've implicitly promised. A satisfying middle is one that develops that promise with specificity and interest. A satisfying ending is

one that delivers on the promise, providing new insight or comfortable confirmation or vicarious happiness.

So, let's start at the beginning as you consider writing your novel. What makes a great opening?

Beginning

The cliché of "A long time ago" actually wasn't a cliché when Laura Ingalls Wilder used it long ago in her now-classic tome. For us, it's a phrase we must mostly avoid. To open our stories, we'll have to reach deeper, try a little harder. Some stories just lend themselves to strong, dynamic openings: the murder mystery that opens with a murder, the police procedural that opens with a chase, the science fiction or epic fantasy novel that opens with a battle, the romance that opens with the protagonist catching their lover having an affair. These are all inherently dramatic openings, with lots of built-in conflict, character development, and emotional resonance as well as action. But not every story brings such an easy opening directly to mind. Sometimes, writers have to work a little harder to craft just the right opening.

There are two key points from earlier chapters we must revisit here: the idea of questions asked and answered—the answers stretched out for pacing over long or short stretches depending, and the promise inherent in the author–reader contract—the promise to deliver on a premise in a satisfying way. Both these things must be established in any good beginning. Kress writes: "In your first scene, your main goal is to keep your reader interested. You do that by focusing not on overall meaning but on the four elements that make a first scene compelling: character, conflict, specificity, and credibility." So, to start, your opening

261

should give readers a person to focus on. Usually this is the protagonist.

In his wonderful sequel to *The Notebook*, titled *The Wedding*, Nicholas Sparks manages to open with his protagonist out front and the story questions asked in the first two sentences:

"Is it possible, I wonder, for a man to truly change? Or do character and habit form the immovable boundaries of our lives?

It is mid-October 2003, and I ponder these questions as I watch a moth flail wildly against the porch light. Jane, my wife, is sleeping upstairs, and she didn't stir when I slipped out of bed. It is late, midnight has come and gone, and there's a crispness in the air that holds the promise of an early winter. I'm wearing a heavy cotton robe, and though I imagined it would be thick enough to keep the chill at bay, I notice that my hands are trembling before I put them in my pockets.

Above me, the stars are specks of silver paint on a charcoal canvas. I see Orion and Pleiades, Ursa Major, and Corona Borealis, and think I should be inspired by the realization that I'm not only looking at the stars, but staring into the past as well. Constellations shine with light that was emitted aeons ago, and I wait for something to come to me, words that a poet might use to illuminate life's mysteries. But there is nothing.

With those words, he establishes the central journey of the protagonist: a search for meaning, a desire to be a better man, and an uncertainty of whether it is possible. The stars and the cold act as physical symbols of his uncertain thoughts and emotions, reminding us, as they do him, of his state of mind. The mention of his wife tells us the focus of his desire to grow, and also introduces another key character for the journey we are about to embark on. It may not be as action packed an opening as a space battle, police chase, or murder, but the search for meaning and the hope that there is more to life, inherent in the questions the protagonist is asking, are universal themes all readers can relate to, questions that call to mind similar journeys we've all made, and the setting of pondering such things while a spouse sleeps and we watch the stars is also familiar. The whole scene, simple and lacking in action though it may be, nonetheless evokes familiarity that connects us with the protagonist as he seeks universal truths we seek ourselves. And that makes this a powerful opening.

Kress writes: "Most successful openings give the reader a genuine character because most stories are about human beings." And so your opening must connect us with a character we will want to know better, want to follow through a story; one who asks the kinds of questions that pique and hold our interest and make us read on. Such questions bring with them implied conflict—potential or existing—that will need to be faced to resolve the question. Again, there's overt dramatic conflict and there's also conflict like we see in *The Wedding*, which involves a man wondering if he is the best he can be and if he can find renewed satisfaction in his marriage and life. No matter what type of conflict lies at the heart of your story, it must be hinted at in the beginning, even though it won't be developed until later, because the hint of that conflict is a hook that catches readers and keeps them reading.

Specificity encompasses the details you use to set the scene and character as well as mood and tone in your opening. The right details give you credibility. They anchor your story in concrete reality, distinguish your opening from others that may be similar, and convince readers you know what you're talking about. The wrong details may lose readers and ruin your credibility right off the bat. Again per Kress, credible details in credible prose convince readers to trust that the author has something to say and knows what they are doing. The sense of trust enables readers to suspend disbelief and go along for the ride, believing the journey will be worth their time and take them somewhere interesting.

Kress suggests several techniques important to credible prose, which I'll summarize here:

1. **Diction**—Know the meaning of words and use them well and correctly, avoiding clichés, and establishing the character's voice, not the author's, clearly and commandingly. If your character would say it—even a cliché—then it belongs, but make sure it is in character and has a point. No words in credible prose are wasted.
2. **Economy**— "Credible prose," Kress writes, "uses only as many words as it needs to create its effects. It doesn't sprawl." Credible pose is concise, with well-chosen words and phrases. Repetition is only used when it is needed to create a powerful effect—a mood, an atmosphere, or a state of mind.
3. **Good Sentence Construction**—Awkward sentences never appear in credible prose. Your sentences may vary from simple to compound, long to short, but every one of them is smooth, unambiguous, and purposeful, moving forward story, character, plot, or theme with every word.
4. **Variety**—Good sentence construction goes hand in hand with sentences of varied lengths. Short sentences can add punch and drama when following longer ones. And longer sentences after short ones will garner heightened attention from readers, who trust that every word counts.
5. **Spare Adverbs and Adjectives**—Credible prose is not overflowing with unnecessary words like needless adverbs and adjectives. Excess modifiers are the work

of amateurs. Strong verbs and nouns are the mark of pros.

6. **Tone**—The tone of credible prose focuses the reader's attention on the story, not the writer, and is never self-indulgent. Resist the temptation to overwrite or to offer needless asides, showy vocabulary, and excessive punctuation. The writing is straightforward and the words shine, not the author or their devices.

So how does all this fit together? Let's look at a couple more examples of strong openings. Here's the opening from Dennis Lehane's *Darkness, Take My Hand*:

> Three days ago, on the first official night of winter, a guy I grew up with, Eddie Brewer, was one of four people shot in a convenience store. Robbery was not a motive. The shooter, Jeff Fahey, had recently broken up with his girlfriend, Laura Stiles, who was a cashier on the four-to-twelve shift. At eleven fifteen, as Eddie Brewer filled a Styrofoam cup with ice and Sprite, Jeff Fahey walked through the door and shot Laura Stiles once in the face and twice through the heart.
>
> Then he shot Eddie Brewer once in the head and walked down the frozen foods aisle and found an elderly Vietnamese couple huddling in the dairy section. Two bullets for each of them, and James Fahey decided his work was complete.

Darkness, Take My Hand is a noir detective novel set in Boston. Now let's go to Bend, Oregon, and this opening from *Frisky Business* by Tawna Fenske:

> Either Marley Cartman had stepped in dog droppings, or the makers of her new lotion had a weird concept of sweet seduction.

265

She dragged the toe of her Jimmy Choo peep-toe across the floor of the Humane Society lobby, thinking it was absurd she'd dressed this nicely to drop paperwork at a business with a goat pen in the foyer.

One detective noir, one romantic comedy, two very different openings, but both excellent examples of the concepts Kress suggested. Lehane starts his story with darkness and tragedy using a matter-of-fact tone, while Fenske's opening is quirky and comedic, much like the novel that follows. The Lehane novel centers on violence, as Boston detectives Gennaro and McKenzie try to protect a local kid from the Mafia, while Fenske's is about romance set around a wildlife sanctuary. Both openings establish character voice, are short on adjectives and adverbs, and are long on sentences of varied lengths, while also establishing setting and tone with economical prose. They are memorable and powerful and draw us in immediately. This is what your novel's opening should accomplish as well.

For readers—and this includes agents and editors—the opening scene or two are all you have to convince them your novel is for them—worth their time and competently written by an author who has something to say and the credibility to say it. If you cannot convince them in the first two scenes, most will put down your novel and walk away. Some won't make it past the first page, to be honest. And the risk is that they may decide never to pick up another book by you again. This is the importance of strong openings. This is why beginnings matter. Find an opening scene that accomplishes all of these things, and follow it with a scene that opens up the character and world a bit more, letting us in on who they are, where we are, and what the problem and central question will be, and you will have our hearts and minds for the next few days or week it takes to read your story. But, of course, then you must deliver on the promise of your strong opening. And that's where the middle comes in.

Middles

The middle of your book makes up its largest section: act two. It is half the book in length generally. This is often the section where writers struggle to find focus and feel bogged down. It helps if you approach your middle (act two) using the Syd Field paradigm we discussed in Chapter 2 on three-act structure, considering it two parts of a whole, divided by a midpoint. Everything after the plot point 1 turning point of act one forms an ascending arc that rises toward the midpoint. Everything after the midpoint forms a descending arc that moves toward the climax. On a chart, it looks something like this:

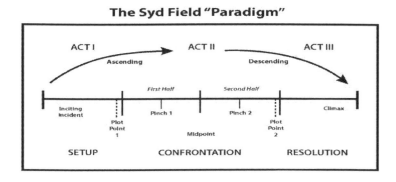

Figure 12-1

The arcs represent the curve of the action, emotion, and character development, which rise in the first half toward the midpoint and then descend after to the climax. Kress writes: "The middle of a story develops the story's implicit promise by

267

dramatizing incidents that increase conflict, reveal character, and put in place all the various forces that will collide at the story's climax." In the first half of act one, it is very much a journey of discovery as the character experiences plot point 1—a call to action—and responds, trying to rise above his or her weakness, overcome obstacles, and gather the clues or complete the steps necessary to be ready to face the antagonist. The midpoint, as we will discuss in a moment, is the point where the character has a revelation that changes him or her in a way that redefines the journey and sends the character on a descending arc toward the final confrontation—possessed of more certainty about where he or she must go and what he or she must do, and more confidence to do it. This is why the midpoint is so important. Although it is not always an overtly dramatic moment, it must always be an internally dramatic one.

The Midpoint

As we discussed in the section on three-act structure, the midpoint is a key turning point where the drama goes from ascending to descending. Something happens that twists the story a bit, either personal revelation for your protagonist or a reveal or an event that changes direction and pushes him or her forward into the second half of act two on the drive toward the final confrontation. Although the turning points at the ends of act one and act two tend to be larger dramatically, this event is still a significant moment. It's the scene where the protagonist and readers stop to take stock of how far they've come and put together many of the pieces, further revealing the map they must follow going forward.

For authors, this is the same opportunity. A chance to look back at what you've done so far and regroup. You've established your setting and significant characters. You've set out your arcs and written one and a half acts. You've described many key things that are recurring themes, settings, and items throughout the story. Ask yourself what you're missing. Did you forget anything? Is anything confusing or unclear? Does anything feel incomplete? What do you need to do to proceed with confidence? Then take the time to tweak a bit and revisit or at least make appropriate notes in these places before continuing, so that you can revisit them later.

One of the common occurrences during a midpoint that is helpful to remember is a shift in driving motivation for your protagonist. The character has changed over the course of what you've written so far in several ways (or should have). At this point, he or she will consider all that's happened and reevaluate the why and how of the rest of the journey. The event, reveal, or revelation that serves as your midpoint is a great spot for them to solidify motivation, or even revise it. For now they see things more clearly, they have more pieces to the puzzle, and they can reevaluate their chosen course and make corrections. Here's where they go from an insecure but determined person forced to embark on a heroic quest to a more confident, deliberate acting hero. Their growth journey is not over, but they are much more sure of themselves, what they are doing, and why. And they have a much clearer sight of the endgame and the stakes as well. This should make them stronger in determination, vision, and even confidence, even if they and we still have doubts about whether they can succeed in reaching their goal. From the midpoint on, the protagonist moves with a new drive forward, even as the antagonist becomes more threatened and desperate in efforts to thwart the hero or heroine.

One of the best ways to work out the next phase is to examine the character and how they've changed so far. What has led to the changes, and have they and we recognized actual change in attitude, approach, confidence, etc.? If not, perhaps work on tweaks that slowly reveal the change, or use the midpoint for a big scene where the change is made manifest and we all realize it. Go back and look at the key scenes that set up that change, then consider where they need to be at the end of the story and imagine scenes you will need to complete the arc and get them there.

You can do the same with every plot and subplot in the story, revisiting key moments for each and planning the next steps needed to carry them to the natural conclusion. By natural conclusion, I don't mean whatever comes. I mean what you envision as the best ending for the story. If you weren't sure before, you should have a better idea what this is by now. Go back and look at your three-act structure outline of your ending. Does the ending you envision still look like what you envisioned at the beginning, or does anything need to be tweaked? Remember, in Chapter 2, I said your outline was just a guideline and could change. This is a good point to reevaluate and restate or revise your goals, so you know where you're headed, what you're working for.

It is also important to examine the antagonist and any main supporting characters the same way. How have they changed? What led them there, and where are they going the rest of the story? Having in your mind a clear sense of what is going on with your story and characters is key to feeling unstuck and prepared to write your second half. Midpoints can often be points where a writer feels stuck and confused about where to go next. So thinking through all these key aspects is a great exercise for escaping that trap and being renewed in vision and confidence to continue with a sense of direction.

What clues and key questions were asked and answered that provided the suspense and plot twists so far? Which are still unanswered that compel you and readers forward? And how will you answer them and in what order? Do you need to rethink any of them? Do you need to add or subtract any?

Taking our earlier example of *Star Wars*: Luke Skywalker has now rescued the princess with Han and finds himself trapped in the Death Star detention block with his companions, fighting against incredible odds. They must find or make a way out, get back to their ship, and then hope Ben Kenobi has disabled the tractor beam. From this point on, act two becomes a chase with Han and Chewie and Leia and Luke separately fighting their way back toward the Millennium Falcon to escape, while C-3PO and R2-D2 do their best to lend whatever aid they can and Kenobi reaches and disables the tractor beam, then faces a confrontation of his own.

Looking at this famous story, it is easy to identify a lot of key moments: from R2-D2 revealing Leia's message to Luke finding Ben to meeting Han to arrival at the Death Star, which all led up to where they are now. Their goal remains clear: to get the plans and the princess back to the Rebel Alliance. And Luke has also learned many skills of the Jedi and how to fight and has gained confidence as a leader and hero that he never had in the beginning. He's never embarked on such an important and dangerous quest before, and he is actually pulling it off. He moves forward with a sense of drive and direction stronger than he had before. This is what good midpoints should do in a story.

Getting Through and Staying Unstuck

Middles are places a lot of writers get stuck. I used to find this a problem, until I started focusing on the throughline—a film industry term for the main plotline, the one that focuses on what happens between the protagonist and antagonist in the story. Since the middle is the core journey wherein the protagonist and antagonist prepare to confront each other and fight out their opposing goals, keeping this in focus can give your middle a sense of direction. Everything that happens should feed this storyline,

271

taking plot and characters toward that ultimate confrontation. In the first half, on the ascending arc, the focus is on preparing the character to know how to confront the antagonist and believe he or she is able to do so. The second half, the descending arc, focuses on final preparations and moving directly and determinedly toward that final showdown as all the necessary pieces are put in place and final preparations taken. If you keep these two goals in focus, it should help shape your middle and allow you to push through any uncertainty that blocks your writing. Additional space in the middle is made up of the various subplots and the scenes required in their arcs. But again, every scene must serve character or plot growth. *Every single scene.* So before you write a scene, figure out what it accomplishes toward the throughline and the character growth necessary to get the protagonist and antagonist to that final confrontation. Knowing that will help you write the scene well and also give you a sense of its belonging in the story. If you have a scene you can't answer this question about, don't write it. It probably doesn't belong yet, though it may be relevant later. You may just be trying to put it in the wrong spot.

Ultimately, if you are blocked, the problem is always internal, not external. Think of it like your character's journey. You have flaws and obstacles to overcome. So, to get past it, you should ask yourself some questions about why you are stuck. Is it fear—fear of failure, fear of success? Is the scene not a good fit for the advancement of plot or character at this point in the story? Have you answered all the questions in your story that led to this scene, or is something missing? Make a list of the next few scenes you envision needing to advance your story, and then consider whether they are in the right order or need to be adjusted. Does the present scene need to shift within that rough outline? That could also be why you are stuck. Your mind may know subconsciously you are not ready to write the scene you sat down to write and you need to go elsewhere first before you can make it work. Another trick is to think through the plots and subplots and ask to which the current scene contributes. Perhaps you have not revisited a certain plotline for a while and need to take a detour there before you can continue with the story, or perhaps a certain scene can contribute to the advancement of multiple plot or character arcs, and writing it that way will free up your mind so you can get to work.

Whatever the answer to these questions, the best approach is to always think in terms of the short term, not the overall, when sitting down to write. Don't think about sitting down to write the whole story but rather the scene at hand. Putting the rest of the task out of mind allows clarity of focus and single-minded attention on the scene at hand, which can unclog any blockage or confusion or at least help reveal answers to the questions that are causing uncertainty. It also can be helpful to set word count goals and mini deadlines for yourself. Most professional writers write whether they feel like it or not and are prepared to completely toss aside a day's output if warranted. They know that the act of writing is like exercise and doing it every day is key to progress, even if the usefulness of the output isn't as equal some days as others. Often the very act of writing can get you over the hump and clear your thoughts, allowing you to regain focus. Sitting and stressing over a blank mind is not the helpful way. The only way to get more story is to write. Sometimes a trigger helps and can be provided by reading another novel with similarities to your work. Something in the subgenre you are writing, perhaps, or something so different it completely takes your mind in different directions. The goal is to unclog your mind and regain clarity and focus. Whatever route works best to get you there is a good route to take.

Some writers use rewards to spur them to write, disciplining themselves to deny the rewards when they don't reach word count or page number goals. Some writers research to break free of the fog, finding it stimulates new ways of thinking and various ideas that can open the mind and free it to write. Many find that discipline is key. For me, when discipline in one area drops, I find it bleeds into others. If I get lazy with exercise, I get lazy with writing, dieting, bill paying, and so much more. So having focus in one area affects the others, and it is key to my writing therefore to maintain a lifestyle of discipline in many areas. Certainly, taking breaks to walk my dogs or exercise is a very good way to unblock by getting my mind on other things and pondering the scene and the questions I need to answer to be able to write. It will be different for every writer, so until you find the best method for you, experimentation may be necessary. But all of this is part of finding the way to write that works best for you.

Whatever you wind up doing, it may also help to have some idea of the climax you are working toward to write the middle that leads there. This is why the structural outlines I suggested in Chapter 2 can be good road maps to help you write. After all, knowing the goal and the destination is often the best way to sort out how to get there. And in fulfilling the promise of a satisfying climax, it is helpful to know where you're going so you can set it up properly with foreshadowing, character growth, plot twists, clues, and the various pieces it will take for everything to fall in place that allow the climax to satisfy us both mentally and emotionally.

So perhaps this is a good time to consider the ending of your story—especially the climax.

Endings—The Climax

A satisfying climax comes from one thing: protagonist confronting antagonist, preferably face to face, and winning. What they win and how depends on the stakes and the goal, of course, but getting the girl, defeating the evil empire, getting the job, stopping the takeover, etc. are all valid and potentially satisfying wins for us. Make them count but give us the satisfaction of watching the win.

That's what all the pacing and suspense has been all about: getting us to this moment. So make sure the moment counts and is emotionally and dramatically rewarding for us. This does not mean every story must have a happy ending, but it explains why many often do.

The climax needs to be played out dramatically. Don't let it happen off screen. We need to witness it. It needs to be the ultimate dramatic conflict that unfolds before us as a scene. Make sure you plan accordingly and write it well. Anything less will be a letdown from all the anticipation you have created. How would you have felt if Luke never faced off with Darth Vader at the end of *Star Wars*? If Frodo had never destroyed the ring in *The Lord of the Rings*? Or if Harry Potter had not confronted Voldemort? I imagine your feelings about any of these stories would be very different. Would you feel satisfied? Seeing the protagonist overcome their imperfections and obstacles and win is a bit part of the satisfaction of good storytelling. And you just don't get the same effect if you tell us how it ended rather than showing us by letting it play out as overt drama. Watching the confrontation is the payoff readers have been waiting for, so give it to them.

In preparing to write your climax, it is important to revisit the earlier story and make sure you have set it up correctly and put all the necessary pieces in place to make it feel satisfying and complete. Go back and look at your setup for major reveals. When, where, and how do you ask what questions? Is there enough foreshadowing? Note areas that need work and potential revisions you can make during editing. Don't stop and do it now. That will interrupt your writing pace. But make sure you correct course in what you write until the end and note what you can go back and fix later to make it better and where to do so. Are your three acts clear in each plotline and arc? Do the characters show growth and change? Double-check to see you are on track and look at how you can improve things for better pacing and suspense in your book both going forward and later in editing.

In addition to looking at the questions, foreshadowing, plot arcs, and character arcs, don't forget to also consider emotional arcs. Because good endings don't just wrap up the pieces logically and neatly on the outside, they also satisfy our inner selves—our emotions. Donald Maass writes in *Writing the Breakout Novel*:

> Why do endings disappoint? Often it is because they are rushed; that is, because the author has written it in a hurry due to fatigue or due to a looming deadline, perhaps both. Climaxes are both inner and outer, both plot specific and emotionally charged. The payoff needs to fully plumb the depths in both ways if it is to satisfy.

The secret, Maass suggests, is to allow your protagonist the possibility of failure until the very end. He goes on to say:

> Construct the plot so that its conflicts, inner and outer, all converge at the same time and place... A great storyteller leaves us in suspense right up to the final moments. Success is never sure; in fact, failure seems the far more likely result.

The satisfaction is in the protagonist rising to the moment and somehow overcoming the odds to succeed. Without that, victory is hollow, the ending emotionally unsatisfying and lacking in depth.

Kress suggests four things good climaxes must accomplish:

1. **Satisfy the view of life implied in your story.**
2. **Deliver emotion.** Readers should feel what the characters feel. If characters feel nothing, the story has not ended yet.

3. **Deliver an appropriate level of emotion**. As discussed in number 2, it's not just any emotion but emotional fulfillment readers are seeking, and that means we need to have been conflicted and unsure until the very end how it might go—if the protagonist can possibly succeed.

4. **The climax must be logical to your plot and story.** This last one may seem obvious, but we've all encountered those endings that were meant to be surprises and twists but that seemed to come out of nowhere, leaving us frustrated and feeling unfulfilled. Kress says, "The climactic scene must grow naturally out of the actions that preceded it, which in turn must have grown naturally out of the personalities of the characters." A satisfying climax is intimately tied to satisfying character arcs—characters we care about, root for, and want to see grow into better people. A climax must not be a coincidence either. It must feel inevitable, even if we doubt it will happen right until the end. Kress suggests asking yourself: "If the protagonist were a radically different person, would this story still end the same way?" The answer must be no if your ending is to be convincing. If it could happen that way for anyone, your ending will fail.

Who else but Luke Skywalker could have used the Force to visualize the exact target and destroyed the Death Star? Who else but Frodo could destroy the ring? I can't imagine those endings coming out any other way, can you? And the same should be true of your climax. Ultimately, the whole story is like an arrow pointing to a specific climax and how you write it ensures that readers' expectations emotionally and mentally follow the arrow to the exact place you lead them. That's the only way you can ensure they'll be satisfied with your climax.

Denouement

Everything after the climax is called the denouement—the wrap-up of the story. In most cases, the denouement is fairly short and concise, providing confirmation of closure for the characters and plot by revealing their emotional and physical fates after the climax. This is especially true for any characters not involved in the climactic scene. The denouement should give readers just enough information about the characters that they feel the story is really over and satisfy reader curiosity. So the denouement is the place to wrap up any pesky unanswered questions still hanging from earlier in a book—all except the few left over to point us to the sequel, that is (if there is one). Readers don't want to be left hanging. They don't want to decide for themselves, either. Readers want to know what happens definitively to the characters they've cared enough about to stick with the story, so make decisions and give it to them.

The general rule is, according to Kress, "The more subtle and low-key the climax in action and tone, the briefer the denouement should be." Don't drag it out and leach all emotion from the climax. Get it done and keep it short so it doesn't seem too anticlimactic. The other key is to dramatize. Show what happens to your characters in action, don't just tell us. But keep it low-key enough that it doesn't detract from the power of the climax.

To demonstrate, let's look at the denouements from two of the stories we looked at in the beginning of this chapter. First, *The Wedding* by Nicholas Sparks:

> Standing on the porch, with autumn in full swing, I find the crispness of the evening air invigorating as I think back on the night of our wedding. I can still recall it in vivid detail, just as I

can remember all that happened during the year of the forgotten anniversary.

It feels odd to know that it's all behind me. The preparations had dominated my thoughts for so long and I'd visualized it so many times that I sometimes feel that I've lost contact with an old friend, someone with whom I've grown very comfortable. Yet in the wake of those memories, I've come to realize that I now have the answer to the question that I'd been pondering when I first came out here.

Yes, I decided, a man can truly change.

Remember the universal questions asked right at the opening: "Is it possible, I wonder, for a man to truly change? Or do character and habit form the immovable boundaries of our lives?" Here we see that the character has found the answer he sought. We've seen it dramatized through events in the story and particularly the climax, but the denouement serves to confirm the character's recognition that he gets it now clearly. He's found the answer.

What about Dennis Lehane's *Darkness, Take My Hand*? It ends as follows:

In the kitchen, we made hot chocolate, stared over the rims of our mugs at each other as the radio in the living room updated us on the weather.

The snow, the announcer told us, was part of the first major storm system to hit Massachusetts this winter. By the time we woke in the morning, he promised, twelve to sixteen inches would have fallen.

"Real snow," Angie said. "Who would've thought?"

"It's about time."

The weather report over, the announcer was updating the condition of Reverend Edward Brewer.

"How long you think he can hold on?" Angie said.

I shrugged. "I don't know."

We sipped from our mugs as the announcer reported the mayor's call for more stringent handgun laws, the governor's call for tougher enforcement of restraining orders. So another Eddie Brewer wouldn't walk into the wrong convenience store at the wrong time. So another Laura Stiles could break up with her abusive boyfriend without fear of death. So the James Faheys of the world would stop instilling us with terror.

So our city would one day be as safe as Eden before the fall, our lives insulated from the hurtful and the random.

"Let's go in the living room," Angie said, "and turn the radio off."

She reached out and I took her hand in the dark kitchen as the snow painted my window in soft specks of white, followed her down the hall toward the living room.

Eddie Brewer's condition hadn't changed. He was still in a coma.

The city, the announcer said, waited. The city, the announcer assured us, was holding its breath.

Progress, Lehane implies, may not change the past, but it bodes well for the future. There is hope. There is a sense of movement in a positive direction. And there is a sense of renewed safety and reassurance that all will be well. For a book that started with the shock of the random shooting of an old classmate, that makes for a pretty decent denouement if you ask me.

CHAPTER 13
EDITING AND REWRITING

I am a firm believer that rewriting is where the magic happens. It's where you take the rough draft you fought through and hone it into a fine-tuned, focused, polished piece. It's where you get the opportunity to finally see your story all laid out and examine its flaws, strengths, and needs in full and set about the work needed to complete it and take it from good to great. To me, the rewriting is when the fun begins, because it is here where things will come together in a way that begins to match the magic vision you've held in your mind for so long and struggled to put into words. Rewriting is an important process, an invaluable opportunity, and I consider it something to look forward to, not something to dread.

Getting to the Rewrite

Now, before you actually start rewriting, it's important to let your manuscript breathe. How long you should do this depends upon you, your level of experience, the deadline, what else you have on your plate, etc. But generally, I agree with those who suggest it should be a minimum of six weeks—six weeks during which you work on anything but this novel, clearing your mind of what has been an obsession, focusing on something new and different, and putting this out of your thoughts to regain some manner of the objectivity required to truly revise well. In *On Writing*, Stephen King writes:

> You're not ready to go back to the old project
> until you've gotten so involved in a new one (or re-

involved in your day-to-day life) that you've almost forgotten the unreal estate that took up three hours of your every morning or afternoon for a period of three or five or seven months.

You're too close to the project, too consumed with it to ever see it clearly and objectively the way one must in order to evaluate it properly, so the time has come to take a break, shut it in a drawer, and resist the urge to return to it for a period of time while you regain perspective.

For me, I usually spend the time on short stories or planning and researching my next book. Sometimes I have some polishes to attend to or an anthology to edit. Other times I have blog posts and marketing and other details I've postponed and ignored for months to catch up on. Whatever it is, the key is to do something else and only something else for a time. You also need to get the distance to emotionally let go enough that you can accept the need to revise and make the book better. Stop coddling your baby enough to see that there are things to be learned and taught and refined about her, and that's okay, it's all part of life and growth, and prepare yourself mentally to undertake the task with the enthusiasm that comes from confidence that it is not a failure but a natural step toward success.

Once you learn to do this, you will find entering the rewrite process to be quite rewarding. You will approach it with renewed focus and energy and the sense of purpose necessary to do it well. King writes:

> If you've never done it before, you'll find reading your book after a six-week layoff to be a strange, often exhilarating experience. It's yours, you'll recognize it as yours, even be able to remember what tune was on the stereo when you wrote certain lines, and yet it will also be like

reading the work of someone else… This is the way
it should be, the reason you waited.

The first step, in fact, before the rewrite actual begins, should be
sitting down with the whole manuscript and reading it line by line,
pen in hand, making whatever notes occur to you as you go, but
not stopping until you've been through it in its entirety, beginning
to end. I do this on paper. It's a great way to rest my eyes, which
spend way too many hours of each day staring at computer screens
or TVs, and it also is a wholly different experience from reading
on a machine. For one thing, the whole page unfolds before you,
not just a portion, and you can see it as a whole in a fresh way that
allows your eyes to take it in differently than they do when you
read on a screen. For another, since you'll undoubtedly spend
hours working it over on screens as you rewrite, it gives you a
chance to take it to the park, porch, etc. and just work with and
read it as readers do, without the demands of the work
environment encroaching. This can be important because you are
seeking perspective and a fresh look, after all. However you
approach it, the trick is to evaluate the whole book before you stop
and do any rewrites, because often themes, tone, arcs, etc. need to
be considered as a whole before you can see their weaknesses and
begin to address them. Chopping it up will disconnect you from
how it all flows and falls together—works or doesn't—and
prevent you from seeing the full perspective needed to improve.

Once you've made your notes, then is the time to go back to
any other notes you might have made as you wrote later chapters
or when your mind just had to make a note during the six-week
hiatus; consider them in light of the fresh reread, and devise an
approach to begin your rewrite. Sometimes, there will be
particular areas you need to address separately: character
development, particular aspects of craft, particular plots or
subplots, theme, etc., and other times you will want to start at the
beginning and work your way through right off the bat. Whatever

the correct approach is is for you to determine, but having a plan is wise, because this is the time for focused effort, not the seat-of-your-pants writing you may have done to finish your first draft. Rewriting is work. Important work that is often inherently different from the initial drafting process, and you have to approach it as such.

The human mind works in funny ways. For example, when we read, our eyes skip the bulk of words, just taking in key words and phrases that allow our minds to assemble the most logical sentence. This allows us to move much more quickly over a page than if we stopped at every word. When you read aloud, however, it forces you to slow down and look at every word. This is why, when rereading your own work, you can skip over missing words, missing conjunctions, typos, homonyms (words that sound alike but have different meanings and spellings), and more. Because we wrote the piece, we already love the characters and subconsciously know so much about them that we assume things that may not come across clearly for others and mentally fill in gaps that aren't on the page, so everything appears okay. This is why we need other eyes to help edit and proof our books. And it's why we need to carefully approach revision with a mind toward objectivity.

The other part of preparing to rewrite is mental. Kat Reed, in *Revision*, suggests a mental checklist that is useful to prepare your mind and attitude for the revision process:

1. **Your first thoughts are not necessarily your best thoughts.** Just today I picked up a project I had struggled with for months and came up with a great new idea that totally helped fix a scene and move it forward, something I had never thought of before. If I had not put it aside, who knows when or if it might have occurred to me. Distance was the perfect aid.
2. **Nothing you write is carved in stone.** Yes, we all love our work. We all are proud of our babies. But

285

face it. No one is perfect. Robert Silverberg told me, "The difference between an old pro like me and a new writer is that I still write crap but I know how to identify it." That is so true. Even then, old pros need editors too because we can always make it better.

3. **It takes revision to turn a loss into a win.** Rejection sucks. So does some criticism. The best way around both is to ensure the book you send out is the best it can be. Period. No other solution.

4. **Shortstop criticism—be your own toughest critic.** Scared of criticism? Dread the bad review? Well, shortstop it by getting there first and giving them as little to criticize as possible. Fix it in revision. Close the gaps, fix the holes, etc. That is your best defense.

5. **If it's worth doing at all, it's worth doing right.** There's really nothing more to say by way of explanation, except if you don't believe this then you are being a special type of fool.

6. **Extra effort closes the distance between you and your audience.** The extra time of revision is your shot to see what readers see and make sure you are communicating as clearly as possible what you intended. It is the chance to make sure what they receive and what you send out most closely match what you hope for in your mental vision of any book.

7. **Revision means survival.** Pretty much without revision, few succeed, and without revision few go far. It is a necessary part of the process, and as I said, I look at it as a positive: where the magic happens. It can truly make a good book great. It is not something to dread but to embrace.

Once you get your mind in the game, it's time to start the read-through and notetaking. Once you've done that, it's time to dig in, so let's look at some common problems you should look for in every manuscript.

Self-Editing Tips for Common Problems

What I am about to teach you is merely an overview of tips you can use to polish your manuscripts and make them more professional when you send them on to a professional editor. In no way will this information qualify you to not *need* an editor nor will it be a guaranteed fix for all the issues in a manuscript. I am an editor and I still need an editor for my writing. So will you. Now the right brain is your creative side. To edit well, you must switch brains and use your left brain. This is why editing should not begin until you've given yourself some time away to gain back a little fresh perspective or objectivity. It is also why techniques such as reading backwards, last sentence first, or reading aloud are very helpful tools to editing and revision.

Saving your editor time and impressing them with your professionalism isn't just about making yourself and your book look good. It's also about maximizing the value you can get from an editor's additional input. The cleaner the manuscript, the less they have to worry about silly basics and the more they can concentrate on the larger, more complex nuances of your writing. And that will allow them to focus on what really makes the difference between a truly great book and a mediocre one.

The 10% Solution Method

The first technique is from Ken Rand's *The 10% Solution.* The basic premise is this: by taking your word count and reducing it by 10 percent, you can and will eliminate a lot of fat to tighten up and add sparkle and confidence to your manuscript. As you develop as a writer, you will come up with lists to check in editing of your most overused words, most misspelled words, etc. These are often key areas for eliminating 10 percent, but here are some others. Use the following table:

-ly	very	smell
Of	about	saw
That	-ing	taste
Said	and	touch
Was	but	windows
Were	like	aloud
By	-ion	bed
His	felt	her
Hear		

Take these words and insert them one by one on your find-replace feature of your word-processing program and highlight the results. Then go through and look at them one by one, asking yourself three questions:

1. Do I keep it as is?
2. Do I change it?
3. Do I delete it?

Then ask yourself if the sentence is accurate, clear, and brief before and after. If it is accurate, clear, and brief before, you likely will choose one and keep it as is. If not, changes are warranted.

For "-ion," it is the last three syllables of many long words. Here you may just need to consider substitutes. Instead of "intoxication," does "drunk" work better? For "conflagration," what about "fire"? For "rationalization," how about "excuse"? Remember, writing is about communication. The simpler, the clearer it is. If it is the vocabulary of a character, that is one thing. Some characters have different social and educational levels and styles and that should be represented, of course, but in general use of language, the simpler, clearer choice is usually better.

Repeat this until you've gone through the entire list. These are generally the most overused and abused words by authors, and there are reasons for them, from passives like "was" and "were" and "felt" to repetitive words like "said," "that," and "but" to weak intruders like "saw," and more. Applying this technique will help you identify many weaker sentences you need to polish and words you need to eliminate to make your prose stronger. Following are some more tips.

Intruder Words

The next tip is to find and identify intruder words in your manuscript. Intruder words lend a feel of passive writing or structure to the narrative. Use them only when consciously aware of doing so, not as a fallback or style. The more active way to state things is to just flat out state it. Ken Rand writes in *The 10% Solution*, "When you show the world filtered through a character's senses, you distance your reader one degree from sensing the story environment themselves." It's like reading through an interpreter, which takes you out of immersion to a step removed. The most common intruder words are "knew," "know," "felt," "wondered," "thought," "mused," "debated," and "saw."

> **Example 1:** He wondered what kind of food she was cooking as he pushed on the front door and released a hearty aroma.

> **Better:** He pushed on the front door and released a hearty aroma. What kind of food was she cooking?

> **Example 2:** He saw orange lanterns, lights, green umbrellas, and heard the music of violins when he crested the top of the hill.

> **Better:** When he crested the top of the hill, orange lanterns illuminated the twilight. Green umbrellas rose up

289

from cozy tables. All around, the music of violins created a sweet harmony.

Commas and Compound Sentences

Next, let's make sure we examine comma usage and compound sentences. The best way to do this is using the following mnemonic: FANBOYS, for "for," "and," "nor," "but," "or," "yet," and "so." When using one of the FANBOYS words to combine thoughts, this forms a compound sentence. Comma placement is commonly seen after the conjunction word. Or neglected. In short, it's rarely in the right place. The simple rule: Break the sentence at the conjunction. If they form two separate sentences, a comma is mandatory. The comma comes *before* the conjunction.

Example 1: I went to the party and ate until I was sick.

Break it: I went to the party | ate until I was sick

The sentences cannot stand by themselves as two separate sentences. Therefore, a comma is not inserted.

Example 2: I went to Johnny's and I fell in love at first sight with the puppy on the stoop.

Break it: I went to Johnny's | I fell in love at first sight with the puppy on the stoop.

Both are single separate sentences and can stand by themselves. Therefore, a comma is required: *I went to Johnny's, and I fell in love at first sight with the puppy on the stoop.*

Basic Passive Voice

Passive voice can almost always be identified with "-ing" words, especially when used with a "to be" verb. But "-ing" isn't the problem. It is the *was* + "-ing" form of passives that is the problem. Nix the structure, and use the straight past form of "-ed."

Example:

He was walking across the room with his shoes off.
He walked across the room with his shoes off.

Don't eliminate every use of "was"—it is often necessary. Eliminate occurrences of "was" + "-ing." Unless your entire story is written in present tense.

Basic Gerund Issues

Virtually anytime "-ing" occurs, it is a gerund structure. And these can lead to gerund conflict. One way to check for conflict is a very simple method. Ask yourself, "Can the action be done at the same time?"

Example 1: Smiling, he answered the phone.

Yes, these two actions can take place at the same time. This is an okay structure.

Example 2: Running around the chair, he entered the back lawn.

No, you cannot run around the chair at the same time you enter the back lawn. One action comes before the other. This structure is incorrect.

More examples:

Having finished the assignment, the TV was turned on.

Correct: Having finished the assignment, Jill turned on the TV.

Having arrived late for practice, a written excuse was needed.

Correct: Having arrived late for practice, the team captain needed a written excuse.

In both examples, the doer of the action must be named correctly in the sentence. Dangling modifiers modify words not clearly stated in the sentence.

Dangling Modifier Issues

Comma usage is frequently an area where writers struggle. Another common comma issue is dangling modifiers. The action set apart in commas must relate to the subject that is making the action.

Example 1: Having been born with three legs, it is obvious the cat struggled with balance.

In this example, "having been born with three legs" modifies the pronoun "it." But what it is supposed to modify is "the cat". Therefore, it needs to be adjusted:

Example 2: Having been born with three legs, the cat struggled with balance.

Example 3: Wanting something warm and cozy, the colorful quilt gave the cat a place to sleep.

The clause before the comma modifies "the quilt," when the intended recipient is "the cat." Rearrange the sentence:

Correct: Wanting something cozy, the cat fell asleep in the colorful quilt.

Repetition

As you go through your book, if you didn't on the read-through, be sure and note words and phrases you repeat a lot, especially on the same page. Make a list and go back and ask yourself the following questions: Is the word really necessary? If it is, what are other ways to say the same thing? Then adjust accordingly. While repetition as a tool for emphasis is valid, unintentional repetition can become annoying and distracting. Nothing stands out to readers more readily than constant repetition. So eliminate as much as you can.

Dialogue Tags

When you have finished the tips I just provided, go back and review your dialogue tags using the tips I offered in Chapter 7: Dialogue. Make adjustments accordingly.

Characters, Plot, and Theme

The order in which you review various aspects of craft as you revise is up to you, but the one thing this phase has that the writing did not is the advantage of seeing the book as a whole and examining how and if the various parts work well together. In *On Writing*, Stephen King writes:

> Every book—at least one worth reading—is about something. Your job during or after your first draft is to decide what something or somethings yours is about. Your job in the second draft—one of them anyway—is to make that something even more clear. This may necessitate some big changes and revisions. The benefits to you and your reader will be clearer focus and a more unified story.

Things emerge as you write, such as themes which may not have been obvious from the beginning. So now you have the chance to go back through, examine them, and make sure all the elements support and expand the theme in ways that bring out the nuances and add depth.

I generally start with story and structure. I look at my opening and I ask questions about it as I do.

1. Does my story really begin here? Or did I start in the wrong place?
2. Does the opening have the right pacing and length, or did I draw it out too much? Too much description? Too little dialogue and character? Too little emotion?
3. Are the story questions clear?
4. Is the length of the opening proportional to the rest of the story, or is it too elaborate? Too involved?
5. Is my opening interesting? Is it compelling?
6. Does my opening have enough action?
7. Is my opening too flashy such that it affects continuity, or does it flow well into what follows?
8. Is everything clear so readers know who is talking, where they are, and what's happening?

After the opening, I start reviewing my plots and subplots and looking at their scene structure, flow, and arcs. I look at the action and conflict. Is something happening, or is it static? Does every scene take us somewhere further in plot or character or both? Are the stakes clear? Is what my characters want clear? Will readers care? Do the setups lead to payoffs? Are all the questions being answered? Are they being answered at the right time—the best time to aid tension, pace, and comprehension? Is the information I am giving enough to reveal the story to readers as I see it, or did I assume things I failed to impart clearly? How can I make it clearer?

Next, I look at point of view. Is it consistent—no head hopping? Is the chronology clear and understandable? Am I shifting at the right points, or should I rethink? Are there too many shifts or too few? Is the tone consistent? Is the character with the most at stake always the point-of-view character for each scene?

I look at pacing, description, and setting. Does the story start fast enough, or does it drag? Are individual scenes dramatic, and do they start and end at the right spot to keep the tension consistent throughout, or do they peter out? Does the payoff at the end of each scene and chapter justify the buildup? Did I balance showing and telling? Do I describe too much or too little? What details are missing that might be important? Does each setting add to the tension and tone of the scene in a way that makes it stronger, or does it fall flat or detract? Does each scene leave readers feeling that something important has happened? Do I use all five senses at least once every other page, if not more? Where can I add more visceral descriptive cues?

If any place bogs down, I look for places to trim the fat and tighten, not only for pacing and tension but also for clarity. Too much information can overload readers, while too little can leave them confused. The trick is to find the right balance. Does each section function properly in the story, or does anything need to be cut or moved to make the story flow better and stronger overall? This requires some cold efficiency and killing your darlings, but the book will always be better for it, every time, and making your book the best it can be is essential. There is no room here for favorite scenes and characters that ultimately serve no purpose but author egos. "I liked writing that" is not enough justification to leave it in. Save it and try to use it in another book or story. Everything that stays here must absolutely belong and add something important, or it has to go. Now is the time to reorganize scenes and details. If you reveal too much or too little, reveal it in the wrong order, or omit important things, this is the time to find and fix it.

Next, I look at characters. Is each major character complete? Are they original or too much of a stereotype? Are they consistent or wishy-washy? Are they distinctive, or can they be confused with another character? Can anything be added to keep them distinctive? Examine diction and consistency of dialogue and tone—is the character being true to themselves in every word and action they take? Is it believable? What does this character want? What does this character fear? What do they overcome? Does the character grow and change? How? If not, what can be done to fix that? Does each character serve a function in the story, or can they be combined or even cut? As editor, I once made a writer cut an entire character and give all her business to another character because she was a minor character who served no real purpose, whereas one of the major characters needed more agency, and so combining them was the best solution. The writer still complains about it to this day, even though she admits it was the best thing for her book. She was later able to go back in and make that character better and more essential to the next book so she could bring her into the story. Ultimately, only keep characters who matter to the outcome of the story. The rest have to go.

Dialogue

I often do a special pass just for dialogue because dialogue is so important. In this, I look not only at characters' diction but also at the pacing and conciseness of dialogue. I probably trim dialogue and description the most of any parts of any draft. Too much dialogue, dialogue that is too drawn out, not enough action—any of this can be a scene killer and has to go. How can you make the dialogue more dramatic and better paced and less wordy? How can you make even exposition passages feel like they move with action, instead of dragging like info dumps? The trick is to make exposition feel organic and necessary every time by keeping it concise and short. Simple is actually better than complex. Less really is more. Read aloud. Try it out. Do you stumble anywhere? Is it smooth and natural, or does it need refining? Are the characters distinctive from each other? Is it clear who is speaking in each case? Characters should sound like individuals, not clones. Listen hard to them and make sure each character has some unique nuanced turns of phrase or styles. Maybe some speak in complete sentences while others talk in spurts and fragments. Some may discuss things directly while others beat around, especially when it comes to emotions. Whatever the case, all dialogue is transactional in nature: it is about an exchange of something useful between two parties, so make sure something happens in every exchange. Is the dialogue accompanied by appropriate actions and descriptive modifiers to show frame of mind, mood, etc.? Most of all, do they all sound like real people?

Ken Rand writes in *The 10% Solution*:

> We don't just see words when we read. We use other senses. We make mistakes because sometimes the senses we're using right now to read copy may be dulled, distracted, or otherwise not functioning to capacity. The solution is to employ different senses in a systematic manner during the editing phase, to catch on the next pass errors that escaped the last pass.

Reading aloud not only employs your ears but your tongue, your eyes, and your mind and heart in ways different from just reading silently. You will hear the way things sound, rather than imagining it. You will hear repetition clearly, for example, because your ears pick it up whereas your eyes may not have. Hearing how the pacing and flow aid the emotional effect of the prose is also invaluable. It is the best way to give you insight into the reader's experience in time to make fixes. You will hear things that sounded complete in your head but are not—not clear, not complete, not as intended. You will notice sentences that seem to run on or end abruptly. Places where transitions between sentences, paragraphs, or chapters seem awkward or abrupt. And places where characters are speaking but it is unclear who is who. These and such more are things you don't want to overlook, and reading aloud is a great tool to help you find them.

Let's take a look at a passage now and see what it looks like between first and second draft.

"Son of a bitch!" I cursed as I fell forward with a thump onto my desk again, rubbing at the ache in my neck I'd awakened as soon as I sat up. Waking up asleep at one's desk isn't something I'd recommend that often, of course, but I'd spent the previous evening wrapping up a stressful case involving an extramarital affair by the local mortician, and well, needless to say his wife hadn't taken the evidence well, despite the fact she'd hired me herself. In fact, I'd dare say I haven't heard that much blue language out of a lady since I was a cop and assigned to do backstage security for Hillary Clinton. That woman could cuss a mean streak like nobody's business, and the sincerity of her attitude just backed up every word. Hillary reminded me of Mrs. Morgenstern, the old widow who'd been our next door neighbor when I was growing up over in Pomona, Kansas, about twenty miles west of Ottawa, where I now I lived. By the time I was sixteen, I'm pretty sure there weren't a person in Pomona who wouldn't have shot that old hag for five dollars, and about half of 'em woulda tried for free. Mrs. Morganstern was one mean bitch, there's just no other word for it, and you just can't get away with that kinda personality in a small town these days.

Figure 13-1

After a day or two, I went back through the passage and did some tweaking. Here's what it looks like after the polished draft.

"Son of a bitch!" I cursed as I fell forward with a thump onto my desk again, rubbing at the ache~~throbbing, that had started~~ in my neck ~~as soon as~~ I'd awakened ~~as soon as I sat up. Waking up, Falling~~ asleep at one's desk isn't

something I'd recommend ~~that often~~, of course, but I'd spent the previous evening wrapping up a stressful case involving an extramarital affair by the local mortician, and well, needless to say his wife hadn't taken the evidence well, despite the fact she'd hired me herself. In fact, I'd dare say I haven't heard that much blue language out of a lady since I was a cop ~~and~~ ~~assigned~~ to ~~do~~ backstage security for Hillary Clinton. That wom~~en~~an could cuss a mean streak like nobody's business, and the sincerity of her attitude just backed up every word. Hillary reminded me of Mrs. Morgenstern, the old widow who'd been our next door neighbor when I was growing up over in Pomona, Kansas, about twenty miles west of Ottawa, where I now ~~I~~ ~~lived~~lived. By the time I was sixteen, I'm pretty sure there ~~weren't~~twasn't a person in Pomona who wouldn't have shot that old hag for five dollars, and about half of 'em woulda tried for free. Mrs. Morgenstern was one mean ass bitch, there's just no other word for it, and you just can't get away with that kinda personality in a small town these days.

Figure 13-2

You can compare the two and see how I went over the diction and conciseness of voice to tighten or add details as needed to make it richer and clearer, but also to improve the pace at the same time. My goal was to write in a voice that implies a certain Midwest country accent without using any dialect or other tricks. I wanted the voice itself to just slip the accent into readers' minds, but I also want it to be humorous, while still being realistic and gritty yet believable. This is an example of how you might revise a passage.

Words on the Page

There are a few things good writers learn to concern themselves with that beginners often leave to their editors or copyeditors—for example, the way words look on the page. Ken Rand writes: "The very *shape of letters* has a lot to do with whether a reader enjoys or even comprehends the words." This is why choosing fonts is so very important, but additionally, if you have a paragraph with sentences using similar words that appear near each other (in the line above or the line below), this can confuse readers or cause them to get lost as well. You'll also want to look for "widows"— solitary words at the end of paragraphs that hang over solo onto the next line. Typesetters and editors will remove these. Your best bet to be sure it's done the way you want is to find them yourself and see if adding or rearranging words in a sentence can help eliminate them before they ever get there.

I also mentioned earlier in the book that pace and flow of the reading experience come from how pages appear. Too many long descriptive passages with no blank space can make reading difficult and make a book seem slow. Editors and typesetters may want to break these up just for that purpose. It is in your best interest to make breaks yourself to avoid that, so you wind up with the book exactly as you intended. Looking for this will also aid your search for exposition info dumps and overly long description, parts of which you might take out to insert at less busy spots later or just save for another book. Flip through a bound book and notice how the varied flow of paragraphs on pages is pleasing to the eyes as you scan or read, and you'll get the idea of the subconscious psychology involved here. It takes time to learn this well, but it is a very worthwhile skill for any author to learn and allows you to influence parts of the process that tend to move on without you if you don't know about them. After all, it is your book. You are the one who has to live with it. Wasted time and frustration arguing about recombining paragraphs and other details during editing is something that benefits no one, so the more work you do before then, the better your experience will be.

Knowing When to Stop

Everything we've covered so far in this chapter is aimed at one goal: helping you make your manuscript stronger and more professionally polished before passing it on to your editor and publisher. The last tip I want to offer is the answer to a commonly asked question: *How do I know when to stop editing?*

When you start noticing yourself putting back things you already removed, it's time to consider stopping and handing it over to someone else. Don't get stuck in the cycle of endless revision so that you never finish. At some point, you can only make each book as good as you are as a writer at that particular moment. Over time, each book will get better and better, but you do need to learn your limits. And no book will ever be perfect. I usually finish revisions and set the book aside for a day or two before doing another read-through aloud. That gives me a break long enough to rest my eyes and brain and come back ready to hear it fresh again and make any final notes as I go through.

When I've reached a point when I know it is the best I can make it, then I send it to my agent or editor for the next stage: the editorial process.

The Editorial Process

The editor's job is to help us identify and fix any remaining grammatical, story, character, or other problems before publication so readers never see them. There are three main types of editing authors encounter: developmental or story editing, line editing, and copy editing. Developmental or story editing looks at the overall story from plot to characters, structure and arcs to themes, style, and even meaning. It looks for issues with plot, characters, logic, and more. Line editing looks at grammar, word use, repetition, style, voice, and technical accuracy such as sentence and paragraph length, pacing, and flow. Copy editing looks at grammar and repetition as well as fact-checking. All three serve different purposes and come at different stages of the process, but all three are special skills that are invaluable for authors wanting to professionally publish.

When you get back pages from an editor, they will typically look something like this:

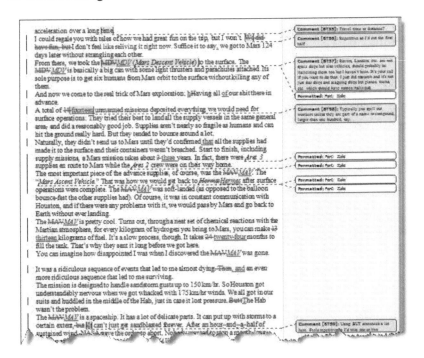

Figure 13-3

There will be corrections in the text as well as notes along the side. These will address everything from grammar and spelling to overused words, formatting, story elements, characters, sentence structure and length, etc. In the copyediting phase, there will also be notes on factual errors and research accuracy as well as other concerns, such as if there are real people with similar names living in the location used in your book and names that need to be changed for legal purposes, etc., as well as notes on house style and formatting that must be complied with for that particular publishing house.

Figure 13-4

Your editors are generally assigned by the publisher as in-house employees or regular freelancers. Usually once you've worked with an editor, they will follow you through every book in a series, but sometimes editors leave for various reasons and changes can occur. The idea is to keep people familiar with the entire series arc, author voice and goals, etc. by working on the subsequent books, so the series as a whole can have the most consistency, as well as to preserve the work of relationship building and partnership between editors and authors. Copyeditors are brought in after the book is ready to go to press, and you will be sent copyedit notes as they prepare the book for printing. The final stage before publication are galleys, which will have notes from proofreaders; this will be your last chance for changes before seeing the book in print.

Now, if you are an indie, the process may be a little different, because you will have to hire your own people to do these jobs. So how do you go about hiring an editor?

How to Hire an Editor

If you need to hire an editor on your own, you will need to do some research. For information on standard rates, check the Editorial Freelancers Association for a list of average rates here: https://www.the-efa.org/rates/. For individual editors, they should have their rates on their website as well as a list of clients they have worked with and even quotes recommending them. For me, I'd ask some of the clients about them as well as friends to see what kind of reputation they have in the community. Then, most editors usually offer a sample edit to demonstrate their skills for free (usually a page or two, maybe a chapter). Submit your work to several editors for samples and then compare them when you get them back. You can also reach out via social media to authors you admire asking for recommendations. Most of us have been there and will be happy to point you in the right direction toward finding a good, reliable editor—one we've worked with or who has worked with friends. Be sure and search bookstores and online for books in print that they've edited, and check the quality and who published them. This kind of information tells you their level of success and skill as well as their taste, which can be important, and their knowledge of genres. You definitely want someone knowledgeable in the genre in which you are writing to help you navigate market expectations, tropes, and other genre-specific concerns.

Once you've found an editor or two you are interested in, ask for full quotes and discuss their cancellation fees, time frame and deadlines, and how they deal with cost overruns, if any. You'll want to be sure in advance you are not charged for extra time without permission, whether they do extra passes or just one, etc. Then choose your editor and get a contract. Make sure the contract outlines guarantees to you, not just to the editor. Usually there will be clauses about payment schedules, how they deal with non- or delayed payments, etc., as well as a delivery timetable. All of this is important to have in writing to avoid conflict later, as these tend to be the areas where most misunderstandings and conflict occur between freelance editors and clients.

After that, you send them your book and get started.

I would expect a decent editor to need between three and six weeks to edit the average novel well (80,000 to 130,000 words)— more if your book is longer. I would also expect them to send you regular updates on the progress and even provide the first half around the time any second payment is due, so you can get an idea of the quality of their edits, usefulness, etc. Editors work for you in this case, not a publisher, so you have total control over what you do with their edits. That's why it's very important to hire an editor you trust and enjoy working with, then trust their judgment enough to use their advice. Your editor's job, whether freelance or in-house, is to help you make your book the best it can be. If you succeed, they look good, too, but most of all, you look good, because your book is your reputation, your calling card. The editor has no motivation to ruin your book with bad advice or to sabotage or hurt it. So the advice they give is always intended to help, whether it hurts your feelings or not. There is a need for your editor to be somewhat blunt—though most try to point out strengths as well as weaknesses and use a sense of humor in doing so to soften the blow—so that you get a sense of how readers will react and can really dig into the issues properly. Remember, it is not personal nor is it an attack. They are all about helping you. They are on your side. Take their comments seriously, ask questions as you have them, and try to find a way to make the editor's suggestions work if at all possible, never dismissing them entirely out of hand.

There will be times when you disagree. Some of those will be over things that are per choice, up to you. Personal taste or preference may play a part. Good editors will admit this and explain their reason for making the editorial suggestions. These are the edits you should decide if you agree with and want to do. In other cases, edits are absolutely necessary. These usually are edits about clarity and understanding, facts, character motives, story holes, story pacing, mood, tone, emotion, etc. and should be considered very carefully and every attempt made to find a solution you can both agree on, even if it is a compromise. Remember that we all have weaknesses and strengths, and the writing process is a journey. Everyone wants the best book possible and is working toward that goal, because a great book makes us all look good. Keeping that in mind should make it easier to take criticism, even when it stings, and put you in the right mindset to trust and work with your editor as a partner, not an opponent.

Once your book is edited, it is ready to go on to formatting, copyediting, and proofing. And those stages will involve more edits generally focused on repetitive words or phrases, grammar and spelling errors that slipped through, italics and underlining, house style, punctuation, etc. If the items are house style, they are nonnegotiable. Everything else can be discussed and considered, but, of course, if the grammar is wrong unintentionally or you have misspellings, you need to fix them. Accuracy matters to readers and critics. It is about professionalism and presentation.

I find the editorial process with some clients can be like pulling teeth, but with many it is pure joy. I enjoy very much watching writers gel with their material as things come into clearer focus, get stronger, and take on that sparkle they always envisioned in their minds. There's real joy in watching a good book become great and seeing the pride the author takes in it and the success that follows. I feel very much a part of that, as will any editor, and if you find a good one, hold onto them and treasure the relationship. It is like finding gold.

CHAPTER 14
FINAL THOUGHTS

Do you still wanna write a novel? Still have that story that just has to be told? Remember when I said it would be a lot of work? I think you have a pretty good idea now of what goes into it. The only thing left to do is to do the work. You may have hoped I'd give you a step-by-step instruction manual, but the truth is it's not that simple. Everyone writes differently. And trying to force a method on you might leave you frustrated to the point of giving up. The actual writing part is something you have to figure out. Find the approach that works best for you and then refine it as you go, learning and incorporating new things. Some of you can hold a lot in your heads and will be able to memorize lots of research and craft and just keep it there as you write. Others will be referring back to this and other books time and again to help you. Some of you may do passes just for characterization, just for dialogue, just for description, etc. because those are areas you really struggle in. There's absolutely nothing wrong with that. I used to do it because description doesn't come naturally to me. I'd leave a lot of sparse notes and fill it in during later drafts because I just wanted to get the story down. But as time went on and I read and studied craft and wrote a lot, I learned to do it, and now I do most of it as I go—though I always find things to tweak and improve in revision, of course. If someone tries to tell you there's only one way to do it, that is the first sign they don't know what they're talking about, so all I can offer is detailed lessons on the elements of craft and how various people approach it and then leave you to it.

I hope you've learned a lot in this book. I quoted from 50 popular (or semipopular) novels from all different genres to give you examples from books you have heard of and genres you like of the principles I am teaching put into action. I quoted from 24 writing books that I find really helpful, and I have listed at least twice that many more in the References and Recommended Reading. The tools are here. You just have to take them and put them to use. I wish you the best at it. I truly wrote this book with great passion to help you succeed. I'd love to be a part of your success, and I'd love to hear how you take this information and run with it and see many wonderful books come out of it. That would be a dream come true: best gift ever!

I've taught it the way I have because it is the best way I know how. Hopefully, your learning styles are compatible, so it is accessible to you. I use a lot of examples and visual examples, etc. because people learn in different ways. I have learned that in 20-plus years of teaching and writing instructional manuals. But no matter what I do or how hard I try, you will have to work. Some of this stuff just won't come easily. For some, various elements will be natural and almost instinctual. Those are the lucky ones. (*We hate them.*) For the rest, it is like going back to school, but when it's something you truly want and want to do well, it should be a lot more fun than regular old school, and a lot more rewarding, too!

Before I go, let me address one final thing: marketing and social media.

A Little Obligatory Bit on Marketing

Marketing cannot be done justice in a simple chapter. It is a complex craft of its own, worthy of entire books and then some. But because it is so key to any author's success, especially the indie author so common today, I'd be remiss if I didn't at least say a bit about it. Now you may be thinking what does marketing have to do with writing fiction? Isn't that the publisher's job? And in the old days, it was. But not anymore. All authors are tasked with marketing these days, even those with big publishers like Harper and Macmillan, but especially those who are self-published or work with small presses. The fact is, if you wait to start marketing yourself until your book comes out, you are not only behind, you are setting yourself up to fail.

Your marketing begins now. You should be starting social media accounts and building your network and community for years before you get published, because when you are published, then you will need to leverage it for all its worth to publicize. But it is worthless for that if you haven't laid the groundwork and established the relationships and goodwill that social media marketing depends on. So figure out which social media platforms you want to use—which make you most comfortable: Facebook, Twitter, Pinterest, blogging, etc.—and get them set up now. Then start supporting other creators and getting to know people. Be a cheerleader for a while and make interesting conversation. Then, when the time comes that those people you have bonded with can help you, they will likely be willing to do so without a lot of pressure.

Most agents and editors today look at a prospective author's social media profile and web presence in deciding which to offer contracts, so this is an important part not just of your marketing but also of your brand and credibility. Decide what side of yourself best sells you, and share that but not the rest. For example, religion and politics, unless they are heavily tied to your writing, are losing prospects for most people. They cause controversy and often are divisive and push as many people away as they bring in. Use with care. It does not mean you cannot care about the issues and the world, but preaching politics and religion is not the best way to market yourself. Instead, focus on other things. Then the occasional post about those passion issues should be okay. But I emphasize the word *occasional*. You also should decide how much of your personal life to share, from family photos to who your family is, what life is like, where you live, hobbies, etc. Remember, authors are public figures. And as such, certain rights to privacy go away. People will attack you for seemingly no reason just to feel powerful or push their own agenda and win support. And it will behoove you to be ready and protect what privacy you can when that happens. Almost every author I know has dealt with it, and some more often than others. So don't reveal things you don't want to come back on you and be repeated over and over. The internet is never private, no matter what your settings. I cannot tell you how many times things I posted to "friends only" found their way to people not in my friends via screenshots, etc.

In addition to social media, marketing involves building relationships with bookstores and vendors at conferences. That can start now too. Get to know them, be likeable, and be helpful. And then when the time comes, you can give them advanced copies of your book and ask them to consider carrying the book. Offer to autograph stock regularly and give them your contact information so they can call if a customer wants a signed copy. The more goodwill you engender with stores, the more they are inclined to hand-sell your book for you, and believe me, hand-selling makes a huge difference. For bookstores, it helps to make a sell sheet for each book to hand out to bookstore staff. I explain this process on my blog at http://bryanthomasschmidt.net/write-tip-how-to-get-the-most-out-of-your-book-sell-sheets/. A sell sheet is a simple publicity summary of the book's plot, attributes, any blurbs, and key information that is designed to intrigue stores and pique their interest in carrying your book. I also offer 9 Free Ways to Market Your Book (http://bryanthomasschmidt.net/write-tips-9-free-ways-to-market-your-book/). Just a few tips to get you started.

When it comes to marketing, not enough can be said about how much *covers matter*. I personally am often turned off by books with amateurish covers. I assume, often rightly so, that if the author or publisher cares so little about the outside of the book, they have put as much into the inside, and it won't be professional either. Many book buyers feel the same. Publishers certainly do. So, get people who know what they are doing to either do your cover or advise you on it and trust them. Believe me, it makes your book stand out if it looks like a slick, New York–published book rather than some self-made, amateur effort. Yes, sometimes NY makes bad covers. It is true. And they can sink a book. But this happens far more often in small presses and self-publishing, and it is worth the time and money to get right. This means both professional design and professional art. And you may not be the best judge. What you like is not the sole arbiter, though having a cover you like does matter. But it also must meet the standards of bookstore buyers and other professionals as well as readers who make buying decisions. So, find someone who has done successful covers and get their help and advice.

Another thing tied to covers are blurbs. Blurbs are endorsement quotes from other authors that you can print on your cover to help sell your book. You need to seek these at least six months ahead of publication, earlier if possible. It will take busy authors a while to read the book and decide if they can endorse it, and usable blurbs will need to be submitted to your publisher several months ahead of release in time to be added to the cover before the book goes to the printer. Don't be afraid to ask your favorite authors. But remember, favors are limited. So, spread the wealth from book to book. And ask early. All they can do is say no. That doesn't mean they won't say yes in the future—as long as you don't overask for favors and keep a good relationship with them. Many readers buy books based on blurbs from favorite authors, so the bigger the names, the better. And it takes a while to establish the credibility that will get these people to be willing to take a chance on your book, so this goes hand in hand with your social media campaign and starts years before you get published. Follow and support other authors, and when the time comes, they may help you out. They often do.

The last element, which is key, is learning to talk about your work well. I know it can feel like bragging to talk about yourself. But talking about yourself and talking about your writing are not the same thing. Art is art. People are people. You need to work on an elevator pitch that is concise—two or three sentences—as well as a paragraph or two summaries that you can share with people when asked or when the opportunity arises. It takes time to learn this well, so practicing in front of a mirror is helpful. Also, key is learning when to take the cue that is an invitation to talk about it and when not to, because there is nothing worse than being that obnoxious author who forces their book on everyone they meet. Believe me, as a professional editor and one who has done acquisitions, that is a big turnoff. It does not impress me. Also important is learning not to sound arrogant. Comparing your work to famous novels is dangerous. Saying, "I have the next *The Martian*" or "I have the next *The Lord of the Rings*" really sets a high bar, and most people will automatically assume you are a complete idiot who doesn't know what they are talking about. Most of the time your work won't live up to that standard either. Sorry to say. Be careful which comparisons you choose, and be humble while at the same time learning to sell. Authors and artists are known for social awkwardness and also for being cocky, but it's better to come off a little awkward and shy than cocky. You will win far more interest that way. No one knows your book better than you. Find the things that connect with people and use those to interest them in your book. The human-interest angle is always the best sell, and if their interests with genre and such also align, use that as well. It takes practice and a little research, but done well, hand-selling is the best way to move your books. Asking someone to read your words is asking them to let you in their head, and people want to spend time with an author they like. So be funny, charming, and humble but also passionate.

Your marketing planning should start long before your book is even done. It has to, or you will be woefully behind before you ever begin. Just as writing a book is work, marketing is a full-time job, and because it is so dependent on the goodwill of others and networking, you really have to start putting the pieces together long before your book is ready to slide onto shelves at stores. You'll also need to do much of your own publicity. Will you do a blog tour? Where? Will you seek blurbs? Will you do interviews? Where? Identify podcasts, blogs, and media you want to approach. You will need good press releases. Can you write them yourself, or do you need help? They require a special kind of writing, so if you are not familiar with it, get at least someone to revise and advise you on them. If you've begun networking well, you probably know a few people already or know who to ask. Also research where and how to submit the releases well. Identify especially your local radio and TV stations and newspapers. Networking can help with that too. Also look for tie-ins to help promote. Is your book tied to any holiday or theme you can time with to market? A major event or sport? Perhaps even write up some interview questions and answers you can send as samples or make available for use by others if they so desire. I'd ask others what they would ask rather than just devising the questions yourself. That way you get more of a sense of an outsider asking questions. Think about author photos. You'll need a professional headshot. And you need a professional bio or two—usually one short and one longer. Also a list of publications and contact information. All of this will make up your press kit.

Sound like a lot of work? There's a reason we saved this until you have finished your first draft. It's a good distraction for getting your mind off the book while waiting for objectivity to return before you edit. Throw yourself into this for a while, and you'll be perfectly set to do good revision with an objective eye. Your marketing materials need to be available both in print and electronically these days, so prepare both, and, if possible, put your electronic press kit up on your website as a page or download links. To find an example, go to your favorite author's website and see what they have. Almost everyone has one.

There are numerous websites and books out there focused on book marketing. I've listed some in the References and Recommended Reading at the end of this book, but there are plenty more. If you need help, ask your publisher, and see what they can provide. Usually they can at least give you poster blowups of the cover of your book and bookmarks, but sometimes also postcards and other materials as well. Often review copies of your book are available as well to send to readers at least in electronic, if not paper, form. All of these are things you'll want to explore once you sign with a publisher and maybe even negotiate as you settle your contract. Regardless, no author today can rely solely on their publisher. Too much rides on your book's success, including future contracts with that publisher but also bookstore orders of future books, which are based on sales of your previous books, and even which stores will carry your book. Marketing, no matter what your path to publishing, is about to become an essential part of your life. Most authors spend at least two to three hours a day working on it. Some spend even more, depending upon their release dates, tour schedule, etc.

Final Thoughts

Congratulations on taking the first step toward finishing your novel. Whether it is your first or your fifth, writing a novel is a big accomplishment—one that not many achieve. I hope you enjoy the process and journey you are embarking on. I hope this book is a helpful part of that. Regardless, I wish you the greatest success, and thank you for taking time to read *How to Write a Novel*. It was written for you.

REFERENCES AND RECOMMENDED READING

Writing Books Quoted

The 10% Solution by Ken Rand

Beginnings, Middles, and Ends (Elements of Fiction Writing) by Nancy Kress

The Breakout Novel by Donald Maass

Characters and Viewpoint (Elements of Fiction Writing) by Orson Scott Card

Checking on Culture by Lee Killough

Conflict, Action & Suspense (Elements of Fiction Writing) by William Noble

Description (Elements of Fiction Writing) by Monica A. Wood

Dialogue (Elements of Fiction Writing) by Lewis Turco

The Emotion Thesaurus by Becca Pugliosi and Angela Ackerman

Writing the Breakout Novel by Donald Maass

How to Write a Damn Good Novel by James N. Frey

How to Write a Damn Good Novel II by James N. Frey

How to Write Dazzling Dialogue by James Scott Bell

Million Dollar Outlines by David Farland

On Writing by Stephen King

Plot (Elements of Fiction Writing) by Ansen Dibell

Revision (Elements of Fiction Writing) by Kit Reed

Screenplay by Syd Field

Setting (Elements of Fiction Writing) by Jack W. Bingham

Storycraft by Jack Hart

Theme and Strategy (Elements of Fiction Writing) by Ronald B. Tobias

Voice & Style (Elements of Fiction Writing) by Johnny Payne

The Way of the Writer by Charles Johnson

Novels Quoted

About That Fling by Tawna Fenske

The Adventures of Huckleberry Finn by Mark Twain

Assassin's Code by Jonathan Maberry

Bad Monkey by Carl Hiaasen

The Big Sleep by Raymond Chandler

The Black Echo by Michael Connelly

The Book of Changes by Robert Silverberg

The Cold Dish by Craig Johnson

The Fix Up by Tawna Fenske

The Handmaid's Tale by Margaret Atwood

Les Misérables by Victor Hugo

The Lion, the Witch, and the Wardrobe by C.S. Lewis

Little House on the Prairie by Laura Ingalls Wilder

The Lord of the Rings by J.R.R. Tolkien

Lord Valentine's Castle by Robert Silverberg

The Martian by Andy Weir

Making Waves by Tawna Fenske

Memory Man by David Baldacci

Naked in Death by J.D. Robb

The Name of the Wind by Patrick Rothfuss

Parallel Lines by Steven Savile

Patient Zero by Jonathan Maberry

Pretties by Scott Westerfeld

Queenpin by Megan Abbott

Rot and Ruin by Jonathan Maberry

Rule of Prey by John Sandford

Safe Haven by Nicholas Sparks

Sandry's Book by Tamora Pierce

The Shining by Stephen King

Simon Says by Bryan Thomas Schmidt

Skinwalkers by Tony Hillerman

A Song of Shadows by John Connolly

Sayonara by James Michener

Tell No One by Harlan Coben

A Time to Kill by John Grisham

The Wedding by Nicholas Sparks

The Worker Prince by Bryan Thomas Schmidt

Touched by an Alien by Gini Koch

True Grit by Charles Portis

Wager of My Heart by Claire Ashgrove

Wife by Wednesday by Catherine Bybee

Other Writing Books I Recommend

Aliens and Alien Societies (Science Fiction Writing Series) by Stanley Schmidt

Body Trauma: A Writer's Guide to Wounds and Injuries (Howdunit Series) by David W. Page

Cause of Death: A Writer's Guide to Death, Murder and Forensic Medicine (Howdunit Series) by Keith D. Wilson

Daily Life in Colonial New England by Claudia Durst Johnson

Deadly Doses: A Writer's Guide to Poisons (Howdunit Series) by Serita Deborah Stevens and Anne Klarner

Drawing on the Power of Resonance in Writing (Million Dollar Writing Series) by David Farland

The Elements of Style by William Strunk, Jr.

English Through the Ages by William Brohaugh

Everyday Life Among the American Indians: 1800 to 1900 (Writer's Guide to Everyday Life Series) by Candy Moulton

Everyday Life During the Civil War (Writer's Guide to Everyday Life Series) by Michael J. Varhola

Everyday Life in the 1800s: A Guide for Writers, Students & Historians (Writer's Guides to Everyday Life Series) by Marc McCutcheon

Everyday Life in the 1800s: A Guide for Writers, Students & Historians by Marc McCutcheon

The First Five Pages: A Writer's Guide to Staying Out of the Rejection Pile by Noah Lukeman

Forensics (Howdunit Series) by D.P. Lyle

Get Known Before the Book Deal by Christina Katz

Guerilla Marketing for Writers by Jay Conrad Levinson, Rick Frishman, Michael Larsen, and David L. Hancock

How to Get Happily Published by Judith Appelbaum

How to Write A Book Proposal by Michael Larsen

How to Write Action Adventure Novels (Genre Writing Series) by Michael Newton

How to Write Horror Fiction (Genre Writing Series) by William Nolan

How to Write Mysteries (Genre Writing Series) by Shannon O'Cork

How to Write Romances (Genre Writing Series) by Phyllis Taylor Pianka

How to Write Science Fiction and Fantasy (Genre Writing Series) by Orson Scott Card

How to Write Western Novels (Genre Writing Series) by Matt Braun

I Have This Nifty Idea... Now What Do I Do with It by Mike Resnick

Jeff Herman's Guide to Book Publishers, Editors and Literary Agents: Who They Are, What They Want, How to Win Them Over by Jeff Herman

Manuscript Submission (Elements of Fiction Writing) by Scott Edelstein

Million Dollar Book Signings (Million Dollar Writing Series) by David Farland

Negotiating a Book Contract: A Guide for Authors, Agents and Lawyers by Mark Levine

On Writing Well by William Zinsser

Police Procedure and Investigation (Howdunit Series) by Lee Lofland

Private Eyes: A Writer's Guide to Private Investigating (Howdunit Series) by Hal Blythe and Charlie Sweet

Scene and Structure (Elements of Fiction Writing) by Jack W. Bingham

Scene of the Crime: A Writer's Guide to Crime Scene Investigation (Howdunit Series) by Anne Wingate

The Science of Science Fiction Writing by James Gunn

The Writer's Digest Handbook of Short Story Writing (Vol. 1) by Dickson, Smythe

The Writer's Guide to Everyday Life from Prohibition Through World War II (Writer's Guides to Everyday Life) by Marc McCutcheon

The Writer's Guide to Everyday Life in Colonial America: From 1607–1783 by Dale Taylor

The Writer's Guide to Everyday Life in Regency and Victorian England: From 1811–1901 by Kristine Hughes

The Writer's Guide to Everyday Life in Renaissance England: From 1485–1649 (Writer's Guide to Everyday Life) by Kathy Lynn Emerson

The Writer's Guide to Everyday Life in the Middle Ages: The British Isles from 500 to 1500 by Sherrilyn Kenyon

The Writer's Guide to Everyday Life in the Wild West (Writer's Guide to Everyday Life Series) by Candy Moulton

Writer's Guide to Psychology: How to Write Accurately about Psychological Disorders, Clinical Treatment and Human Behavior by Carolyn Kaufman

ACKNOWLEDGMENTS

First of all, thanks to Ali Albazaz and all at Inkitt for the opportunity to finally write a published nonfiction book. I adore teaching and I learn as much from it as my students. Lauren Burns, Laura Valeske, editor Amy Thomas, and Ruben Daymon, thanks.

Thanks to my author friends for rallying around me and being willing to pitch in: Jonathan Maberry, Steven Savile, Tawna Fenske, Claire Ashgrove, Gini Koch, Andy Weir, and Peter J. Wacks. To Jaleta Clegg for helping with last-minute diagrams. My Facebook friends for recommending excerpts, sending some to me as scans when I couldn't find my copy, and for recommending some writing books.

Thanks to my beta readers: Jace Killan and Martin Shoemaker.

Peter J. Wacks for late-night brain picking (I said "brain," not nose, people).

My dogs for endless patience and extra kisses despite Daddy's odd insomnia-like hours when he is on a writing gig, my parents, and my own writing teachers: Arthur Giron, Barbara Sackrider, Ted Dale, Dex Westrum, Laura Reiter, Mary Chapman, Mike Resnick, Robert Silverberg, and David Spangler. If I forgot anyone, apologies.

AUTHOR BIO

Bryan Thomas Schmidt is a Hugo-nominated author and editor. His anthologies include *Shattered Shields* with Jennifer Brozek; *Mission: Tomorrow*, *Galactic Games*, *Little Green Men—Attack!* with Robin Wayne Bailey; *Joe Ledger: Unstoppable* with Jonathan Maberry; *Monster Hunter Tales* with Larry Correia; *Infinite Stars*; and *Predator: If It Bleeds*. His debut novel, *The Worker Prince*, achieved Honorable Mention on Barnes and Noble's Year's Best SF of 2011. It was followed by two sequels in the Saga of Davi Rhii space opera trilogy. His short fiction includes stories in The X-Files, Predator, Larry Correia's *Monster Hunter International*, Joe Ledger, and Decipher's WARS, along with original fiction. He edited *The Martian* by Andy Weir, among other novels. His work has been published by St. Martin's, Titan Books, Baen Books, and others. He lives in Ottawa, Kansas. Find him online as BryanThomasS at both Twitter and Facebook or via his website and blog at www.bryanthomasschmidt.net.

Made in the
USA
Lexington, KY